The Edinburgh Companion to
Hugh MacDiarmid

T0386735

Edinburgh Companions to Scottish Literature

Series Editors: Ian Brown and Thomas Owen Clancy

Titles in the series include:

The Edinburgh Companion to Robert Burns
Edited by Gerard Carruthers
978 0 7486 3648 8 (hardback)
978 0 7486 3649 5 (paperback)

The Edinburgh Companion to Twentieth-Century Scottish Literature
Edited by Ian Brown and Alan Riach
978 0 7486 3693 8 (hardback)
978 0 7486 3694 5 (paperback)

The Edinburgh Companion to Contemporary Scottish Poetry
Edited by Matt McGuire and Colin Nicholson
978 0 7486 3625 9 (hardback)
978 0 7486 3626 6 (paperback)

The Edinburgh Companion to Muriel Spark
Edited by Michael Gardiner and Willy Maley
978 0 7486 3768 3 (hardback)
978 0 7486 3769 0 (paperback)

The Edinburgh Companion to Robert Louis Stevenson
Edited by Penny Fielding
978 0 7486 3554 2 (hardback)
978 0 7486 3555 9 (paperback)

The Edinburgh Companion to Irvine Welsh
Edited by Berthold Schoene
978 0 7486 3917 5 (hardback)
978 0 7486 3918 2 (paperback)

The Edinburgh Companion to James Kelman
Edited by Scott Hames
978 0 7486 3963 2 (hardback)
978 0 7486 3964 9 (paperback)

The Edinburgh Companion to Scottish Romanticism
Edited by Murray Pittock
978 0 7486 3845 1 (hardback)
978 0 7486 3846 8 (paperback)

The Edinburgh Companion to Scottish Drama
Edited by Ian Brown
978 0 7486 4108 6 (hardback)
978 0 7486 4107 9 (paperback)

The Edinburgh Companion to Sir Walter Scott
Edited by Fiona Robertson
978 0 7486 4130 7 (hardback)
978 0 7486 4129 1 (paperback)

The Edinburgh Companion to Hugh MacDiarmid
Edited by Scott Lyall and Margery Palmer McCulloch
978 0 7486 4190 1 (hardback)
978 0 7486 4189 5 (paperback)

The Edinburgh Companion to James Hogg
Edited by Ian Duncan and Douglas Mack
978 0 7486 4124 6 (hardback)
978 0 7486 4123 9 (paperback)

The Edinburgh Companion to Scottish Literature 1400–1650
Edited by Nicola Royan
978 0 7486 4391 2 (hardback)
978 0 7486 4390 5 (paperback)

Visit the Edinburgh Companions to Scottish Literature website at
www.euppublishing.com/series/ecsl

The Edinburgh Companion to Hugh MacDiarmid

Edited by Scott Lyall and Margery Palmer McCulloch

Edinburgh University Press

© in this edition Edinburgh University Press, 2011
© in the individual contributions is retained by the authors

Edinburgh University Press Ltd
22 George Square, Edinburgh

www.euppublishing.com

Typeset in 10.5/12.5 Adobe Goudy
by Servis Filmsetting Ltd, Stockport, Cheshire, and
printed and bound in Great Britain by
CPI Antony Rowe, Chippenham and Eastbourne

A CIP record for this book is available from the British Library

ISBN 978 0 7486 4190 1 (hardback)
ISBN 978 0 7486 4189 5 (paperback)

The right of the contributors
to be identified as authors of this work
has been asserted in accordance with
the Copyright, Designs and Patents Act 1988.

Contents

CONTENTS

To John Manson,
and in memory of Kenneth Buthlay and Duncan Glen:
all pioneers in MacDiarmid studies

Abbreviations and Notes

Abbreviations of work by Hugh MacDiarmid

CP1   *Complete Poems: Volume I*, ed. Michael Grieve and W. R. Aitken (Manchester: Carcanet, [1978] 1993).

CP2   *Complete Poems: Volume II*, ed. Michael Grieve and W. R. Aitken (Manchester: Carcanet, [1978] 1994).

CSS   *Contemporary Scottish Studies*, ed. Alan Riach (Manchester: Carcanet, [1926] 1995).

L   *The Letters of Hugh MacDiarmid*, ed. Alan Bold (London: Hamish Hamilton, 1984; Athens, GA: University of Georgia Press, 1984).

LP   *Lucky Poet: A Self-Study in Literature and Political Ideas, Being the Autobiography of Hugh MacDiarmid (Christopher Murray Grieve)*, ed. Alan Riach (Manchester: Carcanet, [1943] 1994).

NSL   *New Selected Letters*, ed. Dorian Grieve, Owen Dudley Edwards and Alan Riach (Manchester: Carcanet, 2001).

RT1   *The Raucle Tongue: Hitherto Uncollected Prose, Volume I: 1911–1926*, ed. Angus Calder, Glen Murray and Alan Riach (Manchester: Carcanet, 1996).

RT2   *The Raucle Tongue: Hitherto Uncollected Prose, Volume II: 1927–1936*, ed. Angus Calder, Glen Murray and Alan Riach (Manchester: Carcanet, 1997).

RT3   *The Raucle Tongue: Hitherto Uncollected Prose, Volume III: 1937–1978*, ed. Angus Calder, Glen Murray and Alan Riach (Manchester: Carcanet, 1998).

SE   *Scottish Eccentrics*, ed. Alan Riach (Manchester: Carcanet, [1936] 1993).

SP   *Selected Prose*, ed. Alan Riach (Manchester: Carcanet, 1992).

Notes

Line references for A Drunk Man Looks at the Thistle have been appended
to the CP1 page references (not given in the published CP1 text) to help
readers situate citations in the long narrative of the Drunk Man's journey,
and as an aid to readers using an edition of the poem other than that in CP1.

For clarity throughout this collection of essays, and except where otherwise stated, Grieve (and his numerous pseudonyms) has been standardised to
MacDiarmid.

The volume editors would like to thank Carcanet Press Ltd and the
MacDiarmid Estate for their kind permission to quote from the Carcanet
MacDiarmid 2000 series.

Series Editors' Preface

The third tranche of this series has as a common theme, one that underlies the whole series, the re-evaluation of the nature of Scottish literature. The volume on Hugh MacDiarmid places him not simply within the traditional setting of the so-called Scottish Literary Renaissance, but in the far wider and more internationally significant Modernist movement. Seen in that light, it is clear why MacDiarmid's work retains an international importance often elided when it is assessed only within a Scottish context. The volume on Scottish Romanticism likewise sheds a distinctive Scottish light on an internationally significant literary movement. It reveals a number of key perspectives including the relationship of the literature of the period to other art forms and the significance of Romanticism in relation to Scottish literature in Gaelic. It also argues clearly and persuasively for recognition of the relationship of Scottish Romanticism to the Enlightenment in a fresh and innovative way. The volume on Drama takes on squarely the canard that somehow Scottish drama was suppressed for long periods. The evidence it provides is conclusive in showing that so far from drama being generally suppressed in Scotland it showed variety, vitality, vibrancy – and resilience against attempts at suppression when they existed. It appears in the earliest records and asserts itself through many forms including folk drama, drama in schools and professional theatre and in all Scotland's languages, including the Latin of George Buchanan's internationally highly influential renaissance drama.

The Edinburgh Companions continue to challenge restrictive perceptions of the richness of Scottish literature. They also open up to scholars and students fresh ideas that will change readers' understanding of the range and depth of the topics under discussion.

Ian Brown
Thomas Owen Clancy

Brief Biography of Hugh MacDiarmid

'Hugh MacDiarmid' was born Christopher Murray Grieve on 11 August 1892 in Langholm in the Scottish Borders. His father James was a postman, his mother Elizabeth caretaker of the local library. Grieve was taught by the composer Francis George Scott at Langholm Academy and in 1908 himself embarked on teacher training in Edinburgh, but left without taking a qualification. Having entered journalism, he worked for a series of local newspapers in Scotland and Wales before World War One. During the war Grieve served as a non-combatant with the Royal Army Medical Corps in Salonika and France. When he was demobilised, he returned to Scotland and married Margaret Skinner. The couple settled in Montrose where Grieve worked for the *Montrose Review*, becoming also a town councillor and Justice of the Peace. It was in Montrose in 1922 that Grieve created MacDiarmid, the most famous of his many pseudonyms, and it was from the Angus town that he launched the movement popularly known as the 'Scottish Renaissance'. As editor and publisher he produced the anthology *Northern Numbers* (1920–2), and the magazines *Scottish Chapbook* (1922–3), *Scottish Nation* (1923) and *Northern Review* (1924). His first published work as author, *Annals of the Five Senses*, a collection of avant-garde short stories and poetry, appeared under his family name of Grieve in 1923. However he found his true voice as the poet Hugh MacDiarmid when, influenced by Jamieson's *Etymological Dictionary of the Scottish Language*, he began to write experimental lyrics in Scots. *Sangschaw* (1925) and *Penny Wheep* (1926) brilliantly exemplified his 'Synthetic Scots' style, while the 2,685 lines of *A Drunk Man Looks at the Thistle* (1926), also in Scots and often regarded as MacDiarmid's greatest poetic achievement, combined the form and influences of international modernism with philosophical searching and reflections on the state of modern Scottish culture. *Contemporary Scottish Studies* (1926), essays first appearing in *The Scottish Educational Journal*, and *Albyn; or Scotland and the Future* (1927), illustrated his ambitious cultural and political aims for Scotland. Grieve became a member of the newly-formed National Party of Scotland in 1928, but left Scotland for London the following year to work for Compton Mackenzie's radio-magazine *Vox*. Neither the magazine nor his move to England was a success, and the venture ended in his unemployment and in the breakdown of his marriage. His personal difficulties during this period – he was hospitalised in 1935 after suffering a nervous breakdown – are reflected in *To Circumjack Cencrastus* (1930) and in 'Ode to All Rebels' (deleted from the first edition of *Stony Limits* in 1934).

In 1933 Grieve moved to the Shetland island of Whalsay with his second wife Valda Trevlyn. His *First Hymn to Lenin* (1931) had demonstrated a deepening radicalism that saw him expelled from the National Party of Scotland in 1933, and he joined the Communist Party of Great Britain in 1934. *Second Hymn to Lenin* was published in 1935, but this was followed by his expulsion from the Communist Party in Scotland for nationalist devia-tion in 1938. *Scots Unbound* (1932) was his last sustained use of the Scots language in his poetry; with *Stony Limits* (1934) he moved to scientific ter-minology and erudite dictionary English, most effectively in 'On a Raised Beach', which also reflected the geological sparseness of his new island envi-ronment. From Shetland he published the prose works *Scottish Scene* (1934), co-authored with Lewis Grassic Gibbon, *Scottish Eccentrics* (1936) and *The Islands of Scotland* (1939). *Lucky Poet*, his fiery autobiography, appeared in 1943; a second volume of personal recollection, *The Company I've Kept*, in 1966. Much of his later poetry, notable amongst which is *In Memoriam James Joyce* (1955), had been written by the time he left Shetland in 1942 to work in munitions in Glasgow. *A Kist of Whistles* (1947), *Three Hymns to Lenin* (1957), *The Battle Continues* (1957) and *The Kind of Poetry I Want* (1961) preceded his first *Collected Poems*, published in 1962. Continuing to 'aye be whaur / Extremes meet' Grieve rejoined the Communist Party in 1957 and listed his hobby in *Who's Who* as Anglophobia. He died on 9 September 1978, the year his *Complete Poems* was issued. Some formerly undiscovered poems were published amidst controversy in 2003 as *The Revolutionary Art of the Future*.

Introduction

Scott Lyall and Margery Palmer McCulloch

Hugh MacDiarmid (1892–1978), most famous pen-name of Christopher Murray Grieve, is a challenging poet, not only in the range and nature of that poetry, but in the form and content of its engagement. The lyric poet who turned to epic, the Scottish nationalist who was also a communist, the reviver of Scots who went on to write in Global English: MacDiarmid's work lives at the apex of such contradictions. By his own admission, he was a poet of extremes. After the failure of his first marriage and a time of physical and mental problems in the 1930s, he would describe himself revealingly in his autobiography *Lucky Poet* (1943) as 'an absolutist whose absolutes came to grief in his private life'. 'I may have paid in pain for my insights into the universe,' he tells us, 'but the pain has gone – the insights remain' (pp. 44–5).

Such insights penetrated his poetry from the very beginning, but they were insights won hard in ways other than through the experience of emotional trauma. MacDiarmid was a lifelong autodidact who began to read omnivorously as a boy in Langholm. The local library, in which his mother worked, was upstairs of the Grieve family home in Parliament Square, and the young Chris Grieve would plunder it for books, filling a big washing-basket. Langholm Library, he would later claim, 'was the great determining factor' (*LP*, p. 8). MacDiarmid's reading-matter remained central to his work as a poet, and he would dredge dictionaries for many of the lexical arrangements in his poems. Yet the seedbed of his Scots poetry in particular was surely also what he described as the 'racy Scots' (*LP*, p. 16) spoken in the Langholm of his childhood. Such Scots infuses his first lyric collections *Sangschaw* (1925), meaning song-festival, and *Penny Wheep* (1926), or 'small ale', and continues in *A Drunk Man Looks at the Thistle* (1926) and *Scots Unbound* (1932).

MacDiarmid was one of a group of outstanding writers who worked in the decades immediately after World War One to create the revival in Scottish literary culture known in its own time as the 'Scottish Renaissance', but which is now increasingly being recognised as a Scottish contribution to international literary modernism. To a significant extent MacDiarmid was the instigator, and in the 1920s in particular the leader, of this movement.

It was his energy and acumen, and his skill and contacts as a journalist, that brought the poetry anthologies *Northern Numbers* and his short-lived but mould-breaking little magazines such as *The Scottish Chapbook* and *The Scottish Nation* into being, thus providing a new forum for discussion of Scottish and international literary and cultural topics. As early as January 1921, the poet and journalist William Jeffrey used the term 'renaissance' in the title of his review of the first *Northern Numbers* anthology, and by the mid-1920s, the terminology 'Scottish Renaissance' was regularly used in reviews and discussions of the new work.[1] Writing in the magazine *Nineteenth Century* in July 1926, Lewis Spence commented that MacDiarmid 'was among the first to recognise that post-war Scotland was ripe for a new literary dispensation. Although then almost unknown, he seized upon the situation with coolness and address and soon dominated it'. Spence singled out for special mention his advancement of 'an enthusiastic claim for the status of the Scots vernacular as a language, advocating its enlargement from the condition of *patois* [. . .] by the revival of older forms, the creation of new ones, and the amalgamation of its several dialects into a species of "generalised" or "synthetic" tongue' for literary use.[2]

MacDiarmid wanted *A Drunk Man Looks at the Thistle*, the long Scots-language modernist poem often considered his masterpiece, to be compared with William Dunbar's 'Seven Deidly Sins' and Robert Burns's 'Tam o' Shanter'; and just as in retrospect Dunbar and Burns are now seen as marking a movement to expand and exploit the possibilities within Scottish language and culture in their own particular periods, so MacDiarmid himself has become the signifier and representative figure of a new revitalising movement in early twentieth-century Scottish literary culture. MacDiarmid's work emerges from this deeply Scottish context, but he wanted ultimately to internationalise Scottish literary culture and his work should be read together with that of modernists such as Yeats, Pound, Eliot and Joyce. His poetry from the 1930s onwards, in particular *In Memoriam James Joyce* with its 'borrowings' from diverse generally unspecified sources, could be seen to continue his life-long pursuit of the expansion of human consciousness through the creative potential within language, while at the same time appearing to anticipate a later postmodernist preoccupation with the 'death of the author'.

This new volume on MacDiarmid's work has the provocative but stimulating task of looking freshly at his achievement from the perspective of the end of the first decade of a new century. Over the years since the publication of the first major collection of his poems in 1962 by Macmillan of New York, there has been a considerable amount of published material on his work, including collections and reprints of primary sources in poetry and prose, and biographical and critical books and essays. The most comprehensive reprint project is that undertaken by Michael Schmidt of Carcanet Press under the general editorship of Alan Riach, which has already brought most of the prose work back into print, and is now working towards an annotated reprint of the *Complete Poems*, which was first published without any critical guidance for readers in 1978. While having such an amount of primary source material now readily available is of enormous help to the general reader as well as the specialist researcher, it can also be daunting and potentially overwhelming for both. Edwin Morgan referred to MacDiarmid's 'mosaic method of composition' in his late poetry, 'using "hundreds of thousands of newspaper cuttings"',[3] and the present-day writer on his poetry, trying to find a way through the mass of material now available, faces a not dissimilar compositional dilemma. This book aims to offer possible routes through the diversity of his oeuvre to writers and readers alike.

Much of the early critical writing on MacDiarmid's poetry was concerned with understanding and 'explaining' this new poetry, helping readers to come to terms with his synthetic literary Scots, and relating it and its author to a previous tradition of Scots-language writing. At the same time it had to deal with an apparently very different poet and poetry appearing in the 1930s, which seemed to have, formally, little connection with any previous Scottish tradition: the 'Marxist Poet' endorsed by a critic such as David Craig in the *Festschrift* edited by K. D. Duval and Sydney Goodsir Smith in 1962, and the poet of fact and knowledge in his later English-language work, explored by poets such as Edwin Morgan in that same *Festschrift* and by G. S. Fraser in *A Critical Survey* (1972). In such early criticism there often appeared to be a division between those who saw the early Scots-language poetry as the essential MacDiarmid, such as Iain Crichton Smith in his essay 'The Golden Lyric'; and those prepared to explore the later poetry in the context of changing times. Many of these early commentators were themselves poets who had been inspired by MacDiarmid's early achievements: poets such as Sydney Goodsir Smith who learned to write Scots as a second language, and looked back to the period of Dunbar and Henryson for his inspiration; Helen Cruickshank, from MacDiarmid's generation of Scots-language writers; and Alexander Scott and George Bruce who led a new movement for poetry in Scots in the 1940s and 1950s. *The Age of MacDiarmid: Essays on Hugh MacDiarmid and his Influence on Contemporary Scotland*, published in 1980, and edited by P. H. Scott and A. C. Davis, both strong campaigners for national independence, examined his work and his life predominantly in its various Scottish contexts, and this preoccupation with a 'Scottish' MacDiarmid and his relationship with Scottish nationalism has been a feature of much later critical writing, both positive and negative, especially during the 1990s when the campaign for a devolved Scottish parliament was gaining momentum, and when, coincidentally, theoretical discussions of diasporic, anti-colonialist and other forms of cultural and political nationalisms were fashionable in academic research. Nancy Gish's *Hugh MacDiarmid: Man and Poet* of 1992, a joint publication between Edinburgh University Press and the National Poetry Foundation, University of Maine, and with its American and Scottish contributors, succeeded in keeping the 'beyond Scotland' MacDiarmid in sight, with chapters from a new generation of scholars, bringing him together with Eliot, Joyce and Olson, and discussing him in interview with Seamus Heaney, as well as having his Scots-language poetry explored in fresh ways by Harvey Oxenhorn, perhaps with an American audience in mind.

One might say that the mark of an outstanding writer of any period or culture is the openness of his or her work to fresh interpretations in later periods and in the context of new intellectual or social and political ideas. This is certainly true of Shakespeare where latent preoccupations in his plays, not foregrounded in the culture of his own time, have surfaced to speak to the concerns of playgoers and readers in later ages. This has certainly been true also of Burns, whose work and personality have gone through many critical and cultural transformations in relation to changing times from his early identity as the 'heaven-taught' ploughman poet, held up by the philosophical followers of the German Herder as an example of the good life of the simple peasant, to his recent reincarnation as a Scottish radical socialist reformer. Similarly, this new volume on MacDiarmid has to find a way to resituate his work for a new technological and information age, while at the same time bringing together with these fresh perceptions both the inseparable international and national dimension, and the formally experimental element that were so central to his poetry, as they were to the literary movement in which he played a leading part.

The perception of MacDiarmid's poetry dominant in this volume is of its unity, from the early modernist Scots-language lyrics (and even before that in the English-language work of *Annals of the Five Senses*) to his 'vision of world language' poem *In Memoriam James Joyce*. This is brought out by the opening essay in the collection, Roderick Watson's 'MacDiarmid and International Modernism', and is supported by Dorian Grieve's analysis and discussion of his language interests and uses, not only in the more familiar area of Scots, but also in his later refashioning of literary English. Grieve's discussion of the nature of MacDiarmid's 'adventuring in dictionaries' is itself supported and expanded into new areas by Michael H. Whitworth's exploration of the use of science in MacDiarmid's later poetry, which takes the previous source identification work carried out by Kenneth Buthlay and others into new territory by showing the necessity behind the 'borrowing' practices, so often condemned in earlier criticism, and, perhaps even more important, the transformative nature of the resulting work. Louisa Gairn similarly takes the reader into new territory by discussing MacDiarmid's Shetland poetry in the context of current ecological issues, a discussion which itself interacts with the geological imagery of the Whitworth chapter. Scott Lyall's chapter on MacDiarmid's communist poetry discusses this political work in the context of the British political poetry of the 1930s, emphasising MacDiarmid's difference from writers such as Auden and Spender, while considering it also in relation to MacDiarmid's committed stance in his poetry generally. All chapters on the poetry have the aim of paying attention to the formal details of the poetry itself, to *how* it is written, as well as to *what* it is about. And in discussions of early Scots-language poetry, attention has been given also to themes and work which have perhaps been less often discussed previously, as, for example, in the chapter 'Transcending the Thistle in *A Drunk Man and Cencrastus*', where Margery Palmer McCulloch and Kirsten Matthews explore the less familiar ontological theme of *A Drunk Man*, and the poet's attempt to transcend this pessimistic, philosophical journey in *To Circumjack Cencrastus*. In addition to such chapters on new approaches to MacDiarmid's poetry, Alan Riach considers his contribution to Scottish letters as editor and essayist, ranging from the short-lived magazines of the early 1920s to his wider contributions throughout his life to newspapers and magazines not edited by himself. Carla Sassi shows how MacDiarmid challenges the ideological borders of totalising political structures and explores the Scottish national identity question in his work through the prism of contemporary postcolonial theories, while Jeffrey Skoblow offers a 'transatlantic MacDiarmid' in which he speculates about what MacDiarmid himself saw when he looked westwards across the Atlantic, and also discusses what his American students make of MacDiarmid when they meet him in the company of other world writers in their senior graduate classes. MacDiarmid has always had an air of controversy and contradiction surrounding his persona and his work, and he himself thrived as poet on his polyphonic identity. In a chapter consciously designed to interact with Sassi's consideration of MacDiarmid's attempt to (un)make the Scottish nation, David Goldie examines Grieve's most famous persona, Hugh MacDiarmid, and questions some of MacDiarmid's more uncomfortable positions and the negative effects of these on perceptions of his work. The collection closes with a more general assessment of MacDiarmid's ambitions for his own poetry and for the literature of his nation, together with a discussion of his legacy and that of the movement he inspired, and his own personal reputation as poet in the new century.

CHAPTER ONE

MacDiarmid and International Modernism

Roderick Watson

'To bring Scottish Literature into closer touch with current European tendencies in technique and ideation' – so declared Christopher Murray Grieve ('Hugh MacDiarmid') as part of 'The Chapbook Programme' on the title page of his new journal *The Scottish Chapbook* in August 1922. The time was right. Joyce's *Ulysses* had been published in book form that February; *The Waste Land* appeared in the October issue of *The Criterion*; and Proust's search for lost time had finally ended with his death in November. This chapter will examine in further detail MacDiarmid's claims for the modernity of his cause, with particular reference to the early Scots lyrics, the phenomenon that was *A Drunk Man Looks at the Thistle*, and how these texts might be said to relate to the later poetry of, for example, *In Memoriam James Joyce*. There were many 'modernisms' in the early twentieth century, so how 'international' and how 'modernist' can these poems, whether in 'braid Scots' or as a 'vision of world language', really be said to be?

Modernism in Scots

MacDiarmid announced his aims in 1923 with 'A Theory of Scots Letters', which he published under his real name over three issues of the *Chapbook*, taking care to stress the modernity and the breadth of his ambition with references to Joyce, Lawrence, Proust, Spengler, Nietzsche, Tolstoy and especially Dostoevsky (1821–81). The Russian connection was emphasised and indeed MacDiarmid proposed a 'Russo-Scottish parallelism' which argued that Scotland could learn from the Russian writers and critics of the nineteenth century who had exploded onto the European scene with a radical remaking of Russian identity and dynamic new spiritual and psychological insights. (Dostoevsky was much discussed in British literary circles in these years especially in A. R. Orage's avant-garde weekly periodical *The New Age*, to which C. M. Grieve had first contributed in 1911. The Russian's influence was suddenly contemporary because of Constance Garnett's English translations, which appeared between 1912 and 1920.) In the aftermath of British imperialism's high period and World War One Grieve hoped for a similar renewal in what he saw as a now deracinated and bankrupt Scottish culture. To add weight to his cause he conflated the Belgian literary revival's slogan 'Soyons nous-mêmes' with Nietzsche's more philosophical challenge from The Gay Science to 'Become what you are' (SP, p. 28).

This was not MacDiarmid's first involvement with modernist ambitions, however, for in 1920 he had produced Annals of the Five Senses (published in 1923 under the name C. M. Grieve), as a series of 'psychological studies' in experimental prose, to trace what he called the 'cerebral sense' as it appeared in his various characters. Written during MacDiarmid's own war service in Salonika and Marseilles, where he had suffered a bout of cerebral malaria, the focus of these prose pieces is mainly psychological, not to say pathological, in their invocation of excited mental states. Each study in Annals is imbued with a sense of self-aware mental movement, charged with an almost hallucinatory intensity. The effect is very similar to the impressionistic modernist studies of Virginia Woolf (1882–1941) in Monday or Tuesday (1921), which she had theorised in her essay on 'Modern Fiction' from 1919: 'Let us record the atoms as they fall upon the mind in the order in which they fall, let us trace the pattern, however disconnected and incoherent in appearance, which each sight or incident scores upon the consciousness.'[1]

MacDiarmid's experimental aims are further marked by the fact that the pages of Annals are sprinkled with passages taken from other texts without a specific provenance being given, and not always easy to trace. The method is acknowledged in a preface to explain that this was his way of catching 'the current reading and cultural conditions of the characters involved', which is followed by a list of the authors whose material he has appropriated. Annals also contains ephemeral passages from local newspapers and lines taken from the letters of his friend and mentor George Ogilvie. It is possible to see this as a form of plagiarism, not dissimilar to the extensive borrowing that reappeared in the later long poems. On the other hand, MacDiarmid's proposal that his characters 'are discernible almost entirely through "a strong solution of books"' (a phrase itself taken from Oliver Wendell Holmes) can justifiably be seen as an early apprehension of intertextuality.[2] Whatever the final judgement on the later work may be, the narrative method of Annals was a declared and creative decision. Equally striking in these studies is the author's fascination with polyphony, intense mental states and the flux of subjectivity – all of which were to reappear in A Drunk Man Looks at the Thistle.

MacDiarmid's interest in experimentally modernist writing was evident from the start, but his 'Theory of Scots Letters' adds a new component to the mix – namely his engagement with the Scots language and Scottish cultural identity.

His commitment is doubly notable because only a few years earlier he had been of the opinion that Scots was irredeemably tainted by its long association with the nostalgia and petty sentiment of the Kailyard. No doubt a factor in this change of direction was the success of lyrics by 'Hugh M'Diarmid', but in fact the poet's case for Scots in 'A Theory of Scots Letters' was not at all incompatible with the modernist thrust of his early work, despite the fact that it might be thought to be introducing a more conservative and nationalist element to the agenda: 'It is a different matter, however, if an effort is to be made to really revive the Vernacular – to encourage the experimental exploitation of the unexplored possibilities of Vernacular expression' (SP, pp. 19–20). MacDiarmid went on to trace those 'unexplored possibilities' by arguing that the Doric has 'certain qualities which no other language possesses and qualities at that of consequence to modern consciousness as a whole' (SP, p. 20). He found these qualities suggested in G. Gregory Smith's *Scottish Literature: Character and Influence* (1919).

From the medieval makars to Walter Scott, Smith's study set out to isolate the 'persisting traits' of Scottish literature, and in particular what he took to be the literary culture's penchant for 'actuality' and 'realism' along with 'the zest for handling a multitude of details', the final effect of which was a sense of 'movement'. However, Smith believed that this 'grip of fact' was countered and indeed contradicted by an equal taste for the fantastic, the grotesque or the uncanny. He coined the now notorious phrase 'the Caledonian antisyzygy' to describe this 'combination of opposites' and the 'jostling of contraries' in Scottish cultural production, especially marked by a 'freedom in passing from one mood to another'.[3] Taking his cue from Smith, MacDiarmid went on to argue in 'A Theory of Scots Letters' that the Scots language was notable for its 'insistent recognition of the body, the senses' and the 'reconciliation it effects between the base and the beautiful, recognising that they are complementary and indispensable to each other'. In this way Scots could also 'telescope' 'diverse attitudes of mind' into 'single words or phases' (SP, pp. 22, 24). Qualities such as these, according to MacDiarmid, were what a modern or even a modernist Scots literature could offer to the world: 'Our Vernacular enables us to secure with comparative ease the very effects and swift transitions which other literatures are for the most part unsuccessfully endeavouring to cultivate' (SP, p. 19). 'Antisyzygy', movement and perpetual contradiction became central to MacDiarmid's creative programme, and the means by which he was to redefine himself as specifically modern, and also as part of an older Scottish tradition.

Following Smith, MacDiarmid went on to argue that this combination of opposites was evidence of a specifically 'Scottish psychology'. Few critics today would condone an argument based on such manifestly essentialist terms, but they were commonly used in the cultural and scientific discourse of the 1920s, which frequently invoked the characteristics of race when talking about what contemporary theorists would see as cultural construc-tions. Having recognised this, however, and despite MacDiarmid's claims and his nationalist agenda, the credibility of the concept of antisyzygy, and its proper significance in modernist terms should be divorced from 'national character' and seen primarily and more properly as a matter of technique in a creative poetics of 'swift transitions', contradiction and instability. In this way MacDiarmid, like many modernist artists of the time, sought to challenge the status quo of social, cultural and textual authority by recognising and celebrating life as a process of flux, change and Bergsonian perpetual 'becoming'. The books of French philosopher Henri Bergson (1859–1941) were enormously influential among modern-ist artists at this time. His thoughts on the ever-changing inner flow of subjective experience, and his concepts of intuition and 'duration' gave a metaphysical dimension to the age's interest in psychological states and 'stream of consciousness' writing.[4]

In pursuit of these values, MacDiarmid was also influenced by the existen-tial stance of the Russian philosopher Lev Shestov (1866–1938) who spoke for 'life' and creative doubt rather than 'reason', celebrating intuition, audac-ity and the concept of chaos as 'unlimited possibility'.[5] MacDiarmid had cited Shestov in support of creative inconsistency in the very first *Chapbook* editorial of 1922, accommodating these views to the concept of antisyzygy, and frequently acknowledging him as his 'master' in the later *Lucky Poet* (1943).

Just as significantly, in 'A Theory of Scots Letters' he saw Scots itself as an expressive medium with a rare psychological force and much needed physical vigour, whose words and phrases 'embody observations of a kind which the modern mind makes with increasing difficulty and weakened effect' (*SP*, p. 24). He also found a 'moral resemblance' (*SP*, p. 20) between Joyce's *Ulysses* and Jamieson's *Etymological Dictionary of the Scottish Language* with exciting implications for the use of the Doric. What MacDiarmid saw in *Ulysses* was a tour de force of high-flown experimental prose that still had not lost touch with an inexhaustibly vulgar oral energy, and what he found in Jamieson's dictionary was a 'storehouse' of images and idiomatic sayings that the more polite anglophone tradition seemed to have lost. Issues of language and sensibility had been raised by T. S. Eliot in his 1921 essay on 'The Metaphysical Poets', which outlined what he saw as a 'dissociation of sensibility', a gap between thinking and feeling in English poetry since the seventeenth century. Although MacDiarmid never cited Eliot's concept, his hopes for Scots as an expressive medium are part of this debate. Edwin Muir, on the other hand, was to take the opposite view in 1936, arguing in *Scott and Scotland* that the Scots tongue had become a language solely of sentiment and feeling incapable of dealing with the 'whole mind'. MacDiarmid, in contrast, saw the language's creative potential as

> a vast unutilized mass of lapsed observation made by minds whose attitudes to experience and whose speculative and imaginative tendencies were quite different from any possible to Englishmen and Anglicized Scots today. It is an inchoate Marcel Proust – a Dostoeveskian [sic] debris of ideas – an inexhaustible quarry of subtle and significant sound. (SP, pp. 22–3)

When MacDiarmid's poem 'Gairmscoile' appeared in *The Scottish Chapbook* at the end of 1923 (footnoted as 'Braid Scots: an Inventory and Appraisement') he saw the Scots language as a way of accessing chthonic powers and primal urges deep in the collective unconscious. These 'forgotten shibboleths' (*CP1*, p. 74) – the 'scaut-heid / Skrymmorie monsters few daur look upon' – will call up the 'spirit o' the race' (*CP1*, p. 72) by ancient powers and sounds, long thought extinct, which will descend on the 'hapless cities' of civilisation, like a herd of rough cattle, or a 'dour dark burn that has its ain wild say' (*CP1*, p. 73) to confound all those who thought the language dead or, worse still, confined to sentiment, nostalgia and the dictionary.

In the aftermath of Nietzsche's attack on conventional morality and rationality, apocalyptic primitivism, like the violent iconoclasm of the Italian Futurists, had become a significant part of the modernist ethos, just as J. M. Synge had declared in the preface to his posthumous *Poems and Translations* (1909) that 'before verse can be human again it must learn to be brutal'.[6] MacDiarmid's vision of a necessary 'barbarian' cleansing and renewal in 'Gairmscoile' is part of this tendency, and very much in keeping with Alexander Blok's long Slavophile poem *The Scythians* (1918), which imagined how the Russian tribes of eastern Europe would sweep away the decadent and bourgeois West. A similar view of the downfall of Europe was taken up by Hermann Hesse in his collection of essays *Insight into Chaos* (*Blick ins Chaos*, 1920), cited by Eliot in *The Waste Land*.

Also taking his cue from Nietzsche, Oswald Spengler's two-volume study *The Decline of the West* (*Der Untergang des Abendlandes*, 1918–22) had heralded the end of Classical Apollonian values in favour of 'Faustian' (Dionysian) disruption, and Grieve's 'Theory of Scots Letters' had quoted this along with Nietzsche's 'Become what you are' on the grounds that 'true' Scots culture was essentially 'Faustian' in Spengler's terms, hence 'dominated by the conception of infinity, of the unattainable [. . .] ever questioning, never satisfied' (*SP*, p. 27). Such were to be the defining characteristics of MacDiarmid's Drunk Man.

Here, then, was MacDiarmid's project, and Scots was to be its ideal vehicle in a language that rings, as 'Gairmscoile' (1926) put it, '*Wi' datchie sesames, and names for nameless things*' (*CP1*, p. 74).

The Expressionist lyrics

MacDiarmid commenced to prove his case with the Scots poems that were eventually published in *Sangschaw* (1925) and *Penny Wheep* (1926) – lyrics which, according to Iain Crichton Smith, 'cannot be duplicated anywhere else in literature'.[7] Many of these poems combine the broad conviviality of the Scots language with more or less traditional metrics and an essentially rural setting ('Crowdieknowe', 'Focherty', 'Sabine', 'Jimsy: an Idiot'); but they also have a metaphysical bias, engaging with much vaster perspectives of space and time as, for example, in 'The Bonnie Broukit Bairn', 'The Innumerable Christ', 'Au Clair de la Lune' and 'Sea Serpent' – all with what Kenneth Buthlay called a 'cosmogonical eye'.[8] David Daiches saw this combination of the domestic and the cosmic as 'the midden heap linked to the stars, and *both equally there*'.[9] Much more striking, however, is how MacDiarmid infused every one of these poems – domestic and cosmic alike – with an intensely death-conscious energy that is one of the characteristics of European expressionism.

The 'Dionysian' element in much modernist art has long been recognised,[10] and in particular it was German expressionist writing and painting that embraced the creativity of primitive states in both feeling and technique, using expressive distortion and the collision of images to convey internal anxiety and all the stress and exhilaration of modern life. Such art embraces discontinuity, emphasising instinct, feeling and internal turmoil over reason, coherence and order. In the same vein, MacDiarmid's Scots lyrics – and much of the spirit of *A Drunk Man* – generate an extraordinary combination of what he himself had seen as the 'spiritual' and the 'pathological'.

Consider, for example, the closing lines of 'Somersault', in which the poet evokes his delight in 'the stishie / O' Earth in space':

> The West whuds doon
> Like the pigs at Gadara,
> But the East's aye there
> Like a sow at the farrow.

Sunset and dawn, the diurnal round, are characterised in startlingly original terms that yet remain grounded in a farmyard vernacular. The planet Earth is personified and 'breenges' by, while the sea gives a 'gallus glower' to set an oddly intimate tone (*CP1*, pp. 47–8). Yet there is a darker implication in the simile, for it suggests that every day ends with death and a kind of madness, as in the casting out of devils in the New Testament tale of the Gadarene swine in Mark 5:13, while each new day is born in a pigsty only to be possessed in its turn. And there is an echo of Spengler, too, as the West destroys itself to make way for a resurgent East. In twelve lines, the poet celebrates the cosmic whirl with a mixture of uncanny glee, colloquial grotesquerie and millennial foreboding. It is a memorable effect, typical of these poems.

Kenneth Buthlay noted a certain similarity to the 'Metaphysical' images of John Donne, whose reputation was indeed being reassessed in the 1920s, via Herbert Grierson's editorial work and Eliot's essay on the Metaphysical Poets. Buthlay also observed that the Scots lyrics could be used to illustrate the principles of Imagism as proposed by T. E. Hulme, Ezra Pound et al. in London in the years between 1909 and 1913.[11] MacDiarmid's familiarity with *The New Age* meant that he almost certainly encountered Hulme's 'Complete Poetical Works' – all five poems – when they were published in that periodical in 1912, as well as his writing on Bergson's work, which Hulme translated. Buthlay did not pursue the point about Imagism, but it is well made, and in fact the Imagist 'rules' from this period are rather better realised by MacDiarmid's lyrics than they were by some of the movement's founders.

> An 'Image' is that which presents an intellectual and emotional complex in an instant of time [. . .] It is the presentation of such a 'complex' instantaneously, which gives the sense of sudden liberation; that sense of freedom from time limits and space limits.[12]

The subtly altered ballad-like forms and rhyme schemes of MacDiarmid's poems, along with his use of Scots, might also be said to meet the Imagist requirements for composing 'in the sequence of the musical phrase, not in the sequence of the metronome' and, most especially: 'To use the language of common speech'.[13]

Imagism, at least according to its proponents, was an attempt to refresh, renew and concentrate poetic expression at a time when verse had become prolix and predictable. And certainly the main impact of MacDiarmid's early lyrics is to be found in their sudden conceptual leaps and vividly physical ideation. Thus the world is overturned like a spinning top in 'Moonstruck', to make the moon a crow on a signpost while everything stops and 'Time' (that duly capitalised and very abstract conception) 'Whuds like a flee' (*CP1*, p. 24); or the Earth becomes an 'Eemis Stane' (or a gravestone, indeed) whose primal message is obscured by the accretions of history, characterised as 'fug' and 'hazelraw', and by the driven snow of the poet's own eerie memories (*CP1*, p. 27). Then there are the stormy waves of 'Hungry Waters' like old men with seaweed hair, howling and licking their lips as they chew mountains to sand; or the bereft lass with a dead baby in 'Empty Vessel' who becomes a metaphor for all human pain, or (if we read it a different way) for the indifference of the cosmos: 'The licht that bends owre a'thing / Is less ta'en up wi't' (*CP1*, p. 66). In 'Servant Girl's Bed' the wax of a guttering candle invokes the fallible mortal 'creesh' (*CP1*, p. 65) (a wonderfully liquid rendition of human flesh) that is the body of a young woman consumed by the very chemical processes that give it life and heat; or trees gobble like demented turkeys in black whirlpools of shadow in the atmospheric turmoil of 'Sunny Gale'; or the physical world is transmogrified once again into febrile animal life in 'On an Ill-Faur'd Star' where the seas screech like owls, and the land shivers like a skinny cow in the dust of Time. In 'Overinzievar' a landscape in Perthshire is no less nightmarishly tormented where undifferentiated farm-workers, hens, pigs and insects stand stunned on crumbling soil under forked lightning that cracks like a whip.

Such rural scenes are not so very unfamiliar in themselves, for they were the topoi, after all, of hundreds of popular poems in the Doric throughout the nineteenth century. But MacDiarmid's expressionist intensity has transformed, not to say entirely destroyed this tradition, as poem after poem is haunted by powerful currents of terror, creative energy and death. Moments of tenderness in poems such as 'Empty Vessel', 'The Watergaw' and even 'Scunner' are all the more powerful for being set in such a quickened and turbulent landscape.

Nor is the poet's Scots so comfortably 'Doric' in the end, for in amalgamating dialect words, idioms and phrases from all round Scotland (often taken from the pages of Jamieson's Dictionary), and in using them so originally, MacDiarmid had in fact 'defamiliarised' the very tradition he was seeking to renew, or rather he had succeeded in making it into something entirely new. The Russian Formalist critic Victor Shklovsky (1893–1984) argued that the purpose of all art was to 'defamiliarise' the mundane world around us in this way, by foregrounding its literary form, thus increasing the difficulty and length of perception – so that we see both the world and the text itself as if with fresh eyes.[14] Such must have been the impact of these lyrics in the early 1920s, when even readers fluent in Scots would have felt a little adrift in MacDiarmid's lightning-riven landscapes, while for anglophone readers, then as now, the Scots lexis itself generates an interestingly or dauntingly estranging effect. Whatever the context, domestic or cosmic, metaphysical or expressionist, the one factor that all these poems have in common is their overwhelming conceptual and verbal energy, the final result of which is the celebratory and uncanny glee of the likes of 'Ex vermibus', 'In the Hedge-Back', 'Wheelrig', 'Country Life', 'In the Pantry', 'Whip-the-World', 'Locked', 'Thunderstorm', 'The Widower' and 'Morning'.

Here again is the central paradox of MacDiarmid's modernism – that it should so fluently bring the voice and subject matter of an essentially rural dialect into contact with imagist intensity, expressionist distortion and existential daring. What could possibly follow?

A Drunk Man Looks at the Thistle

MacDiarmid's most famous long poem is a modernist masterpiece on a par with *The Waste Land*, yet it is seldom mentioned in any account of Anglo-American or European modernism. Tracing its critical reception furth of Scotland and outside the field of Scottish literature would not take long, and MacDiarmid's name rarely appears in company with Yeats, Pound, Eliot and Carlos Williams. Yet, like them, he is a system-builder with the same ambition to refresh poetic language and somehow transcend lyrical utterance in longer and ever more challenging works.

In the first instance, however, the spirit of *A Drunk Man* might seem to be closer to late Romanticism than it is to the dislocations of modernist expression, although late Romanticism and early modernism arguably have much in common. Nor does MacDiarmid share the overwhelmingly pessimistic bias of Yeats and Eliot. Yeats in 'The Second Coming' may deplore the fact that the 'centre cannot hold' but for the Scots poet (pupil of Shestov and the 'unlimited possibility' of chaos) this is a liberation. There is no doubt that the Drunk Man wrestles with alienation and despair, but the energy, mobility and sheer stamina of the contest, in many different registers and poetic forms, mixing satire, tenderness, vulgar humour and metaphysical speculation, is its own pharmacon (poison and medicine) and ultimately the saving grace of both character and poem.

In this and some of the later poems in Scots, in their epic scope, colloquial flow and vitalist optimism, MacDiarmid has more in common with Walt Whitman (1819–1892) than he does with Yeats and Eliot. MacDiarmid was fond of quoting from Whitman's 'Song of Myself': 'Do I contradict myself? Very well, then I contradict myself. I am large, I contain multitudes', and in the opening pages of *A Drunk Man* he famously committed his persona to be always 'whaur / Extremes meet' (*CP1*, p. 87, ll. 141–2) in pursuit of 'Thomas Hardy's definition "that literature is the written expression of revolt against accepted things"'.[15] On the other hand, like Yeats and Eliot, MacDiarmid's writing is dense with both canonical and arcane allusions including, as we have seen, a theory of letters and a larger literary programme to address what he, too, saw as a contemporary condition of cultural crisis. Except that this crisis will be met by embracing its condition and contradictions, not by seeking to remove or repair them; if this response has its roots in a 'Caledonian antisyzygy', so much the better for Scotland's contribution to the modern world.

The colloquial speed of *A Drunk Man* was more than matched by the symbols, images and the imaginative energy of MacDiarmid's verses; less concentrated than was the case with the early lyrics, perhaps, but gaining an extra dimension from the poem's much broader argument. The opening

MACDIARMID AND INTERNATIONAL MODERNISM

pages take the reader directly into a debate, or rather a rant, about the 'croose London Scotties' at Burns Suppers where the poet's memory is travestied in lines that simultaneously cite and parody T. S. Eliot's own satirical accounts of smart society:

> It gets my dander up to see your star
> A bauble in Babel, banged like a saxpence
> 'Twixt Burbank's Baedeker and Bleistein's cigar [. . .]
> The sumphs ha'e tae'n you at your wurd, and, fegs!
> The foziest o' them claims to be a – Brither! (*CP1*, p. 85, ll. 70–6)

In lines such as these MacDiarmid gives early notice of how wildly his poem will mix registers and cultural references ranging from a modernist poet to a famous *Punch* cartoon about the penny-pinching Scot who had not been in the capital 'abune half an 'oor, when bang went saxpence!' Within the next dozen pages the Drunk Man will make direct or indirect references to a nursery rhyme, Jesus Christ, a Wordsworth sonnet, Oswald Spengler, James Hogg, G. K. Chesterton, Nietzsche, Burns's 'Epistle to J. Smith', 'Ode to a Nightingale', Jekyll and Hyde, Frankenstein, Expressionismus, de Sade, von Sacher-Masoch, Scottish tourist trinkets, *The Waste Land*, the *Odyssey*, Freud, Mephistopheles and Gregory Smith's definition of antisyzygy as a 'Grinnin' gargoyle by a saint' (*CP1*, p. 96, l. 426). The same pages also deliver versions of poems by Alexander Blok, Georges Ramaeckers, Zinaida Hippius and Else Lasker-Schüler, all done into Scots.[16] Along the way MacDiarmid's metaphors are even more striking in the imaginative violence of the collisions they generate between 'munelicht' and 'leprosy', or the devil's laughter and that virtually untranslatable mixture of inspiration and ecstasy that is the Welsh hwyl, while the Drunk Man's face flies 'open like a lid', even as his brains swell like seaweed bladders on an incoming tide only to lie, when inspiration fails, like 'runkled auld bluid-vessels in a knot' (*CP1*, pp. 94–5, ll. 374–80). Here the startling expressionismus of the lyrics has been recruited to a much longer and more complex argument that will be sustained in vividly colloquial Scots at breakneck pace for the full 2685 lines of the poem.

Like Yeats, and certainly like Whitman, MacDiarmid sought to speak for his nation, and in *A Drunk Man* he attempted to enact, or indeed to *become* a new vision of his nation through his chosen persona. There is no doubt that the poem shares Whitman's Romantic solipsism ('Lay haud o' my hert and feel / Fountains ootloupin' the starns / Or see the Universe reel / Set gaen' by my eident harns', *CP1*, p. 99, ll. 501–4). But at the same time, as with 'Song of Myself', the poem is equally deeply engaged with issues of social and national import. Not the least important element in *A Drunk Man*, after all, is its many satirical attacks on then contemporary Scotland and its attempt to envisage or even to generate new paradigms for cultural identity. However, it is the poem's metaphysical dimension that is most applicable to the context of modernism.

It is useful to think of the scope of A Drunk Man as an expanding cone: from the focal point of the individual poet, to the wider circumferences of society, the nation and ultimately the universe. The poem opens by reflecting on the dilution and bowdlerisation of Scottish cultural and political identity ('Sic transit gloria Scotiae', CP1, p. 84, l. 33), a theme it will return to and regularly satirise, before going on to cast a critical eye on the protagonist's own condition. The speaker is haunted by visions of elusive beauty and symbolically feminine mystery in verses such as 'At darknin' hings abune the howff' (CP1, p. 88, l. 169); 'I ha'e forekent ye!' (CP1, p. 90, l. 240); and 'O wha's the bride . . .' (CP1, p. 102, l. 612). The first two of these visions of the 'silken leddy' were taken from early poems by Alexander Blok (1880–1921) to convey his own haunting desire for some otherwise unattainable Platonic ideal. For MacDiarmid's Drunk Man, these symbolist moments of fleeting beauty contrast with brutal reflections on his own sexuality – 'It's queer the thochts a kittled cull / Can lowse or splairgin' glit annul' (CP1, p. 101, ll. 583–4) – and the pain and futility of childbirth (CP1, p. 103, ll. 636–9). Nevertheless, such moments, gross or tender, are a door that opens to wider questions about the nature of existence and what it means to be a thinking creature forever subject to desire under the eye of eternity.

MacDiarmid moves across all such elements of sexual and metaphysical longing with complete freedom, as the poem progresses by a series of dizzying expansions and contractions. In the same way the symbol of Scotland's national plant, the thistle, speaks successively or simultaneously for the thorn of desire and frustration to which all human flesh is subject. It also symbolises Scotland's grim Calvinist history, the constraints of language itself and finally the inescapably limited nature of physical being:

> The need to wark, the need to think, the need to be,
> And a' thing that twists Life into a certain shape
> And interferes wi' perfect liberty –
> These feed this Frankenstein that nae man can escape.
>
> For ilka thing a man can be or think or dae
> Aye leaves a million mair unbeen, unthocht, undune,
> Till his puir warped performance is,
> To a' that micht ha' been, a thistle to the mune. (CP1, p. 91, ll. 265–72)

Caught between the 'rose' of the flower and the prickles of the stem, the poet wrestles with the ambiguity and mystery of this many-headed and elusive symbol as it morphs into his own skeleton, or the octopus creation, or a sea-serpent in the deep that he is doomed to pursue, just as Ahab sought Moby Dick, another symbol of the horror and mystery of the universe and humanity's unreasoning rage to embrace or destroy it.

The poem is remarkable for the fluidity of these images, perpetually shifting and changing shape, as they do, under the dual influence of moonlight and whisky, symbols in their turn of the deceptive nature of perception and the transports of intoxication, inspiration and madness. From late Romanticism to early modernism, the Dionysian aspects of this are clear to see, as in Rimbaud's letter to Paul Démeny in 1871 in which he argued that the poet must become a 'seer' by 'a long, immense and systematic derangement of all the senses'.[17] But there are older and more specifically Scottish elements here, too, for the setting of MacDiarmid's poem inevitably invokes the opening of Burns's 'Tam o' Shanter' and the uncanny journey into other worlds that its equally drunken protagonist will make between the tavern and his wife at home. Another precursor to the Drunk Man's imaginative voyage can be found in the ballad of 'Thomas the Rhymer', asleep on Huntly bank, enchanted by the fairy queen and fated to be changed forever by the experience.

Such intertexts, like Smith's theory of antisyzygy, confirm MacDiarmid's commitment to the reconstruction of Scottish identity and the literary tradition, but the fluidity and extreme dynamic restlessness of the poem's narrative voice (or rather voices, so various is the protagonist's utterance) generates something entirely new. At one level, of course, the work is an extended poetic monologue and many of its metrical forms are relatively conventional, with a notable preference for abcb quatrains. Yet it is driven by an extraordinary polyphonic restlessness, which mixes spiritual anguish, satire, gross colloquial humour and aching desire in successive passages, or indeed successive lines, for page after page. The effect is to marry the grotesquerie of Bakhtinian carnival with Bergsonian inner flux to generate a psychological *Walpurgisnacht* of violently colliding narrative positions, concepts and images.

Nevertheless, underneath the turmoil, there is almost always a speculative and metaphysically inclined mind at work, albeit entranced by its own plurality – like the protagonists of *Annals of the Five Senses*. The strikingly expressionist images of the early short lyrics – which stood alone and implied so much – have now been recruited to a wider argument of loss and longing:

O hard it is for man to ken
He's no creation's goal nor yet
A benefitter by't at last –
A means to ends he'll never ken,
And as to michtier elements

The slauchtered brutes he eats to him
Or forms o' life owre sma' to see
Wi' which his heedless body swarms,
And a' man's thocht nae mair to them
Than ony moosewob to a man, [spider's web]
His Heaven to them the blinterin' o'
A snail-trail on their closet wa'! (*CP1*, pp. 129–30, ll. 1470–81)

[. . .]
I tae ha'e heard Eternity drip water
(Aye water, water!), drap by drap
On the a'e nerve, like lichtnin', I've become,
And heard God passin' wi' a bobby's feet
Ootby in the lang coffin o' the street. (*CP1*, p. 147, ll. 2056–60)

The Drunk Man is haunted by mortality and the vastness of time, and most of all by the thistle, which symbolises everything that stands between himself and final wholeness and full expression – a condition from which there is no escape. This longing for the Other (whether imagined as woman, nation or universe), like the drive for full linguistic expression, is founded, like all desire, on lack, and hence by definition it is fated always to fail.[18] Yet, paradoxically, this is also the source of all our creative drives.

MacDiarmid explored this concept more specifically in 'The Impossible Song':

We are like somebody wha hears
A wonderfu' language and mak's up his mind
To write poetry in it – but ah!
It's impossible to learn it, we find,
Tho' we'll never ha'e ony use again
For ither languages o' ony kind. (*CP1*, p. 508)

This poem was part of 'Ode to All Rebels' originally planned for *Stony Limits* (1934), but its anguish lies at the heart of *A Drunk Man*. It would be interesting to revisit *The Waste Land* with this formula in mind, for in that poem and in *Four Quartets*, for example, Eliot also longed for the impossibility of full expression. But where Eliot came to withdraw from the struggle to seek the 'still point of the turning world',[19] MacDiarmid's protagonist *becomes* the struggle and accepts it as the nature and prerequisite of being alive. In keeping with Shestov's existential insights, the Drunk Man *embraces* chaos and perpetual change in himself and the universe alike:

I am the candelabra, and burn
My endless candles to an Unkent God.

I am the mind and meanin' o' the octopus
That thraws its empty airms through a' th' Inane. (*CP1*, p. 148, ll. 2093–6)

'Candelabra', 'octopus', 'thistle': whatever the model of multiplicity and many-branchedness where light meets monstrosity, duality and national identity, such an identification with the cosmos ultimately drives Romantic solipsism to defy alienation:

Darkness comes closer to us than the licht,
And is oor natural element. We peer oot frae't
Like cat's een bleezin' in a goustrous nicht [tempestuous]
(Whaur there is nocht to find but stars
That look like ither cats' een). (*CP1*, p. 148, ll. 2109–13)

The recursive problems of introspection and interpretation have rarely been so concretely and vividly realised. Lines such as these, both abstract and concrete, with their colliding images, differences of scale and their mixture of high and low registers, remind us of the vital part the extreme colloquial mobility of Scots plays throughout the poem, and justify MacDiarmid's earlier claims for the language in 'A Theory of Scots Letters'.

A *Drunk Man* belongs to the modernist canon in its confrontation with desire, incompleteness and alienation, but uniquely among its peers, it accepts the chaos of desire via the mobility of its many modes and moods, and in doing so overcomes, or at least resists, the siren song of despair, defeat and disaffection. It remains modernist in its intellectual ambition and in the endlessly changing mobility of its utterance, even if that utterance is in largely conventional metrical forms. But then again, it does something entirely new by tackling such large themes in a democratically colloquial language, charged to the utmost degree with so much oral energy.

Above all, it is the heteroglot nature and the unstable socio-linguistic status of Scots, matched to the psychological and dialogical mobility of MacDiarmid's use of it in the Drunk Man's mouth that allows his poem to join *Ulysses* and *The Waste Land* as a challenge to the literary canons of the day. MacDiarmid's Scots can tackle any and every subject, however 'high' or 'low', with a vulgar familiarity, an intellectual irreverence and a final deep seriousness that is ultimately political in its implications. For MacDiarmid, that political dimension was specifically linked to his nationalism and his hopes for a Scottish literary revival. For the Russian theorist Mikhail Bakhtin, however, the political implications of dialogical discourse, ripe with polyphony and charged with the vulgar energy of the carnival, make a broader, but still from MacDiarmid's point of view, very relevant challenge to all forms of vested monological, linguistic and cultural authority.[20] And yet, after the frenetic, intoxicating, spiritual and pathological whirl of the poem itself, it is all the more appropriate, perhaps, and entirely and wonderfully in keeping with the spirit of the piece, that *A Drunk Man* should end with a shrug ('I'll tak' it to avizandum', *CP1*, p. 166, l. 2650) and a throw-away joke about a less than cosmic silence.

Far from embracing silence, however, MacDiarmid continued to write prolifically. The more directly autobiographical dimension of *Scots Unbound* (1932) and other poems of this period celebrated Scots and the Joycean flow of 'Water Music' from his boyhood in Langholm, while the direct address of the *Hymns to Lenin* introduced a new and harsher polemic to British political poetry of the 1930s. The spirit of his undoubted masterpiece from this period, 'On a Raised Beach' (1934), is sterner, calmer and existentially unrelenting by comparison, and can lay claim to being one of the finest philosophical poems of the century. 'On a Raised Beach' is written in English, yet the opening and closing passages are so deeply defamiliarised as to be almost incomprehensible as a way of conjuring up the austere and forever unapproachable world of stones. It was this spirit, and the discursive anglophone voice heard in *Stony Limits*, that was to develop into a new kind of modernist epic that MacDiarmid was to work and rework for the rest of his writing career.

A Vision of World Language

In Memoriam James Joyce was begun by 1939 (although not published until 1955) as part of a longer poem sequence to be called *A Vision of World Language*, which, with *The Kind of Poetry I Want* (1961) and other titles, were to be part of the multi-volume, never-to-be completed long poem *Mature Art*. There are parallels here with Pound's forty-year commitment to the unfinished *Cantos* and, like Pound, MacDiarmid's aim was to publish a modernist magnum opus that would redefine what we understand poetry to be. *In Memoriam James Joyce* could not be more different from the fevered explosive and expressionist power that characterised the early lyrics and *A Drunk Man*. MacDiarmid now sought 'a poetry of fact' (*LP*, p. xxxii).

Having turned to scientific and Marxist materialism in the 1930s, MacDiarmid was determined to forge a poetry that could illuminate a world of material facts without recourse to the Romantic solipsism of Coleridge's 'esemplastic power', the very same image-making power that had so characterised *A Drunk Man*.[21] It is as if he has relinquished the traditional role of the poet as maker/makar/god-like author in favour of a cooler and more neutral relationship between himself, the text, the reader and the surrounding world. Nevertheless, his new project is still connected to the poetic pursuit of the 'octopus creation' in *A Drunk Man*, and the 'curly snake' in *To Circumjack Cencrastus* (1930). The metaphysical mystery of the many-headed thistle in *A Drunk Man*, also seen as the sea serpent, or as Yggdrasil, the tree of the cosmos from Norse mythology, has now been reimagined in terms of an accumulated coral reef of material information, couched in epic rather than lyrical terms, looking back, indeed, to the naming of the boats on the beach at Troy in Homer's *Iliad*. By such an accumulation of 'facts' the poet's aim was still to find a way towards ultimate wholeness: 'a symbol of the reality / That lies beyond and through the apparent' (*CP2*, p. 821).

A significant feature of the work from this period is its use of extensive quotations, only very occasionally acknowledged, from a host of different and frequently arcane sources. This is a return to the method of *Annals of the Five Senses*, however this time its intention is not to catch the endless complexity of internal 'cerebral' states – in what one of its characters saw as the ideal of a 'great music' which will achieve a 'logical yet ever new unfolding, the embodiment in the whole composition of richest variety with completest unity'[22] – but rather to do the same for the entire physical universe and the multitudinous forms of specialised and esoteric knowledge by which we seek to live in it and know it.

The controlling metaphor of *In Memoriam James Joyce* is language itself, and the poem's 'vision of world language' is a vision of the world *of* language, and also of the world *as* language. From this position MacDiarmid will 'speak' the world in epic and esoterically erudite poems, making innumerable references to the natural realm and as many again to the delights to be found in the most arcane reaches of the encyclopaedia and the dictionary. Thus the passage beginning 'We must look at the harebell as if / We had never seen it before' (*CP2*, p. 844) *describes* the many plants on a hillside, and *lists* the many varieties of sheep that might be seen there, too. The lyric and creative imperative to 'imagine' the scene, then to defamiliarise and 'make it new' again, has given way to a kind of taxonomy and a librarian's imperative to catalogue it. Thus the poet's celebration of Joyce's genius praises a mind that 'Opens and shuts smoothly and exactly / Like the breech of a gun' or displays the 'unquenchable radiance' of Mozart's *Marriage of Figaro* (an astonishing combination of unlikely epithets), before going on to cite the arcane skills of skiing, fencing and Zen archery as further icons of this ideal in a long passage dense with specialised vocabulary from each art (*CP2*, pp. 826–8). In I. A. Richards' terms, the vehicle has quite overtaken the tenor in this kind of writing, which is a mutation of the epic simile by which the secondary terms of comparison have completely overwhelmed the initial subject of the trope. In fact these secondary terms – endlessly elaborated – have become the whole point and purpose of the poem. Metaphor has been replaced by metonymy and the 'kind of poetry I want' has become a metapoetry that accumulates an infinite regression of similes without ever quite reaching or becoming a single, final utterance in itself. The effect is reminiscent or, rather, prescient of Jacques Derrida's concept of *différance*, hence MacDiarmid's confession in the opening pages of *In Memoriam* that 'all this here, everything I write, of course / Is an extended metaphor for something I never mention' (*CP2*, p. 745). Lacking that final unmentioned transcendental signifier, the new poetry of fact exists in an empty space of endless deferral that it can never fill, and the achievement of full expression, completion, wholeness and silence that so haunted the Drunk Man is further away than ever before: 'We know that total speech is impossible, of course, / Like a too big star that therefore could transmit no light' (*CP2*, p. 742).

Nevertheless, MacDiarmid continued to make the effort, admiring how Charles Doughty revelled in the most esoteric of vocabularies, by which the world is both made known and estranged: 'The tilts of a camel-litter, / The nombril of a shield, / The burdon of a pilgrim [. . .] Making language at once more rich and more precise, / And passionate for naming particular things / And particular parts of things' (*CP2*, p. 740). The power of language is still at the heart of the enterprise, but the expressionist intensities of the Scots lyrics and the psychic savagery of the '*datchie sesames*' in 'Gairmscoile' have given way to a patient, monk-like enumeration:

> They are not endless these variations of form
> Though it is perhaps impossible to see them all.
> It is certainly impossible to conceive one that doesn't exist.
> But I keep trying in our forest to do both of these,
> And though it is a long time now since I saw a new one
> I am by no means weary yet of my concentration
> On phyllotaxis here in preference to all else,
> All else – but my sense of sny! (*CP2*, p. 758)

'Phyllotaxis' is the study of the spiral structures by which plant leaves are arranged on a stem, while 'sny' is the slow upward and inward bend of, for example, planks curving on the hull of a wooden ship.

This is a new and entirely different kind of modernist poetic engagement, and although the catalogue of the universe is endless, and final completion and closure must always and ultimately be beyond reach, at their best these later poems still have their own prosaic, intermittent and strangely powerful music:

> The gold edging of a bough at sunset, its pantile way
> Forming a double curve, tegula and imbrex in one,
> Seems at times a movement on which I might be borne
> Happily to infinity. (*CP2*, p. 758)

– Yggdrasil indeed.

CHAPTER TWO

MacDiarmid's Language

Dorian Grieve

Shortly before his death in 1978, Hugh MacDiarmid was asked whether he preferred reading his Scots poems or his English ones. He replied:

> I think the better ones are all in Scots. And it comes easier to me. I relapse into the kind of speech I had as a boy and in my youth, and I find it easier than English . . . because Modern English is so clippit, the essence seems to have gone out of it.[1]

This assessment would have been a surprise to the young, ambitious C. M. Grieve of the early 1920s whose poetic interests revolved around international modernism and who was keen to distance himself from any taint of parochialism. Many aspects of his political and poetic persona were already in place: his nationalism, internationalism, intellectual elitism, his opposition to the English cultural hegemony and his passion for literary obscurantism. Writing to his friend and one-time English teacher, George Ogilvie, in March 1922, he claims to have written a number of sonnets which

> deal with foreign subjects – Russian, French, Italian, Spanish, Bulgarian – for the most part: and are largely unintelligible to those who are not thoroughly familiar with the modern literatures of these countries [. . .] In one sonnet the ceremony of Cursing and Expulsion from a Jewish synagogue is used as a basis. No one can understand this sonnet who doesn't know what a Sharof is, etc. (*L*, pp. 71–2)

Scots would seem to be far from his compass.

Nonetheless an increased interest in Scots was in the air, with a number of poets, such as Violet Jacob (1863–1946) and Marion Angus (1866–1946), making successful use of regional Scots dialect to provide an integrity that the supra-regional, post-Burnsian Lallans no longer possessed. Scholarly interest too was burgeoning. James Murray, an editor of the *Oxford English Dictionary*, had produced *The Dialect of the Southern Counties of Scotland* in 1873; a

Scottish Dialect Committee had been instigated by W. A. Craigie – another
OED editor – in 1907 with the aim of laying the groundwork for a new
Scottish dictionary; and in 1920 the Vernacular Circle of the London Robert
Burns Club was formed with its object 'the consideration and adoption of
methods for the preservation of the oral and literary language of Lowland
Scotland'.[2] Nor was MacDiarmid opposed to Braid Scots literature – he had
indeed included Scots work by John Buchan (1875–1940) and Violet Jacob
in the first of his *Northern Numbers* series (1920).

It was the report of a paper given to the Vernacular Circle by J. M. Bulloch,
'The Delight of the Doric in the Diminutive' (1921), a celebration of small-
ness and sentiment, which first provoked MacDiarmid to state his position
on the subject of Doric literature. He finds that the language has 'insuperable
spiritual limitations' and that for 'the most part the Doric tradition serves to
condone mental inertia – cloaking mental paucity with a trivial and ridicu-
lously over-valued pawkiness'.[3] He goes on to produce a catalogue of quotable
prose to the effect that Doric, frozen in a rural past, and, in literature, largely
sustained by a retrogressive sentimental impulse, is not fit for the purpose of
dealing with the concerns of modern, urban society. His attitude remains,
nonetheless, inclusive, insisting only that quality is the test to which all
literature must submit itself, Doric not least.

When he comes to pen his own first poems in Scots from a clutch of unfamiliar words in Sir James Wilson's *Lowland Scotch* and under the cautiously
pseudonymous 'Hugh M'Diarmid', it is not a complete volte-face; rather, he
has discovered how his own brand of vernacular literature may fit with interests already his own. From the first he draws comparison between his own
practice and that of Joyce's *Ulysses* (1922), published some months before:

> We have been enormously struck by the resemblance – the moral resemblance
> – between Jamieson's *Etymological Dictionary of the Scottish Language* and James
> Joyce's *Ulysses*. A *vis comica* that has not yet been liberated lies bound by desue-
> tude and misappreciation in the recesses of the Doric.[4]

He notes also a 'distinctively Scottish *sinisterness*' and a 'Doric economy of
expressiveness'.[5] His view of the utility of Scots for the purpose of literature
does, however, require rapid adjustment and he is quick to write on the topic,
partly to create a theoretical space for his work, and partly, one suspects, as a
goad to his ambition. The Scottish vernacular is now

> the only language in Western Europe instinct with those uncanny spiritual and
> pathological perceptions alike which constitute the uniqueness of Dostoevesky's
> [sic] work. [As such, it is a] vast storehouse of just the very peculiar and subtle
> effects which modern European literature in general is assiduously seeking [. . .]

It is an inchoate Marcel Proust – a Dostoeveskian [sic] debris of ideas – an inexhaustible quarry of subtle and significant sound.[6]

The strange effects and economy of expression had also been recognised by writers in the eighteenth century who employed the term 'energy' for the increased immediacy, density and vitality that they recognised in Scots over a polite, refined and relatively passionless Standard English: the very symptoms, indeed, that were producing a modernist sense 'of the imminence of linguistic aridity and imaginative death'.[7] In the year that brought Eliot's *The Waste Land*, Joyce's *Ulysses* and Rilke's *Duineser Elegien*, MacDiarmid's own solution was found in the leaves of Jamieson's Dictionary.

So much for the European crisis of language, but what of the rustic nature of Scots? Clearly the desuetude into which Scots had fallen would be somewhat repaired by MacDiarmid's dictionary use, but his plan initially seems to suggest that Scots must also develop high-register vocabulary and terms for modern contrivances from its own internal resources, 'to give it all the illimitable suggestionability it lacks (compared, say, with contemporary English or French), but *would have had if it had continued in general use in highly-cultured circles to the present day*'. 'What,' he asks,

> is the Doric for motor-car? It is futile to say 'mottor caur'. The problem that faces a conscientious literary artist determined to express himself through the medium of the Doric is to determine what 'motor-car' would have been in the Doric had the Doric continued, or, rather, become an all-sufficient language.[8]

His practice, however, does little to bear out this approach. While he stretches the meaning of words, occasionally to breaking point, and uses a broader range of vocabulary than had recently been seen in Scots poetry, he is little interested in creating new terms, whether in Scots, or out of Joycean experimentation. David Murison identifies *wan-shoggin'* ('ill swinging') as one of the few constructions that MacDiarmid may have originated.[9] Employing the productive Scots reversing prefix *wan-*, it is notable rather for its conservatism than its innovation. Although content to experiment with language at the level of the poem, for the words themselves he prefers to have linguistic security and he quietly shelves this initiative. When he does come to extend Scots vocabulary in this direction, the path he follows is the same as that of Burns: he uses English. The situation, of course, is not that simple. A high-register Latin borrowing such as *obsequious* has had as long an existence in Scotland as it has south of the border, but owing to its presence in Standard English is somehow viewed as less Scottish. The disparity is exaggerated by the fact that Scots dictionaries to date, for reasons of time and cost, have concentrated solely on words that are not found in Standard English, or that possess a sense distinct from their English counterparts. Jamieson's, therefore, would provide no solution.

Beyond the basic Anglo-Saxon word stock this common element is indeed subdued in the early lyrics, suggesting caution on MacDiarmid's part. We find *immensity* with an end stress, thus asserting its Middle Scots nature, and a few recently formed words, such as *mammoth* and *mastodon* in 'Gairmscoile'. While the concerns of the early lyrics are not exactly rural, neither do they reflect a post-industrial society, and *factory* makes its way in only by virtue of its appearance in a translation of Rudolf Leonhardt's 'The Dead Liebknecht' (1926). When he turns from lyric to epic, however, his vocabulary becomes more heterogeneous, and A *Drunk Man Looks at the Thistle* (1926), while remaining distinctly Scots, makes far more use of words found in both lan-guages: *cryptic*, *epileptic*, *emerge*, *eternal*; as well as newer arrivals: *zoologically*, *cyclone*, *hormone*, all first recorded after 1800. However, while Burns occa-sionally exploited the implicit shift in register between Scots and Standard English in, for example, 'To a Mouse', where the second verse turns from Scots to mock-serious, high-register English: 'I'm truly sorry Man's dominion / Has broken Nature's social union',[10] MacDiarmid avoids this device, instead presenting a self-sufficient Scots and, in A *Drunk Man*, one that is capable of moving from the colloquial to the serious without switching idiom. While it might be said that the Drunk Man's very drunkenness provides a distanc-ing strategy that licenses this admixture, by the time of 'Ex-Parte Statement on the Project of Cancer' in *Stony Limits* (1934) it is clear that the whole of English has in some sense become subsumed by MacDiarmid's Scots:

> – The arrangement o' achromatic scotopic vision
> In a hauf-light wi' its primitive rod apparatus,
> As compared wi' chromatic photopic vision
> In sunlight by means o' the cone mechanism. (*CP1*, p. 445)

This, though, is in the nature of an experiment, when MacDiarmid's interests were already moving to English as his preferred medium of expression. None of this is to imply that MacDiarmid's poems did not obtain much of their freshness from playing Scots against type. Given his dismissal of Bulloch's praise of the diminutive as 'Doric infantilism', it is not a surprise to discover that diminutives do not play a large role in MacDiarmid's Scots poetry. His most diminutive-rich poem, 'O Jesu Parvule', from *Sangschaw*, derives its sense of danger from the brooding power of the infant Jesus, the 'bonnie wee craturie' (*CP1*, p. 31), in opposition to the small, familiar and naive world conjured by those diminutives.

Returning then to his use of dictionaries, for his first Scots poem, 'The Watergaw', Sir James Wilson's *Lowland Scotch as Spoken in the Strathearn*

District of Perthshire provides, in Wilson's orthography, *aanturin, chittur* and *Dhur'z nay reek ee laivruk's hoos dhe-nikht*, and, in the second half of a word list of weather-related terms on page 169, provides not only *yow-trummul, waatur-gaw, oan ding*, but also *weet nikht*, and, on the same page, in a collection of words related to time, *foarnuin*.[11]

> Ae weet forenicht i' the yow-trummle
> I saw yon antrin thing,
> A watergaw wi' its chitterin' licht
> Ayont the on-ding;
> An' I thocht o' the last wild look ye gied
> Afore ye deed!
>
> There was nae reek i' the laverock's hoose
> That nicht – an' nane i' mine;
> But I hae thocht o' that foolish licht
> Ever sin' syne;
> An' I think that mebbe at last I ken
> What your look meant then. (*CP1*, p. 17)

He does not take the words precisely as he found them, extending *chitterin'*, 'shivering', to refer to light where it might more normally be applied to a person, and invigorating and deconstructing an old metaphor by suffixing it with 'an' nane i' mine'. Perhaps surprisingly, given the manner of its composition, the poem is less, not more, contrived than his earlier poetry in English. MacDiarmid's dictionary Scots seems to provide his language with enough mettle – and enough baffle – to allow him, however temporarily, to leave Poundian language-stretching and allusion and produce work in a more fluid vein.

More importantly, the poem inaugurates a compositional method that MacDiarmid was to employ throughout his career, reacting to and transforming lists of interesting Scots words culled from Jamieson's *Dictionary*, Watson's *Roxburghshire Word-Book*, Colville's *Studies in Lowland Scots* and, later, similarly curious English words from *Chambers's Twentieth Century Dictionary* and elsewhere. 'Egypt herrings' which are '*Eelyin*' in an emeraud sea' in 'Ex ephemeride mare' (*CP1*, p. 45), or a man who 'sits *oolin*' ower the fire', with eyes like 'twa *oon* eggs' in 'Blind Man's Luck' (*CP1*, p. 46; my italics), owe much to the proximity of these words in Jamieson. In later poems in Scots and English, a predominance of unusual words beginning with the same letter, or from the same part of the alphabet is also testament to this practice. Edwin Morgan notes incisively that

> many of these words will have no apparent semantic connection with the theme that's being dealt with, but they are given relevance by the ingenious

way they're worked in – often by a brilliantly unexpected use of metaphor. So a purely chance connection of rare words is transformed into an apparently and of course temporarily ordered and meaningful connection.[12]

Elsewhere a process of selection is perhaps more evident. For example, the highly alliterative beginning of 'Water Music', from *Scots Unbound* (1932), with its clear emphasis on sound, is comprised nonetheless of words that are both meaningful and relevant to the purpose of the poem: an evocation of the rivers of Langholm:

> Archin' here and arrachin there,
>   Allevolie or allemand,
> Whiles appliable, whiles areird,
>   The polysemous poem's planned. (*CP1*, p. 333)

(Which, sticking closely to dictionary definitions, might tentatively be rendered: 'hesitating here and snatching there, giddy or in a courtly style, sometimes pliant, sometimes in disorder . . .')

It is not just the words, their juxtapositions and definitions, but also the illustrative quotations and even the critical apparatus of the dictionary that might provide MacDiarmid with the impetus for a poem. 'O Jesu Parvule' owes its inspiration to its epigram '*Followis ane sang of the birth of Christ, with the tune of Baw lu la law*. GODLY BALLATES' (*CP1*, p. 31), found in Jamieson's under *balow*. Jamieson's speculative etymology for *ressum*:

> A small fragment, *There's no a ressum to the fore* [. . .] A. S. *reasn*, a beam, or Su.G. *ris*, a twig? The phrase may have been borrowed from a ruined house, of which there was not a beam or wattle left standing[13]

provides the stimulus for 'The Currant Bush' (1926), beginning 'There's no' a ressum to the fore / Whaur the hoose stood' (*CP1*, p. 46).

In his autobiography, *Lucky Poet*, he reflects on the practice:

> Like Mallarmé I have always believed in the possibility of 'une poésie qui fut comme deduite de l'ensemble des propriétés et des caractères du langage' ['a poetry which was as if drawn from the totality of the properties and characteristics of language'] – the act of poetry being the reverse of what it is usually thought to be; not an idea gradually shaping itself in words, but deriving entirely from words. (*LP*, p. xxiii)

It is worth noting, however, that precisely the same could be said of the least successful poetry and prose of the Whistlebinkie, Kailyard and Lallans movements, where works are composed around a limited and hackneyed Scots vocabulary, to convey a similarly hackneyed range of emotions. MacDiarmid is using interesting and evocative words, but, to the extent that he is successful, he is also applying an inventive poetic intelligence and genuine craftsmanship to produce his effect.

Kenneth Buthlay, Ruth McQuillan and David Murison, among others, have provided detailed studies of MacDiarmid's linguistic sources and shown that following words back to their original sources often provides new angles that enrich our understanding of his poems. For example, 'On a Raised Beach', with its array of geological and stone-related terminology, contains the following lines: 'I pledge you in the first and last crusta / The rocks rattling in the bead-proof seas' (CP1, p. 430). Of these, McQuillan notes that only by reference to *Chambers's Twentieth Century Dictionary* will we find that *crusta* means not just 'a gem, prepared for inlaying', but also 'a cocktail served in a glass, its rim encrusted in sugar'; that prayer is the original meaning of *bead*, and that *bead-proof* is 'of such proof or strength as to carry beads or bubbles after shaking, as alcoholic liquors'. She continues, 'the whole passage is a marvellous running fall of meaning and allusion, and you can't even enjoy it properly without access to the dictionary MacDiarmid used'.[14]

While that may be true, lack of a dictionary does not preclude enjoyment of the poems. In 1924, in the pages of *The New Age*, MacDiarmid is found praising Lewis Carroll's 'Ballad of the Jabberwocky' alongside a range of modernist movements, including those 'which seek to devise a language with audible and visual but no intellectual values'; two years later, in the same journal, he argues that 'comprehensibility is error: Art is beyond understanding'.[15] This is of relevance when we approach works such as 'Water Music', or this from 'On a Raised Beach':

I study you glout and gloss, but have
No cadrans to adjust you with, and turn again
From optik to haptik and like a blind man run
My fingers over you, arris by arris, burr by burr,
Slickensides, truité, rugas, foveoles,
Bringing my aesthesis in vain to bear,
An angle-titch to all your corrugations and coigns,
Hatched foraminous cavo-rilievo of the world,
Deictic, fiducial stones. (CP1, pp. 422–3)

He writes poems that may be interrogated by the intelligence, puzzled out, found to be comprehensible, but their initial enjoyability relies on something different that seeks to outflank rational response. This angle of approach to the MacDiarmid of *Sangschaw* (1925) and *Penny Wheep* (1926) has much to recommend it also. The lexis is strange, yet the result is inviting rather than alienating. Although trawled from dictionaries the words are not invented, so while their rational meaning is in some cases opaque, the phonaesthetic effect of the words is still available to us because they are some part of our language structure. Somewhat later, J. R. R. Tolkien achieved similar effects using Old English lexis to give us 'Mordor' and 'Shaddowfax'. For a reader not acquainted with Scots, 'The Eemis Stane' (1925) is still effective poetry and, when 'The warl' like an eemis stane / Wags i' the lift' (*CP1*, p. 27), it is the 'quarry of subtle and significant sound'[16] that makes it so, just as it would if it were to 'gyre and gimble in the wabe'.

The tendency to focus on MacDiarmid's lexical adventures can obscure the fact that a great deal of the effect he achieves in Scots is in the sound. Although the first line of 'The Innumerable Christ' (1925), 'Wha kens on whatna Bethlehems / Earth twinkles like a star the nicht' (*CP1*, p. 32), may be translated into English without any lexical difficulty, it would be hard to argue that it is in any real sense translatable without losing its eerie significance. The Scots sandhi, where sounds are dropped at the boundary of two words, *i' the, o' the*, provides MacDiarmid an opportunity for a denser line, a more flowing sound and the use of a device no longer in fashion in English poetry. The halting triple stresses of 'The Eemis Stane', 'I' the how-dumb-deid o' the cauld hairst nicht' (*CP1*, p. 27), compared, say, with the diabolic rhythm of 'There's teuch sauchs growin' i' the Reuch Heuch Hauch / Like the sauls o' the damned are they' ('The Sauchs in the Reuch Heuch Hauch', *CP1*, p. 18), illustrate the increased metrical diversity MacDiarmid also gains by his use of Scots.

Beyond basic Scots vocabulary, it is difficult to show that any of MacDiarmid's more curious words are the result of a boyhood in Langholm. While *ringle-eyed* may be heard in Langholm to this day, its first occurrence in a MacDiarmid poem alongside other difficult *r* words makes it next to certain that the dictionary was his source. Indeed, he spoke a very standard Scottish English all his adult life. He insists, nonetheless, that 'English [. . .] is not my native language', and that it is impossible to convey

> the tone of my being, in a language in which, for example, '*Egypt*' spells *ee, gee, wy, pee, tee*, whereas in the speech of my boyhood (and in which all my best poetry is written) the spelling of '*Egypt*' is (I know no English equivalent for the sound and therefore use the pronunciation of the French word '*oeil*', which gives it exactly) *oeil, joeil, woeil, poeil, toeil*. (*LP*, pp. 34–5)

And well he may, because what Langholm certainly did give him was his broad-vowelled Border accent and an ear for his own Scots. MacDiarmid reads his own Scots poetry marvellously and the free availability of some of his recordings on the internet is an opportunity to experience his poetry as he himself heard it.[17]

In the 1926 author's note to *A Drunk Man Looks at the Thistle*, MacDiarmid states that the 'whole thing must, of course, be pronounced *more Boreali*' and this is clearly his intention for all of his work in Scots.[18] The 'teuch sauchs growin' i' the Reuch Heuch Hauch' are singing their Scots origin in the repetition of the shibboleth Scots gutturals, [x, ç], but *growin'* too will distinguish itself with a diphthong [grʌu], a near rhyme for *growl*, against Standard Scottish English [gro]. Kenneth Buthlay observes that by the 1970s the isogloss for *brough* between a northern pronunciation [brʌx] and a southern one [brʌf] runs north of Langholm, and asks us to consider the rhyme: 'But rings it maistly as a brough / The mune, till it's juist bricht enough (*CP1*, p. 143, ll. 1946–7).[19] MacDiarmid reads it with a southern pronunciation and is, as Buthlay notes, remarkably reluctant to use the guttural sound in readings, happily winding up both his recordings of *A Drunk Man* '– "And weel ye micht," / Sae Jean'll say, "efter sic a nicht!"' (*CP1*, p. 167, ll. 2684–5) – with standard *might* and *night* [mait, nait]. However, these instances, and in particular the standard spelling of *enough* as against *eneuch*, say nothing about how MacDiarmid intended the words to be pronounced. 'The Eemis Stane' contains the sole instance of MacDiarmid employing the form *thaim*, which he uses to rhyme with *fame*. The rhyme, however, is just as clearly present in 'I Heard Christ Sing', where *them* rhymes with *came* (*CP1*, p. 19), and, again, in the rhyming triplets towards the end of *A Drunk Man* where we find *same*, *them* and *Hame* (*CP1*, p. 165, ll. 2626–8).

In common with many other poets writing in Scots from the eighteenth century onwards, MacDiarmid will occasionally utilise standard pronunciation to preserve rhyme or assonance. For example, in *A Drunk Man* we find a Standard English *death* rhyming with *Nazareth* (*CP1*, p. 88, ll. 166–8). Other instances are less clear. The final line of 'The Watergaw' has *meant* which one may wish to read as a standard pronunciation to preserve assonance with *mebbe*, *ken* and *then*: 'An' I think that mebbe at last I ken / What your look meant then' (*CP1*, p. 17). While it is interesting to note that in all of MacDiarmid's recordings of the poem he says *meent*, we must cling to the primacy of the text, as MacDiarmid's readings, although rich and atmospheric, are a trifle cavalier in detail, on the one hand refusing a Scots pronunciation and failing to rhyme *cairry it* and *vary it*, on the other refusing a standard pronunciation and failing to rhyme *no'* and *grow*. Langholm and the surrounding area does possess a pronunciation of *it* with a distinct high front vowel *eet*, and we can perhaps detect a trace of MacDiarmid's Border origins in his reading of 'Empty Vessel' where he produces a pure rhyme between *sweet* and *wi't*.

The Scots orthography that MacDiarmid employs in his early lyrics and *A Drunk Man* is inconsistent and there is perhaps little value in any detailed investigation of it. While he prefers *guid*, we also find *gude* and *good*, *change* is found with *cheenge*, *death* with *daith*, and so on. He does, however, tend to avoid *-ow-* spellings where a monophthong is intended, so *doon* varies with *doun*, but *down* is found only once. In common with other poets in the first wave of the Scottish Renaissance, MacDiarmid exhibits a marked preference for forms containing what has since come to be known as the apologetic apostrophe, that is, forms that supply an apostrophe where the Scots word 'misses' a sound which is present in its Standard English cognate: *ha'e* for *have*, *fu'* for *full*, *sparin'* for *sparing* and so on. This practice, which was unknown in earlier Scots, began with writers of the eighteenth century either as an attempt to render the text comprehensible to a readership accustomed to reading English, or simply because it seemed correct to the writers themselves. Although the apostrophe in particular was singled out on these grounds by a younger generation of Scots language proponents in the mid-twentieth century as a type of linguistic cap-doffing incompatible with a self-confident national literature, there was little frisson associated with it in the 1920s; indeed, these forms might be said to have constituted something of a standard in Scots orthography.

For MacDiarmid, considerations such as these were a distraction from the main, creative, goals of the Renaissance and would 'not detain for two seconds any but orthographers run to seed'.[20] Nor was his resistance to orthographic reform altogether passive. Rejecting James Wilson's proposals for a quasi-phonetic writing system for Scots, he notes that 'literature appeals to the eye as well as to the ear, and there are traditional and associative values not to be lightly discounted'.[21] Late in life he appears to have had a change of heart and was persuaded to place a notice in *The Scotsman* to the effect that he desired any subsequent collection of his poems to be respelled in accordance with the Scots Style Guide. Although he did survive till the proof stage of his *Complete Poems*, this was not, in the event, carried out, and John Weston's 1971 edition of *A Drunk Man* was the only work to be submitted to this process.

MacDiarmid's early encounters with contemporary European poetry were from English translations, notably those of Jethro Bithell and, later, those of Deutsch and Yarmolinsky. Perhaps inspired by similar efforts by R. L. Cassie and Alexander Gray, both of whose work he admired, he included a translation of a Stefan George poem in *Sangschaw*. It was an important step, both as a statement of his international interests and as an exercise in the capacity of Scots for this kind of expression. As with many later translations, such as those in *A Drunk Man*, he used an English crib to produce an expressive, rather than a faithful, translation, in line with the kind of practice Ezra Pound had been exhorting.

The Drunk Man's admission, '*I ken nae Russian*' (*CP1*, p. 151, ll. 2224–5) applies as much to MacDiarmid himself. While he had some knowledge of French from school, David Daiches is probably correct in his assertion that 'MacDiarmid's *sense of language*, which is subtle and profound, must be distinguished from his knowledge of foreign languages, which is rudimentary.'[22] A *Drunk Man* makes use of German theoretical expressions to stress an awareness of contemporary trends in European thinking and keep pace with Eliot:

> Type o' the Wissenschaftsfeindlichkeit,
> Begriffsmüdigkeit that has gar't
> Men try Morphologies der Weltgeschichte,
> And mad Expressionismus syne in Art. (*CP1*, p. 94, ll. 349–52)

In Memoriam James Joyce (1955) takes this approach several steps further including words and phrases from Sanskrit, Breton, Welsh, Greek, Chinese, Hebrew and many others in a bizarre attempt to create a world language of ideas. Daiches notes wryly that the one Hebrew word he finds in it is printed upside down.[23] As ever, MacDiarmid got his language where he could. Clearly, dictionaries would be of little help in such an endeavour and, indeed, his sources seem predominantly to have been prose. If nothing else, they are a tribute to the length of time and degree of fastidiousness he engaged in accumulating them. While many sources are advertised, elsewhere he is coy. A passage containing a series of technical terms of Chinese calligraphy (*CP2*, p. 819), 'Fighting snakes write wonderful wriggling ts'aoshu ("grass script")', is culled, with the surrounding English, from Lin Yutang's *The Importance of Living*. A, perhaps meaningful, Chinese character, *Jen* (*CP2*, p. 827), comes from I. A. Richards's *Mencius on the Mind* via MacDiarmid's own *Scottish Eccentrics* (1936). A Gaelic phrase, 'Tha cuid de'n sgrìobhadh anns an leabhar so bòidheach ri / leughadh, ach is mòr am beud nach robh na's fearr eolas aig a' / bhan-ughdair air a' chùis' (*CP2*, p. 869), and the passage preceding it, is taken from a review of Isabel Frances Grant's *The Lordship of the Isles* by Ruaraidh Erskine of Mar in the *London Mercury* of May 1935, which also provides a translation: 'some of the writing in this book is pretty to read; but it is a great pity that the authoress has not better knowledge of the subject'.[24] However, his prose sources do occasionally augment the sense of a passage. The first person of *In Memoriam James Joyce* recalls how he liked to hear a girl speak to her father in fluent Greek:

> All in Plato's or Xenophon's style and vocabulary,
> Only borrowing from the modern language
> The few words necessary
> For purely 20th century things,
> And wish I might be found so speaking too [. . .]
> But alas I can speak no Greek

And am now too old to learn
And nil leiyeas ogam air. (CP2, p. 797)

The last line is Irish and, along with another Irish phrase a few lines before (and almost all of the rest of the stanza), is taken, with MacDiarmidian errors, from the *Journals and Letters of Stephen MacKenna*, where it is glossed 'I have no cure for it.'[25] MacKenna himself was a much-lauded translator of the *Enneads* of Plotinus, whose neoplatonic philosophy is one of the elements that underpins MacDiarmid's poem. This source, if we find it, might lead us further back, with a pleasant circularity, to Joyce's *Ulysses*, where Stephen Dedalus is reminded: 'Mallarmé, don't you know [. . .] has written those wonderful prose poems Stephen MacKenna used to read me in Paris,'[26] and we have travelled from the purest classicism to Mallarmé's 'Hamlet et Fortinbras' in a few short steps. The connection may or may not have been MacDiarmid's intention, but it is surely the type of self-education he wished the poem to invite. Lest our hopes for his sources are raised too high, the final line of *In Memoriam James Joyce*, '*Sab thik chha*', a nod to *The Waste Land*'s 'Shantih shantih shantih', is given a footnote: 'The final (Gurkhali) sentence means "Everything's O.K."' and 'indicates that the author shares Werner Bergengruen's conviction of what the German writer calls "the rightness of the world"' (CP2, p. 889). The phrase itself, however, is from John Masters's 1952 novel *Bhowani Junction*: 'Faintly from the back of the train someone shouted "*Sab thik chha*" – the Gurkhali for "Everything okay".'[27]

The inclusive attitude towards the various literary cultures of Scotland with which MacDiarmid started out was given a concrete form in his edition of *The Golden Treasury of Scottish Poetry* (1940). Intended as a Scottish counterpart to Palgrave's *Golden Treasury*, MacDiarmid was aware he held an opportunity to reshape the canon by including selections not just from English and Scots, but also, in translation, from Latin and Gaelic. MacDiarmid undertook the Gaelic translations himself. In distinction to his previous translations, these aimed as far as possible at fidelity to the original, with Sorley MacLean (1911–96) supplying literal translations and detailed metrical notes. In spite of his claim in *Lucky Poet* to have learned a little Gaelic in his early youth, it is likely that this did not go beyond a smattering, and, indeed, MacLean notes, 'He had little Gàidhlig himself.'[28] Nonetheless, MacLean says of MacDiarmid's translation of 'The Birlinn of Clanranald' that it 'preserves the movement, rhythm, resonance, colour and sensuous quality of the original wonderfully'.[29] Other attempts were less successful. However, this remains an important effort better to represent Scotland's literary heritage and to present an image of unity in diversity that MacDiarmid so relished.

MacDiarmid is disarmingly frank in his enthusiasm for language, not just as a tool for poetry-making but often as a major topic of the poems them-selves. While he frequently theorised his practice, it is clear that an abiding curiosity and interest in language was more vital and involving to him than any mere theory. It was as an enthusiast, then, rather than as a pedant, that MacDiarmid experimented with languages other than his own. James Murray observed that Burns commits a solecism in transforming 'the Scotch "Scots 'at hae" into Scots wha hae which no sober Scotchman in his senses ever naturally said',[30] and MacDiarmid, too, is open to such accusations. Ruth McQuillan points out that the herring fisher's cry, 'Come, shove in your heids and growl' ('Shetland Lyrics: With the Herring Fishers', CP1, p. 437), is a mishearing of the diphthong in Scots grow, 'increase'.[31] Kenneth Buthlay comments that MacDiarmid's consistent use of abies to mean 'except' is probably a result of confusion with beis, which does have that meaning.[32] David Purves notes accurately that 'Yin canna thow the cockles o' yin's hert' from A Drunk Man (CP1, p. 83, l. 14) is a back-translation from English, the historically accurate Scots impersonal pronoun being a bodie.[33] It is an accuracy that MacDiarmid may have attempted but that he, nonetheless, set little store by. His defence is modernist in the vein of Mallarmé. Writing of himself in 1924, under the pseudonym J. G. Outterstone Buglass, he says that MacDiarmid

> cares nothing for the opinions of the 'authorities' or of anyone who is more interested in the letter than in the spirit. Professor Craigie and others who are busy dictionary-making and the Vernacular Circle of the London Burns Club he defies with an arrogance which cries: 'A fig for your researches! If I write in a language I invent wholly myself and insist on calling it Scots in defiance of all precedents, nothing you can do can prevent my ultimate success – if I write well enough!'[34]

CHAPTER THREE

C. M. Grieve/Hugh MacDiarmid, Editor and Essayist

Alan Riach

Hugh MacDiarmid's achievement lies not only in the unique courage and generosity of his poetry, but in his immense delivery as an editor, anthologist, journalist and newspaper-man; in these latter capacities he often used his own name, C. M. Grieve. His work was threefold: as poet, journalist and editor. This chapter is concerned only with the last two of these.

As editor he was the creator of a number of periodical publications in which he could choose the contributors, disseminate the information he wanted people to know about, design the format and foster the circulation of little magazines; as editor of anthologies of poetry, he was in charge of making selections of contrasting material and promoting new work not only by publishing it but by placing it alongside more traditional material. This was characteristic of *Northern Numbers* (1920–2), the three anthologies of poetry he edited immediately after his demobilisation from the war, at a time when he was also writing his early poems in English, soon to be followed by his first lyrics in Scots. In these anthologies, he published work by established names such as John Buchan, Violet Jacob and Neil Munro alongside work by younger poets, such as Roderick Watson Kerr, who had just survived World War One. These younger poets were writing out of their experience of the unprecedented proximate horror, the physical carnality of violence of that war, and subsequently out of the industrial degradation of city-life they experienced on their return. Their new poetry sat beside the more traditional poems of an older generation. The message must have been as piercingly clear as it remains. The third of these anthologies was made up of poems by ten men and ten women. It was as if, in that time, the very early 1920s, the editor was already asserting the equal value and validity of the literary and poetic expression of the experience of women with that of men.

MacDiarmid began his post-World War One campaign to reinvigorate Scottish culture in the early 1920s through his journalism and provocative essays. He wrote for three main kinds of periodical, each one having a different purpose and impact. One kind is the journal brought into existence as a self-determined project with a limited, intense life-span: a short run. It is meant to make a big impact, to say something provocative, to engage with orthodoxy vigorously. The result hoped for is a changed scene. Little magazines were important conveyers of exciting new modernist developments in the literary arts. The most famous example is Wyndham Lewis's Vorticist magazine *Blast* which published only two numbers, in 1914 and 1915. Grieve's activities in the early to mid-1920s with *The Scottish Chapbook*, *The Scottish Nation* and *The Northern Review* were similarly intended to enter an established cultural dynamic and confront it with new priorities. These magazines published poems, fiction, short plays and essays, all of which were challenging aesthetic and political conventions. Their aims were explicitly to bring literary engagement to contemporary Scotland, encountering and anatomising cultural, social and political conditions. Where the priorities of Ezra Pound and Wyndham Lewis may be described as pre-eminently aesthetic, moving away from Victorian and Edwardian sensibilities – for example, in breaking regular metrical verse of the sort practised by Tennyson into a 'free verse' of narrative fragments – by contrast, MacDiarmid's agenda was centrally a combination of aesthetic, educational and political ideas, in the national context. In the literary and artistic world where Scotland was fictionalised as a pastoral haven to which exiles may look retrospectively, and a political subsidiary named North Britain, the new Scotland represented by new literature, art and politics, was imagined as a nation-state renewed and reimagined. The work of these periodicals was therefore to politicise Scotland's literature, languages and arts, a legacy that persists into the twenty-first century. The drive was continued from *The Scottish Chapbook* to the American James H. Whyte's *The Modern Scot* (founded in 1930), to which MacDiarmid contributed poems and articles. His final magazine, *The Voice of Scotland*, in its three incarnations at different times, attempted and achieved a longer continuity, but it also had this quality of aggressive intervention in cultural and political affairs.

Second is the journal with an anticipated long-term continuity. It, too, has a definite time-limit, but such magazines can have a healthy life-span, especially if their attention is responsible to the moment, when they evince a sensitivity to emerging writers, established writers, and the changing literary and cultural scene. The purpose of such journals is to represent those dynamics and to direct, nudge, prioritise, move the attention of their writers and readers to what the editor believes really matters. These journals overlap each other in their periods of production – monthly, weekly, quarterly – and gather a reputation for being of particular merit or attending to particular things. One might think here of the intention behind the first magazine devoted to the new technological phenomenon of radio, *Vox* (1929–30), ostensibly edited by Compton Mackenzie but which MacDiarmid worked on and for as a major contributor and acting editor until it folded, after a very short run, leaving him unemployed. Its successor eventually became the longer-lasting *Radio Times*, for which MacDiarmid was still writing in the 1970s.

The third category is that of established newspapers and periodicals: the national press, to which MacDiarmid throughout the 1920s and 1930s contributed syndicated articles on subjects of Scottish cultural interest of all kinds. Newspapers all over Scotland – from *The Dunfermline Press* (where in September 1922 his Scots lyric poems, 'The Water Gaw' and 'The Blaward and the Skelly', also first appeared) to the *Orkney Herald* and *Shetland News* – published his essays on Scottish literature, drama, music, history and other topics under his own name or a variety of pseudonyms. In Montrose, his centre-of-operations throughout the 1920s, he worked as a reporter for the local newspaper, the *Montrose Review*, a job he held down with one short break from 1920 to 1929. As well as the national press, there were long-lived journals with a specific readership. Of the publications Grieve himself was deeply involved with, the following are the key journals.[1]

The first, and most challenging, was *The Scottish Chapbook*. This was published monthly from 1922 to 1923 and announced its programme under the radical slogan of MacDiarmid's modern Scottish Renaissance, 'Not Traditions – Precedents!', which was emblazoned on the cover of earlier issues, beside a bold line drawing of a lion rampant. Only fourteen numbers of this magazine were issued but it was a major influence in Scotland's literary culture, principally through its editorials, the 'Causerie' (or 'Manifesto') essays that were a regular showcase for his arguments. The first issue in August 1922 announced the beginning of a Scottish literary revival, the aim of which was to change the direction of Scottish literary culture, as opposed to recycling familiar clichés about Scottish identity. The third issue of October 1922 introduced the new Scots-language poet 'Hugh M'Diarmid' whose poetry would refashion the Scots language as a modern – and modernist – literary language. Three further editorials from numbers seven, eight and nine, in 1923, comprised 'A Theory of Scots Letters', which argued out the potential literary and social capacities of the Scots language, asserting that this vernacular idiom contained qualities of understanding and expression as unique and various as those to be found in Dostoevsky, D. H. Lawrence or James Joyce. In its programme, the *Chapbook* put forward Scottish points of view in relation to national and international matters in literature and the arts. It was a vital catalyst in early twentieth-century cultural revival in Scotland: national *and* international, constructive *and* destructive. Such double principles informed the entire ethos of *The Scottish Chapbook* and kept it unpredictable and lively in the variety of its contents in different literary genres and in the range of subjects its editorials discussed.

The Scottish Chapbook, as Glen Murray points out in his introduction to the first volume of the *Raucle Tongue* collections of MacDiarmid's prose, was modelled on Edward Marsh's London-published *Chapbook* of 1919, just as *Northern Numbers* had been modelled on *New Numbers* and *Georgian Poets*, influential collections of their time.[2] These were the precedents MacDiarmid was using creatively, not constrained to emulate their conservatism in style or political thrust, but taking their example as modes of address to a literary readership who – in his view – required a big injection of political stimulation. He was profligate in the quantity of his production but strategically-minded in taking advantage of every possible publication outlet available. He would write for specialist journals, national newspapers, local weeklies, intellectual literary and cultural magazines, political periodicals: everything from the tabloid *Daily Record* to the *Cambridge Review*, from T. S. Eliot's *The Criterion* to *Marxism Today*. In the early 1920s, after the interest provoked by his own *Scottish Chapbook* and *Scottish Nation*, he was commissioned by the editor of *The Scottish Educational Journal* (a regular periodical for schoolteachers) to write a series of articles for the journal under the title of 'Contemporary Scottish Studies' (many of which were collected and published as a book in 1926). Here, his subjects ranged across all the arts and education in Scotland, covering literature in its major genres of poetry, fiction and plays, music, painting and sculpture, history and historiography. His witty and controversial attacks on successful writers such as J. M. Barrie (1860–1937) whom he considered 'acceptable only in increasingly homoeopathic doses' and novelist Neil Munro (1864–1930) whose 'popularity [. . .] is simply a commercial phenomenon' (CSS, pp. 15, 19) prompted fierce discussion in the correspondence pages and reputedly among the public.

In 1931 T. S. Eliot published MacDiarmid's important essay 'English Ascendancy in British Literature' in *The Criterion*. This essay took a broad survey of the dangerous ambiguity of the adjective in the phrase 'English Literature'. The core of its argument was that the legacy of political imperialism in the centralised authority of English literature and the English language was disempowering, neglecting and suppressing the value, validity and range of literary expression in other languages and forms within the archipelago of Britain. In contrast, MacDiarmid claims that, 'so far from manifesting any trend towards uniformity or standardization', national literatures around the world are 'evolving in the most disparate ways'. As such, he believes it to be 'a pity that English literature is maintaining a narrow ascendancy tradition instead of broad-basing itself on all the diverse cultural elements and the splendid variety of languages and dialects, in the British Isles' (SP, p. 67):

> Few literatures offer within themselves so rich a range of alternative values, of material for comparative criticism, as does, not English, but British, meaning by the latter that common culture – in *posse*, rather than *in esse* – which includes

not only English (and English dialect) literature, but the Gaelic and Scots Vernacular literatures as well. (*SP*, p. 69)

'English Ascendancy in British Literature' was an important development from the earlier 'A Theory of Scots Letters' of 1923, and a powerful indict-ment of cultural and political anglocentricism. This argument characteristi-cally conflated cultural and political authority and was effectively a defence of literary independence for Scots and Gaelic, and an endorsement of Scotland's multi-lingual literary tradition.

The argument was also continued in 1931 by *Living Scottish Poets*, a follow-up to the *Northern Numbers* anthologies, and a selection of MacDiarmid's contemporaries demonstrating an impressive diversity of style, form and subject, compacted into thirty pages. Lewis Spence's archaic ballad-like Scots in 'The Lost Lyon' rubbed shoulders with Rachel Annand Taylor's poised, eloquent, English-language dialogue 'The Princess of Scotland'; poems in rich Scots by Helen B. Cruickshank, Marion Angus, Pittendrigh Macgillivray and MacDiarmid are set beside English-language poems by Edwin Muir, Margot Robert Adamson and Alexander Gray's bleak but intensely patri-otic 'Scotland'.[3] MacDiarmid himself contributes 'The Irish in Scotland', addressed 'To a Visitor from France', claiming that the authors convention-ally associated with Scotland – Burns, Scott, Carlyle and Stevenson – should be seen in the context of Gaelic Scotland, whose strengths might be reju-venated by 'the branch of Ireland / Growing among us'.[4] By using Gaelic phrases in the poem, and by evoking the Gaelic people of the Highlands and Islands, he is insisting on the diversity of linguistic and social identity that makes Scotland a multi-faceted nation, and opposing the idea of cultural uniformity.

All the journals MacDiarmid brought into existence and edited himself could be seen as contributing to this argument, including the early *Scottish Nation*, which was issued weekly through thirty-four weeks in 1923 and had a tabloid newspaper format, as opposed to the more exclusively literary *Scottish Chapbook*, and *The Northern Review*, a monthly magazine more like the earlier *Scottish Chapbook*, which ran to only four issues in 1924. He also contributed to *The Pictish Review*, edited by the Hon. Ruaraidh Erskine of Mar (1869–1960), which called for a revival of Gaelic cultural identity. The one journal that was continually his principal model in terms of intellectual appetite and range was A. R. Orage's *The New Age* and its successor, *The New English Weekly*. MacDiarmid contributed regularly to *The New Age* through the 1920s. In its pages, writing under the names of Grieve and MacDiarmid, he was in the company of Ezra Pound, Katherine Mansfield, H. G. Wells, Edwin Muir, Bernard Shaw and the composer Kaikhosru Shapurji Sorabji (1892–1988). As with Edwin Muir, the radical Nietzschean ethos of the journal had been an informing influence on his thinking, bringing ideas from Freud and Nietzsche, while his introduction to Marx came from Keir Hardie before World War One, when he was working as a junior reporter during the miners' riots in South Wales.

In the late 1920s and 1930s, MacDiarmid's headquarters moved to London, then Liverpool, then Shetland, but his engaged arguments were maintained through the pages of *The Free Man*, later incorporated with *New Scotland (Alba Nuadh)*. Here he wrote on political issues (communism, fascism, Lenin, Hitler), recent and contemporary Scottish writers (John Davidson, Lewis Grassic Gibbon, William Soutar) and other significant modern writers (D. H. Lawrence, Sean O'Casey). (In 1942 *New Scotland* was to publish his 'Scottish Arts and Letters: The Present Position and Post-War Prospects', in which he claimed that the literary and cultural movement he had conceived during World War One was springing into lusty life during World War Two.) In the late 1920s and 1930s, however, he was also contributing to *The Scots Observer* ('A Weekly Review of Religion, Life and Letters') and *The Modern Scot*, a self-consciously intellectual, modernist, avant-garde quarterly. *The Modern Scot* published his 'Charles Doughty and the Need for Heroic Poetry' (1936), an article central in marking the shift in his aesthetic towards epic poetry, which brought together an appreciation of a neglected and fascinating Victorian English epic poet and the philosophical drive to go alone into a desert world, to find a new language for that experience, whether Doughty's ancient Britain or *Arabia Deserta* (1888), or MacDiarmid's North Sea Shetland archipelago. For all the Romanticism of this quest, in his essay MacDiarmid equates epic poetry with what he sees as the progressive new society being developed by Soviet communism: 'It is epic – and no lesser form – that equates with the classless society' (SP, 126). The work that he himself was engaged on at this time could be seen as heroic. The poetry collected in *Stony Limits* (1934), including arguably the central poem of his career, 'On a Raised Beach', foregrounds a solitary figure who nevertheless represents himself in an eternal confrontation with the elemental cosmos on behalf of all human beings. The vulnerable song of the bereaved mother in 'Empty Vessel', from *Penny Wheep* (1926), or the tears of the child in 'The Bonnie Broukit Bairn', from the 1925 collection *Sangschaw* – in fact, almost all MacDiarmid's early poems in Scots – indicate his faith in, and compassion for, the human centrality in the cosmic story. In the 1930s he carried this further literally, through his own isolation and then ultimately into a sense of connectedness with others, through an endless celebration of human languages and forms of cultural expression, in the epic poems *In Memoriam James Joyce* (1955) and *The Kind of Poetry I Want* (1961). These should be read as coming forward from the context of the 1930s, in which they were most extensively begun, and read also alongside both *The Islands of Scotland* (1939), which gives attention to the unexplored, loneliest places, and the marvellously expansive ruminations of the autobiography, *Lucky Poet* (1943). The essay on Doughty, and his contributions to periodicals throughout the 1930s, 1940s and 1950s, were the hinterland of arguments and ideas informing the major poems.

There was one magazine that MacDiarmid edited for an extended period of time: *The Voice of Scotland*, which appeared intermittently, in three periods, from 1938 to 1939, then after World War Two, from 1945 to 1949, and finally from 1955 to 1958. (Despite shifts in its editor's home-base, every single issue kept its blood-red title on the slate-grey cover.) MacDiarmid spent most of the 1930s in the Shetland archipelago with his second wife Valda and their young son Michael. On 25 October 1933, at Edinburgh University, a young man named Bill Aitken, who was studying English, edited and published an issue of *The Student* magazine (vol. 30, no. 2), commemorating the 350th anniversary of the institution, and he invited MacDiarmid to contribute to this issue. There were birthday salutations from eminent contemporaries in the journal's opening pages: J. M. Barrie, Ramsay MacDonald, John Buchan, Sybil Thorndike, Stanley Baldwin and Winston Churchill all appeared. But at the end of the magazine, MacDiarmid, writing under his family name of C. M. Grieve, threw 'A Stone among the Pigeons':

> Edinburgh University may be celebrating its 350th Anniversary; it is safe to predict that before it reaches its 400th it will have undergone radical changes representing a complete overthrow of all that my co-contributors are so satisfied about, and that its past history and the reputation of its 'distinguished sons' will be subjected to a correspondingly different estimate. [. . .] All our so-called 'progress' has landed Scotland in a mess, the excruciating horrors of which cannot be exaggerated, and any attempt to gloss over our predicament can only be due to wilful or constitutional blindness to all the facts.[5]

For daring to publish this Aitken was emphatically invited to surrender his editorship.[6] He did so proudly. Afterwards the friendship between MacDiarmid and W. R. Aitken was to be fastened and sustained through the rest of their lives. Aitken became MacDiarmid's chief bibliographer and the eident co-editor of his *Complete Poems* forty years later. But the early years of their acquaintance, from *The Student* episode on, led straight to the final magazine under his editorship, *The Voice of Scotland*. Upset at the way Aitken had been treated, MacDiarmid invited him to Shetland, and he visited the family there in the summer of 1937. He found their conditions grim. When, a year later, in 1938, MacDiarmid received an award of £125 from the Royal Literary Fund and his friend, the local doctor on Whalsay, David Orr, agreed to support the new venture of a periodical in which he could express himself freely, Aitken, now working as a professional librarian in Dunfermline, became the business manager, and the journal's first run was printed there. Thus personal circumstance, the bagatelle of contacts, and the disposition of good readers to support work of manifest quality, all helped bring into print a slim but serious journal that otherwise would not have existed.

'This is not a Communist periodical,' the magazine's first editorial began, 'although the editor is a member of the Communist Party. But it will be restricted to left-wing writers, and may be defined as left in tendency [. . .] our principal aim is advocacy of Independent Worker's Republicanism à la John Maclean!'[7]

First conceived of as *Scottish Republic*, the new journal ran through four issues in that first year, in the declared hope that it might, if not 'make a wide appeal', then at least 'influence the important propagandists'.[8] This was the force of its title. *The Voice of Scotland* was not intrinsically intended as a personal, lyrical, singular 'voice' but as a forum for poetry and radical opinion emerging from all parts and aspects of the nation, provided they supported in some fashion the editor's aspiration to socialist republicanism. Nor was it only a platform for polemic and satire; in Glen Murray's words, 'some of MacDiarmid's finest poetry of this period ("The Glen of Silence", "A Golden Wine in the Gaidhealtachd", "Dìreadh 1") [. . .] appeared in it, as well as seminal prose writing such as "The Red Scotland Thesis"', and important pieces reflecting on his relationship with the Communist Party of Great Britain and his disdain for 'The English Literary Left'.[9] Moreover, besides writing the editorial, 'Notes of the Quarter', and book reviews, MacDiarmid also encouraged a variety of authors to publish with him, including William Soutar, Sorley MacLean, Hamish Henderson and Dylan Thomas.

But polemic was irresistible. In the wake of Edwin Muir's *Scott and Scotland* (1936), which had so incensed MacDiarmid because Muir had stated that the only way Scottish literature could advance in the modern world was for it to be written exclusively in English, the second issue of the magazine printed a line-drawing caricature of Edwin and his novelist wife Willa by Barbara Niven, in which a vast female form in a bathing suit sits beside a little, tender-looking lamb. Intended to cause offence, it did exactly that, not only to the Muirs. If MacDiarmid won the argument, in the sense that it is now generally accepted that Scottish literature is rich in a variety of languages, pre-eminently Scots and Gaelic as well as English, then it might also be noted that Muir had a point too: the English-language modern and contemporary Irish authors, most famously Yeats, Joyce and Heaney, are widely read and taught in schools and universities throughout the English-speaking world, to a far greater extent than MacDiarmid or Lewis Grassic Gibbon (1901–35). *Scott and Scotland* had been part of a series of books published by Routledge in the mid-1930s, whose general editorship MacDiarmid had taken over from Grassic Gibbon after the latter's unexpected death.

In these books, leading Scottish writers addressed contentious subjects. Published volumes included Eric Linklater's *The Lion and the Unicorn* (1935); William Power's *Literature and Oatmeal* (1935); Willa Muir's *Mrs Grundy in Scotland* (1936), a proto-feminist reading of sexual suppression in Scotland; Compton Mackenzie's *Catholicism and Scotland* (1936); and most contentious of all, *Scott and Scotland*. As well as publishing the caricature in *The Voice of Scotland*, MacDiarmid responded by editing *The Golden Treasury of Scottish Poetry* (1940), including poems in Scots, English and translated from Gaelic, French and Latin, demonstrating conclusively the multi-lingual character of Scotland's literary tradition. He included nothing by Muir.

MacDiarmid's relationship with William Soutar (1898–1943) was more sustained: they were good friends and MacDiarmid respected and liked Soutar immensely, dedicating a fine long poem to him, 'Tam o' the Wilds and the Many-Faced Mystery', included in *Scottish Scene, or The Intelligent Man's Guide to Albyn* (1934), which MacDiarmid had co-authored with Grassic Gibbon. When MacDiarmid edited Soutar's *Collected Poems* (1948) he began his introduction by deferring to the future a definitive biographical and critical study of Soutar because there remained 'a great body of as-yet-unpublished poems'.[10] It has been suggested that MacDiarmid deliberately omitted some of Soutar's poems from this edition because they were so good that publishing them would have enhanced Soutar's reputation at the expense of MacDiarmid's. This seems extremely unlikely. MacDiarmid was keen to publish and broadcast his praise of work he thought highly of, and to claim it as part of the literary movement he had been leading. Moreover, when he criticised the work of others, he regularly did so openly and often violently. To suggest that he excluded some of Soutar's work as an underhand act of suppression is to misread MacDiarmid's character and to misinterpret the nature of his friendship with Soutar.[11]

The next run of thirteen issues of *The Voice of Scotland* was not printed until after World War Two, when MacDiarmid was living in Glasgow. These issues included comment on the cultural and political events of the time: Joan Littlewood's Theatre Workshop, a by-election, the pretentiousness of the Edinburgh Festival, the insufferable mediocrity of minor Scottish versifiers, the arrival of various international visitors to Scotland, including John Hewitt, the Ulster poet, Jan Kott, the Polish novelist and Shakespeare critic, and the Italians, novelist Alberto Moravia and poet Eugenio Montale, who (in 1948) was 'not unknown already to Scottish literati' through the writing of Hamish Henderson.[12]

The magazine was also publishing the new generation of Scottish poets, including Douglas Young (1913–73) and George Campbell Hay (1915–84), and MacDiarmid was still calling for an independent Scottish republic. He was planning to devote an issue to Irish writing when the second run ended and a six-year break began. MacDiarmid continued writing for a wide range of other periodicals and newspapers, most of all for *The National Weekly: A Weekly Review of National and Local Affairs*, a left-wing nationalist newspaper published every Saturday and the repository of most of MacDiarmid's journalism from 1948 to 1953. After its demise, he was involved with various other magazines, including a position as advisory editor of *Lines Review* (launched in 1952 in honour of his 60th birthday), until the third run of *The Voice of Scotland* began in 1955. Now published from Edinburgh by Malcolm Macdonald, there was less emphasis on Scottish republicanism and the declared purpose of the magazine was 'to contribute to the creation of an independent Scottish Literature'.[13] Thirteen issues appeared.

One of the central debates of this run concerned MacDiarmid's epic poem *In Memoriam James Joyce*. Writing under the alias 'Arthur Leslie', MacDiarmid published the essay 'Jerqueing Every Idioticon: Some Notes on MacDiarmid's Joyce Poem' in which he proposed the kind of questions that might be asked of his own potential readers:

1. Where are the following languages found – Vogule, Efik, Tagalog, Soghdian Xhosa, Kumyk, Avar, Lezghin, Lak, Dargan and Tabagaran?
2. What do you know of the following writers – Andra Lysohorsky, Gjerj Fishta, Avetik Isaakyan?

This sort of challenge was calculated to subvert Scottish parochial nationalism in favour of seeing the reinvented nation in a more bracing international context; indeed, 'Arthur Leslie' argues that with *In Memoriam James Joyce* MacDiarmid 'is constantly bringing his global poem back to Scottish instances'.[14]

In the next issue from April 1956 another essay on *In Memoriam James Joyce* appeared, by David Craig, an engaged but critical reading which compared MacDiarmid unfavourably with Shakespeare, Pope and Blake. MacDiarmid then published his own 'Reply to Criticism' (exercising his rights as the poem's author as well as the magazine's editor), pointing out that such comparisons are ineffective and inappropriate when more closely comparable poetry had been written by his contemporaries Ezra Pound (1885–1972) and David Jones (1895–1974). MacDiarmid attacks the 'too narrow conception of poetry' exemplified by Craig's critique, and reveals that a 'catalogue poem' such as *In Memoriam James Joyce* is 'a plea for a unification of knowledge, a general synthesis', in a period in which civilisation – defined as 'a high level of culture' – is fragmenting (*SP*, pp. 235–6, 237). This critical dialogue reveals much about what MacDiarmid thought he was doing with *In Memoriam James Joyce* and it demonstrates something of the kind of intellectually-engaged argument published in *The Voice of Scotland* and other little magazines of the period. The page proofs of the final, unprinted issue (vol. 9, no. 3) include a review of Kurt Wittig's *The Scottish Tradition in Literature* (1958), the first book of its kind in half a century, and one that exerted considerable influence in Scottish literary criticism. MacDiarmid commented: 'It is in keeping with what has long been the case in other departments of Scottish scholarship – and is still the case – that its author should be a foreigner,' and he hoped that Wittig had

> finally disposed of the old idea that Scottish Literature could be regarded as a tributary to the greater stream of English Literature. On the contrary, it is entirely separate and to treat it as a branch of English Literature – or to pose it against the background of English Literature – is to have a wrong impression of it altogether.[15]

An internationally-minded Scottish republic of letters was being established and this issue is also notable for collecting poems and translations by Edwin Morgan (1920– 2010), who, through the next half century, was to become Scotland's foremost 'man of letters' and one of the country's most distinguished literary critics.

Throughout the 1940s and 1950s MacDiarmid's output continued prodigious, in *Forward*, *The National Weekly*, *Scottish Journal* and *Scottish Art and Letters* (he was guest literary editor, alongside the art editor J. D. Fergusson, on issue 4). *Scottish Journal* and *Scottish Art and Letters* were productions of the Glasgow publisher William Maclellan (1919–96), who saw into print MacDiarmid's *In Memoriam James Joyce*, Sorley MacLean's *Dàin do Eimhir* (1943) and early work by W. S. Graham, among many other major poets of this period. Maclellan published the series of anthology-periodicals *Poetry Scotland* and MacDiarmid guest-edited issue 4 in 1949. *Scottish Journal* published MacDiarmid's 'The Key to World Literature' (1952), which illustrates the Scottish poet's outward-looking internationalism and, in some respects, arguably anticipates the Global English of the contemporary postcolonial era.

In the 1960s and 1970s, MacDiarmid published few sustained series of articles in the same periodical, but he maintained a vast production rate and essays were published in a wide range of places. His last regular columns were for the *Radio Times*, a series of 'Preview' mini-essays (1976–8) in which he discussed the television and radio programmes he intended to watch – or more often, to avoid – in the coming week, reaffirming his commitment to engage critically with popular media. However, in no sense had he lost his radical edge: as late as 1976, the *Guardian* published an article by MacDiarmid on Bertolt Brecht in which he confirmed his view of the lasting value of the Marxist poet and playwright.

If this is a clear indication of the internationalism of MacDiarmid's literary engagement, it is important to emphasise that it arises from the grounds of national identity that MacDiarmid had fought for and reclaimed. In an era when popular available editions of the greatest Scottish writers were almost non-existent, MacDiarmid did whatever he could to bring them into print, editing two selections of poems by William Dunbar (in 1952 and 1955) and three selections of Robert Burns (1926, 1949 and 1962). Like almost all of his younger contemporary poets after World War Two – pre-eminently Edwin Morgan, Alexander Scott, Sydney Goodsir Smith, Sorley MacLean and Iain Crichton Smith – MacDiarmid edited or translated the work of older Scottish poets for a modern readership, and felt a responsibility to reintroduce Scottish literature to contemporary readers in a way that most professional educationalists and cultural authorities had neglected to do or actively shunned.

MacDiarmid's 1973 selection of poems by Robert Henryson (c.1420–c.1490) opened with an introduction arguing that the then little-known Henryson had a significant claim to be Scotland's greatest poet, with a range and depth of human understanding beyond even that of his technically masterful contemporary, William Dunbar (c.1460–c.1520).[16] MacDiarmid's Henryson made the fifteenth-century poet's work available to a wide twentieth-century readership, a feat that was repeated and embellished by Seamus Heaney in his 2009 book of translations from Henryson, *The Testament of Cresseid and Seven Fables*, which published not only Heaney's English-language versions, but also the original Scots-language Henryson poems as well. The virtue of this was evidently to use Heaney's international fame to enhance Henryson's readership. Heaney has often acknowledged MacDiarmid's greatness and the magnitude of his achievement, writing eloquently and perceptively about him.[17] This was evidence of literary intervention using the commodity-fetishism of twenty-first century celebrity culture to promote the work of a major, relatively neglected figure, by virtue of the name of the Irish Nobel laureate.

Engaging the means at hand to further the cause for the good of others is an exemplary act. The work of Hugh MacDiarmid, as editor, for all that it involved at times the sharpest of cutting critiques, remains exemplary for exactly that same reason.

CHAPTER FOUR

Transcending the Thistle in *A Drunk Man* and *Cencrastus*

Margery Palmer McCulloch and Kirsten Matthews

In his discussion of Scottish criticism in *Scott and Scotland*, Edwin Muir (1887–1959) commented that admirers of MacDiarmid praised him 'chiefly for his first two books of lyrics, whereas easily his most original poetry is to be found in the long semi-philosophical poem, *A Drunk Man Looks at the Thistle* [. . .] The result is that a really original Scots poet like Hugh MacDiarmid has never received in Scotland any criticism of his more ambitious poems which can be of the slightest use to him.'[1] Muir wrote this in 1936, but the insecurity that can be brought about by the lack of perceptive critical response can be seen earlier in MacDiarmid's letter to George Ogilvie of 9 December 1926, written shortly after the publication of *A Drunk Man* and the 'sair reading' made by reviews of the work in the Scottish newspapers:

> Many thanks for your kind and reassuring letter. I always suffer from reaction after putting out a book: and am ridiculously sensitive to what reviewers say – even when I know their incompetence and malice. I say to myself: what *can* reviewers be expected to make of a thing like the *Drunk Man* – and yet I am horribly vexed when they make nothing of it or something utterly stupid. (*L*, p. 90)

MacDiarmid's previous letter of 6 August 1926 had stressed his ambitions for his new poem and the efforts he had put into it: 'I realise fully the importance of what you urge in regard to the *Drunk Man*. It will either make or finish me so far as Braid Scots work, & Messrs Blackwood's are concerned. I dare not let them down with a work of such magnitude.' And contrasting this new publication with his previous collections of lyrics, he commented:

> There are poems in the book (which is really one whole although many parts are detachable) of extraordinary power, I know – longer and far more powerful and unique in kind than anything in *Sangschaw* and *Penny Wheep*; but that's not what I'm after. It's the thing as a whole that I'm mainly concerned with, and if, as such, it does not take its place as a masterpiece – sui generis – one of the

biggest things in the range of Scottish Literature, I shall have failed. (L, pp. 88–9)

Present-day readers may well consider the above to be an acute assessment of the nature and achievement of A Drunk Man, continued in its author's additional comment in his post-publication letter to Ogilvie that he had 'set out to give Scotland a poem, perfectly modern in psychology, which could only be compared in the whole length of Scots literature with "Tam O' Shanter" and Dunbar's "Seven Deidly Sins". And I felt that I had done it by the time I finished – despite all the faults and flaws of my work' (L, p. 90). Yet his insecurity was such that in this same letter we find him already putting A Drunk Man behind him and advertising the greater potential to be found within a new project, another long poem to be titled To Circumjack Cencrastus:

> It will be a much bigger thing than the Drunk Man in every way. It is complementary to it really [. . .] But where the Drunk Man is in one sense a reaction from the 'Kailyaird', Cencrastus transcends that altogether – the Scotsman gets rid of the thistle, the 'bur o' the world' – and his spirit at last inherits its proper sphere.

In relation to A Drunk Man, therefore, Cencrastus will be 'positive where it is negative, optimistic where it is pessimistic, and constructive where it is destructive' (L, p. 91).

This chapter will explore the oppositions presented by these two major poems from the early period of MacDiarmid's writing career. In addition to his specifically Scottish references to 'a reaction from the "Kailyaird"', MacDiarmid's comment in his letter focuses on the thistle imagery of A Drunk Man as the 'bur o' the world'. This wider metaphorical (and metaphysical) interpretation of the thistle symbolism will therefore be prominent in the discussion of both poems: in A Drunk Man through an exploration of its pessimism which, as with T. S. Eliot's The Waste Land, is philosophically rooted in the lost certainties of the modern world; and in Cencrastus in its transformation into a search for transcendence through the new symbol of the Curly Snake.[2] The chapter will also assess the extent to which the proposed transcendent 'optimism' of Cencrastus eludes the frustrations of its author's sublunary Scottish context.

A Drunk Man Looks at the Thistle

A Drunk Man opens and closes with its themes strongly centred in a Scottish context, and this Scottish signifier in the thistle imagery weaves itself in and out of the wider discourse throughout the poem. On the other hand, the philosophical and psychological duality explored in the poem, its preoccupation with the nature of human consciousness, and the questioning of human purpose and place in a world where the advances of science (and no doubt the unprecedented catastrophe of the recent European war) appear to have banished the idea of God and of human beings made in His image from the modern world picture, are themes which go beyond any national dilemma. Together with its innovative form and language-use, these are the outstanding philosophical elements which give this poem its place as a major poem of the modernist period.

The poem's speaker, the eponymous Drunk Man, is aware from its outset that his philosophical mission – or his fate – is 'owre continents unkent / And wine-dark oceans [to] waunder like Ulysses' (*CP1*, p. 95, ll. 399–400), and he steps out of character briefly in the poem's initial stages to warn us that although he is beginning with 'what's still deemed Scots, and the folk expect', once he is sure of our attention, he will take us to 'heichts whereo' the fules ha'e never recked' (*CP1*, p. 83, ll. 22, 24). Given the modernist context of the poem, the Drunk Man's reference to Ulysses is most often taken to refer to Joyce, one of his author's linguistic heroes. However, the implications of his later philosophical journey suggest that the comparison might well be also with the nineteenth-century Tennyson's 'Ulysses', whose protagonist, like MacDiarmid's, pledged himself 'strong in will / To strive, to seek, to find and not to yield' – lines specifically quoted by MacDiarmid in *Lucky Poet*.[3] The Drunk Man is also 'strong in will' and he follows Schopenhauer and Nietzsche in his belief in the will as opposed to rationality. His credo is to 'aye be whaur / Extremes meet' (*CP1*, p. 87, ll. 141–2), and this too is the pattern of the ontological journey on which readers embark with him: a journey conducted through imagistic language and through a logic of the imagination as opposed to rational argument.

As discussed also in Roderick Watson's consideration of the poem, its thistle imagery is at the heart of this journey and has various possible interpretations depending on its context at any given time. Sometimes it stands for Scotland, with its spiky leaves and surprisingly beautiful soft purple flowers symbolising Scotland's lost or unrealised potential, its capacity for crucifying its own roses (as we see in the 'Ballad of the Crucified Rose' section); at others this specifically Scottish interpretation expands philosophically to the contrary nature and achievement of human life itself. Sometimes the thistle is a phallus, or the mythical tree Yggdrasil, or even just its everyday botanical self, a spiky growth on the hillside. However, after the specifically Scottish opening of the poem, an increasingly dominant theme and interpretation of the thistle symbolism concerns duality in human life. Duality has been a traditional preoccupation in Scottish writing from the medieval period to Burns and the fiction of Hogg and Stevenson, a moral preoccupation also closely linked to Calvinist religious teaching on the subject of good and evil. On the other hand, what we find in MacDiarmid – and potentially in Stevenson also – is modernity's preoccupation with duality in a psychological as opposed to a religious context, in a way related to a new realisation of the complexities of the human mind and behaviour as explored in the researches of Freud and Jung. Through his own researches, Stevenson's Dr Jekyll came to realise 'that man is not truly one, but truly two [. . .] I learned to recognize the thorough and primitive duality of man'.[4] In contrast to Jekyll's attempt to separate out his opposing identities, MacDiarmid's Drunk Man initially embraces this duality and adopts it as his credo in his intention to be 'whaur / Extremes meet', but his growing recognition of its implications for what it means to be human leads him also to despair.

It is not, however, the more traditional concern with morality, with the religious opposition of good and evil, that concerns the Drunk Man, but the opposition between human potentiality and the inability of individual humans to bring this into being. At a later stage of the poem, when he is struggling to come to some understanding of what human life might mean in a universe without a purpose, the Drunk Man self-mockingly comments that he is *'fu' o' a stickit God'* (*CP1*, p. 134, l. 1632): a description which could be applied equally to his author at this early stage of his writing career. Like many Scottish artists and intellectuals, MacDiarmid rejected the Calvinism that had characterised Scottish Protestantism since the Reformation, but he did not in his earlier years reject religion itself, becoming attracted to Catholicism and publishing 'Catholic Sonnets' in his *Scottish Chapbook* in the early 1920s.[5] Even in the 1930s, when 'faith' in a communist ideology had replaced any form of Christian belief, he could still use Christian imagery as metaphor, as, for example, in his *Hymns to Lenin* and his comparisons of Lenin to Christ.

One of the notable features of the *Drunk Man* poem itself is its direct use of imagery drawn from religious sources, with Burns brought together with Christ in its opening sections as examples of the way in which outstanding human achievement can be distorted and used by others for their own ends: 'an / Excuse for faitherin' Genius wi' *their* thochts' (*CP1*, p. 84, ll. 50–1). As the poem develops, this religious imagery is used in more controversial ways to explore the theme of human duality. Sexuality – a human attribute most often confined to the evil pole in traditional religious teaching, but which MacDiarmid, like Burns, would appear to have found an essential part of his artistic creativity – is brought together with the Christ story in the Drunk Man's exploration:

Said my body to my mind,
'I've been startled whiles to find,

When Jean has been in bed wi' me,
A kind o' Christianity!' (*CP1*, p. 101, ll. 571–4)

His speculations on how 'Man's spreit is wi' his ingangs twined / In ways that he can ne'er unwind' (*CP1*, p. 101, ll. 585–6) leads to the enigmatic ballad 'O wha's the bride that cairries the bunch / O' thistles blinterin' white?', with its implicit linking of sexuality and original sin brought up against the positives of a human relationship:

> *But I can gi'e ye kindness, lad,*
> *And a pair o' willin' hands,*
> *And you sall ha'e my breists like stars,*
> *My limbs like willow wands.* (*CP1*, pp. 102–3, ll. 612, 628–31)

This positive moment is short-lived, however, and his speculation then turns to the opposite pole: 'Millions o' wimmen bring forth in pain / Millions o' bairns that are no' worth ha'en', while the question: 'Wull ever a wumman be big again / Wi's muckle's a Christ?' continues the duality debate through a contrast between the idealised Christ-child story and mundane human reality:

> Mary lay in jizzen
> As it were claith o' gowd,
> But it's in orra duds
> Ilka ither bairntime's row'd.
>
> Christ had never toothick,
> Christ was never seeck,
> But Man's a fiky bairn
> Wi' bellythraw, ripples, and worm-i'-the-cheek!
>
> (*CP1*, pp. 103–4, ll. 636–9, 644–51)

Who is to be blamed for this situation – human beings who cannot develop the creative potential within them, or a God who has created them with a mortal flaw?

> Mebbe we're in a vicious circle cast,
> Mebbe there's limits we can ne'er get past,
> Mebbe we're sentrices that at the last
> Are flung aside, and no' the pillars and props
> O' Heaven foraye as in oor hopes. (*CP1*, p.116, ll. 1026–30)[6]

At one point in his journey the Drunk Man laments that his thoughts 'circle like hobby-horses' (*CP1*, p. 112, l. 897) and this questioning of duality, of human potential and a possible predestined limitation to human development, continues to circle unceasingly in various imagistic manifestations until in the especially despairing speculation that follows on from the failure in 'The Ballad of the Crucified Rose' (or 'Ballad of the General Strike') section, he finally bursts out:

Faither in Heaven, what gar'd ye tak'
A village slut to mither me,
Your mongrel o' the fire and clay?
The trollop and the Deity share
My writhen form as tho' I were
A picture o' the time they had
When Licht rejoiced to file itsel'
And Earth upshuddered like a star.

A drucken hizzie gane to bed
Wi' three-in-ane and ane-in-three. (CP1, p. 126, ll. 1363–72)

This is shocking imagery, but its very violence bursts out of the previous, continually circling self-debate about human potentiality and the inability to realise this; the awareness of a divided nature, and the inability to understand or come to terms with this; and especially, the inability to let go entirely of the traditional religious belief in a meaningful universe created by a God who had also created human beings in His own image, yet the contrary realisation that such a belief appears no longer tenable in the face of nineteenth-century evolutionary, geological and other scientific discoveries, and the intellectual and social realities of the modern world. Charles Darwin himself suffered just such a crisis with regard to his evolutionary discoveries, writing to Asa Gray in 1860 after the publication of *On the Origin of Species* in the previous year:

With respect to the theological view of the question. This is also painful to me. I am bewildered. I had no intention to write atheistically. But I own that I cannot see as plainly as others do, and as I should wish to do, evidence of design and beneficence on all sides of us. There seems to me too much misery in the world. I cannot persuade myself that a beneficent and omnipotent God would have designedly created the Ichneumonidæ with the express intention of their feeding within the living bodies of Caterpillars, or that a cat should play with mice. Not believing this, I see no necessity in the belief that the eye was expressly designed. On the other hand, I cannot anyhow be contented to view this wonderful universe, and especially the nature of man, and to conclude that everything is the result of brute force [. . .] I feel most deeply that the whole subject is too profound for the human intellect. A dog might as well speculate on the mind of Newton. Let each man hope and believe what he can.[7]

In a manner similar to Darwin's earlier struggle with the incompatibility between traditional Christian teaching and the evidence of his biological researches, what might be considered the Drunk Man's blasphemous outburst is a measure of the strength of his former belief as well as of his realisation of its irrelevance to his present search for understanding. It is also a marker of his creator's formal difference from a philosophical poet such as Eliot. While the discourse of *The Waste Land* is also based in the conditions of modern life and the loss of a traditional religious world view, Eliot's modernist method is impersonal, obliquely referential both in relation to a lost past and a distasteful present, yet consistent in the beauty of its formal organisation. MacDiarmid's poem, on the other hand, is expressionistic, alternating between despair and a kind of evolutionary optimism (similar to that of Shelley) which demands energetic searching; a wild satirical comedy and the contrary transcendent beauty of his several lyrical passages; and throughout the poem, the strong, personalised voice of his adopted persona, the Drunk Man, as opposed to the various voices of Eliot's unidentified or impersonal speakers.

After the 'Ballad of the Crucified Rose' passage, with its bleak illustration of the triumph of negative forces in human life (which occurs approximately at the mid-point of the poem), it is the meaning of human life per se rather than its duality that dominates the Drunk Man's ceaseless debate with himself. In some respects his questioning parallels that found in Tennyson's *In Memoriam*, written in memory of his drowned friend Arthur Hallam, and published in 1850 before the appearance of Darwin's *Origin of Species* in 1859 but at a time when contemporary biological and geological researches were already throwing doubt on traditional religious teaching about the universe. After its conventional elegiac opening, Tennyson's poem develops into an anguished reconsideration of religious belief in the immortality of the soul and the nature of the universe which has its similarities with Darwin's own struggle quoted previously. For Tennyson's speaker, God and Nature now seem 'at strife', with Nature no longer Wordsworth's caring foster-mother, but an indifferent natural force 'red in tooth and claw' and careless of both the 'single life' and the 'type': 'From scarped cliff and quarried stone / She cried: "A thousand types are gone: I care for nothing, all shall go!"' On the other hand, although the poem's speaker can now only 'falter where I firmly trod' and 'stretch lame hands of faith', Tennyson was ultimately able in his poem to work through to an acceptance that 'no man understands' and to hold to his emotional faith that there is a caring Power beyond him: 'the heart / stood up and answered: "I have felt."'[8] There is no such way out for the modernist MacDiarmid's Drunk Man, despite his giving a higher place in his search to imagination and the senses than to rationality. And as with his earlier struggle with human duality, it is less the religious loss of belief in God that overwhelms him than the futility of human life in a world without purpose, a life which is not part of a continuing human development:

> What use to let a sunrise fade
> To ha'e anither like't the morn,
> Or let a generation pass
> That ane nae better may succeed.
> Or wi' a' Time's machinery
> Keep naething new aneth the sun,
> Or change things oot o' kennin' that
> They may be a' the mair the same?

And as so often, he turns to a sexual image to carry the burden of a fruitless human existence:

> The wasted seam that dries like stairch
> And pooders aff, that micht ha' been
> A warld o' men and syne o' Gods. (*CP1*, p. 123, ll. 1236–43, 1260–2)

MacDiarmid was influenced by (and, like Edwin Muir, received much of his post-school education from) the ideas circulating in *The New Age* periodical, and especially the writings of its editor A. R. Orage (1873–1934), with whom he shared a belief (which never really left him) in the possibility of the expansion of human consciousness. The nature of human consciousness was a topic of much interest in the early years of the century in relation to the writings of psychologists and philosophers, and it is clear from a reading of Orage's *Consciousness* of 1907 that MacDiarmid was familiar with this work and that it fed into his Drunk Man's philosophical explorations.[9] For Orage, as for the Drunk Man, the human journey 'in search of ourselves [. . .] must be by a series of acts of the imagination. It is an imaginative quest'. His conception of the human mind is 'as a rotating and revolving sphere' (somewhat like the Drunk Man's thoughts 'circling like hobbyhorses') while he sees human thought as being subject 'to the tyranny of the pairs of opposites' in the mind, to the 'inherent duality of the human mind'. These ideas – and many more throughout Orage's book – have their place in MacDiarmid's long poem. Most relevant, however, to the Drunk Man's despair at his inability to bring the potential he feels within him to a lasting fruition, and his observation of similar inadequacies in his fellow humans, is Orage's idea (following Nietzsche) that human consciousness is a process of 'becoming' and that it may be possible 'for the human to transcend the human', and for 'man to become more than man'. Indeed, he finds that this 'consciousness of becoming is, in fact, the distinguishing mark of human consciousness'.[10] Yet Orage believes also that much contemporary speculation about what a 'superman consciousness' might mean is futile, since it seems based on a belief that this would 'merely differ in degree from the consciousness of man', that it would result in 'a sort of perfected man'. In contrast, Orage insists that it would be 'a different kind of consciousness', and therefore a change of being; and he refers to the mystics throughout the ages who pursue 'transcendental things [. . .] above and beyond human things'.[11] Such an idea of a 'superman' would appear to offer little comfort to the Drunk Man who is trying to bring to fruition within his human journey the intellectual and artistic potential he hopes for. Nor is there a place in it for the kind of social and environmental progress envisaged in his author's radical politics. As his thoughts continue to circle around the seeming inability of human life to reach its potential, the Drunk Man is struck also by the utter insignificance of that human life in the infinite space of the universe itself:

> For what's an atom o' a twig
> That tak's a billion to an inch
> To a' the routh o' shoots that mak'
> The bygrowth o' the Earth aboot
> The michty trunk o' Space that spreids
> Ramel o' licht that ha'e nae end,
> – The trunk wi' centuries for rings
> Comets for fruit, November shoo'ers
> For leafs that in its Autumns fa'
> – And Man at maist o' sic a twig
> Ane o' the coontless atoms is! (CP1, p. 130, ll. 1482–91)

In this passage, the philosophical and aesthetic effect is created not by expressionist imagery as so often in the poem, but by the enveloping rhythmic movement of lines that follow each other with hardly a pause for breath, and by imagistic spatial and time contrasts such as an 'atom o' a twig' and the 'michty trunk o' Space' with 'centuries for rings' and 'comets for fruit' which draw the reader or listener into an intuition of the immensity of the universe, defamiliarising it even while we recognise common elements of our known world such as trees and fruit and November showers. Then, after the pause before the penultimate line, we have that final couplet with its terse statement of the utter insignificance of human life in this immeasurable universe, a perception expressed in a relentless tetrameter metre with the iambic first line of the couplet followed by a contrasting dactylic / trochaic line: '– And Man at maist o' sic a twig / Ane o' the coontless atoms is!'

The 'Letter to Dostoevsky' section of MacDiarmid's poem grows out of this deepening crisis of understanding with regard to the nature and purpose of human life in a universe that itself appears beyond human understanding.[12]

As mentioned previously in Chapter 1, discussion of Dostoevsky and his writings was much in evidence in the second and third decades of the twentieth century as a result of Constance Garnett's translations of his work. Reviewing Garnett's translation of *The Eternal Husband* in the *Times Literary Supplement* of February 1917, Virginia Woolf described Dostoevsky as 'this great genius who is beginning to permeate our lives so curiously. His books [. . .] belong for good to the furniture of our minds'. Edwin Muir described him in *We Moderns* as 'a great psychologist' and one 'who depicted the subconscious as conscious'.[13] Very relevant in relation to MacDiarmid's references to him in *A Drunk Man* are the pages of *The New Age* in late 1925 and 1926, preceding the publication of MacDiarmid's poem in November 1926. These pages contain many references to and extracts from Dostoevsky's writings, together with discussions of Russian philosophy and literature. In the issue of 19 November 1925, for example, extract IV of a serialisation of Dostoevsky's 'Grand Inquisitor' chapter of *The Brothers Karamazov* sits side-by-side with a review by MacDiarmid of new verse, while on 17 and 25 December reviews of 'Foreign Literature', this time by C. M. Grieve, appear beside pre-publication excerpts from 'Mme Dostoevsky's Reminiscences' of her husband.

MacDiarmid found much common ground between Dostoevsky's ideas and his own, and the Russian is introduced in his poem as one of the Drunk Man's heroes. Both writers believed that the artist must suffer with the sufferings of his country and both believed in the bringing together of extremes in their work. It is relevant, therefore, that in the *Drunk Man* poem it is to Dostoevsky that its protagonist turns in his trouble and asks 'for a share o' your / Appallin' genius' (*CP1*, p. 138, ll. 1751–2) in order to transcend the philosophical problems that beset him, and also to help him give his country, Scotland, an identifiable place in world history, as Dostoevsky had previously done for Russia. The Scottish theme, which has never been entirely absent during the long philosophical discourse in the middle sections of the poem, therefore begins to become more prominent in the 'Letter to Dostoevsky' section, bringing with it a return of the thistle imagery whose earlier dual symbolism is used increasingly negatively in these later sections of the poem. This movement comes to a head in the 'Farewell to Dostoevsky' passages, when the attempt to draw strength from the connections with the Russian writer seems to have foundered, both in relation to the Drunk Man's attempt to transcend his own subjectivity – to 'be free / O' my eternal me' (*CP1*, p. 142, ll. 1897–8) – and his confidence that his country can give him what he needs to grow artistically. Imagistic language once again creates the atmosphere in this farewell passage, drawing not only on the natural world but also on Scotland's history through the references to ruined cottages and empty glens:

The wan leafs shak' atour us like the snaw.
Here is the cavaburd in which Earth's tint. [heavy snowfall; lost]
There's naebody but Oblivion and us,
Puir gangrel buddies, waunderin' hameless in't.

The stars are larochs o' auld cottages. [ruins]
And a' Time's glen is fu' o' blinnin' stew.
Nae freen'ly lozen skimmers: and the wund [window-pane]
Rises and separates even me and you. (CP1, p. 151, ll. 2220–4)

This is a space and time image of utter desolation and it is followed by stanzas
in which the thistle appears as all that is destructive in human life, a negative
inheritance that cannot be overcome:

The thistle rises and forever will,
Getherin' the generations under't.
This is the monument o' a' they were,
And a' they hoped and wondered.

The barren tree, dry leafs and cracklin' thorns,
This is the mind o' a' humanity
– The empty intellect that left to grow
'll let nocht ither be.

Lo! It has choked the sunlicht's gowden grain,
And strangled syne the white hairst o' the mune. (CP1, p. 152, ll. 2232–43)[14]

The Scottish theme of *A Drunk Man* ends in a semi-jocular manner with
its protagonist undecided about accepting his Scottish place on the Great
Wheel of Life, while his wider ontological search also ends inconclusively
in silence. The few instances of philosophical transcendence throughout his
search – communicated in passages of fine lyric poetry – have been swiftly followed by the realisation that 'Men canna look on nakit licht' (CP1, p. 143, l.
1932), an observation that anticipates Eliot's moment in the rose garden in
'Burnt Norton' and the Platonic realisation that 'human kind / Cannot bear
very much reality'.[15] As in his early lyric 'In the Hedge-Back' (CP1, p. 25),
the fleeting experiences of transcendence in MacDiarmid's poem have often
been achieved through the Drunk Man's sexual union with his wife, Jean,
and the creativity this inspires. And it is with Jean and a potentially creative
Silence – 'Yet ha'e I Silence left, the croon o' a' (CP1, p. 166, l. 2671) – that
his author leaves him at the end of this Scottish modernist long poem.

Art and Life in *To Circumjack Cencrastus*

In *To Circumjack Cencrastus*, as in *A Drunk Man*, MacDiarmid considers the
possibility of transcendent understanding or poetic vision. Unlike the Drunk

Man of the earlier poem, however, the poet in *Cencrastus* does not readily accept the worldly intrusions into his quest for transcendence. *A Drunk Man* might be considered a poem of epistemology – a work that explores the limitations of human understanding.[16] *To Circumjack Cencrastus*, on the other hand, becomes a poem of struggle as the poet voices his increasing frustration with the worldly impediments that prevent him attaining the ideal plane of transcendent vision to which he aspires.

Human understanding is presented in *A Drunk Man* as a paradoxical union of transcendence and earthly experience. Unfettered transcendent vision overwhelms the intellect; and if transcendence is an unattainable ideal, the response of the poet must be to take refuge in material existence, or to allow himself to be silenced by the impossibility of attaining perfect knowledge:

> Men canna look on nakit licht.
> It flings them back wi' darkened sicht,
> And een that canna look at it,
> Maun draw earth closer roond them yet
> Or, their sicht tint, find nocht insteed
> That answers to their waefu' need. (*CP1*, p. 143, ll. 1931–6)

A Drunk Man centres on this paradox; its central image is the thistle – the 'bur o' the world' which 'canna vanish quite' from the poet's understanding (*CP1*, p. 143, l. 1951). *To Circumjack Cencrastus* began as an attempt to refute the *Drunk Man*'s acceptance of such earthly limitations. In his 1926 letter to George Ogilvie (quoted at the beginning of this chapter), MacDiarmid states that *Cencrastus* will cast off the worldly concerns of *A Drunk Man*. 'It will not depend', he promises, 'on the contrasts of realism and metaphysics, bestiality and beauty, humour and madness – but move on a plane of pure beauty and pure music' (*L*, p. 91). When it was published in 1930, however, *To Circumjack Cencrastus* did not reach the arguably unattainable plane of transcendent vision to which MacDiarmid had initially aspired. Instead, *Cencrastus* retains the concern with the 'bur o' the world' that had characterised *A Drunk Man*.

The serpent Cencrastus embodies this tension. As a symbol, it represents both an unattainable, transcendent understanding that lies outside worldly experience, and an underlying, unifying identity that contains all elements of reality. The opening lines of *To Circumjack Cencrastus*, addressing the serpent, present us with a paradigm: a single creature whose 'movement' contains or subsumes every movement in the world:

> There is nae movement in the warld like yours.
> You are as different frae a'thing else
> As water frae a book, fear frae the stars [. . .] (*CP1*, p. 181)

The serpent Cencrastus gathers all the world's diversities into its motion, but is unlike any of them. If the poet in *To Circumjack Cencrastus* initially aspires to capture (or 'circumjack') the serpent in its capacity as unfettered, abstract understanding of the world, he is ultimately forced to have recourse to the second, worldly, significance of his symbol. *To Circumjack Cencrastus*, echoing the symbolic status of the eponymous snake as a binding-together of all worldly experience, becomes a repository for the variety of earthly existence, rather than a vehicle for transcendent thought. In other words, *Cencrastus* as a poem is ultimately defined not by the transcendence that MacDiarmid initially envisaged, but by the extensive use of allusion to numerous sources from the material world.

Cencrastus contains original poetry in a wide range of styles, not all of it written in the first instance as part of this project; it also includes translations, quotations and borrowings from many other texts. *A Drunk Man* may have been similarly allusive in form, but there the disparate materials were bound together by the continuity of the dramatic persona of the Drunk Man. In *Cencrastus* there is no dramatic unity. The presence of Cencrastus – the poem's central symbol – is elusive and inconsistent. In our search for a unifying principle behind *Cencrastus* we are therefore left with the poet himself. This means that, as well as anticipating in terms of form the collage-like structure of *In Memoriam James Joyce* (1955) and *The Kind of Poetry I Want* (1961), *To Circumjack Cencrastus* also looks forward to the autobiographical process of self-examination that came to fruition in the *Clann Albann* project (1931–3) and subsequently in *Lucky Poet* (1943).[17]

MacDiarmid may have written to Ogilvie of his plans for *Cencrastus* from Montrose in 1926, but *Cencrastus* was largely put together in 1930, after MacDiarmid's disastrous move to London to work on the magazine, *Vox. Vox*, an ambitious weekly journal dedicated to criticism of the emerging medium of radio broadcasting, under the general editorship of Compton Mackenzie, collapsed after just three months, leaving MacDiarmid in serious financial difficulties. The move to London had disrupted MacDiarmid's marriage, and the financial hardship worsened the situation. In Easter 1930, Peggy Grieve, frustrated by MacDiarmid's irritability as he engrossed himself in *Cencrastus*, wrote to Helen Cruickshank: 'I sometimes threaten to shut him in a padded room and then to stand screaming outside. Living with or being a friend of a poet is no joke!'[18] In May 1930 MacDiarmid found work in Liverpool, and the resulting separation from his family further added to the breakdown of relations between himself and Peggy.[19]

Against this background, *To Circumjack Cencrastus* was assembled, and the majority of the poem's recent critics have seen its structural inconsistencies as a reflection of the turmoil in the poet's personal and professional life at the time. Catherine Kerrigan, for example, writes: 'the failure of *Cencrastus* was in many ways symptomatic of the condition of MacDiarmid's life in the late twenties'.[20] Harvey Oxenhorn argues: 'A sharp decline in the quality of the writing suggests a poet who is merely going through the motions, who is "utterly exhausted".'[21] Margery Palmer McCulloch concludes her 1982 analysis of the poem with the observation: '*Cencrastus* exhibits MacDiarmid's precarious artistic situation at its rawest. Never again does his poetry bear such an obvious relationship to the problems which faced him in his struggle to continue to write.'[22] The structural weaknesses of *Cencrastus* as a poem, however, are more than a symptom of his personal distress at the time of writing. Increasingly as the poem progresses it becomes self-consciously autobiographical in its exploration of the way in which life intrudes on and dominates art.

It is ironic, but not inconsistent with MacDiarmid's later use of literary collage in his autobiography, *Lucky Poet*, that the most serious and sustained exploration of the conflict between art and life in *Cencrastus* comes not in MacDiarmid's own words, but in translation from *Requiem für eine Freundin*, by Rainer Maria Rilke (1875–1926). The use of English in this section, which stretches from line 540 to line 736 in *Cencrastus* (*CP1*, pp. 197–202) sets it apart from the main body of the poem, which is written in anglicised Scots. The blank verse of the translation looks back to the slightly irregular iambic pentameter of the opening stanzas; but it also highlights the tragic seriousness of the Rilke passage, in contrast to the flippancy of the sections that immediately precede and succeed it. Rilke's original described the death of an artist and friend of the poet, Paula Modersohn-Becker, in childbirth, and on this basis commented on the battle between art and life. The Rilke passage in *Cencrastus* is explicit in casting the artist as the subject of a tragic struggle with the intrusions and necessities of human existence:

> How short your life was, put against the hours
> You sat surrendering all you might have been
> To that blind germ of destiny again.
> O tragic task! O task beyond all power! (*CP1*, p. 201)

The exclamation of the final line here places the artist firmly within a context of tragic self-sacrifice that looks ahead to MacDiarmid's autobiographical preoccupation with the suffering and social exclusion of the poet in the *Clann Albann* poems. Nevertheless, the Rilke translation does not constitute, in literal terms, the voice of MacDiarmid himself. The translation from Rilke's German was made not by MacDiarmid but by J. S. Buist, one of the extended circle of literary acquaintances with whom MacDiarmid was associated in the early 1930s. After the publication of *Cencrastus*, Buist complained in a letter to John Tonge that very little had been altered in MacDiarmid's adaptation of his translation, which at least one review of *Cencrastus* had singled out for praise.[23] Without access to Buist's text, there is no way of measuring the truth of his complaint, but it alerts us to one of the central problems of *Cencrastus* and the autobiographical works that followed it – namely, that MacDiarmid requires us to accept the words and ideas of others as representative of his own poetic identity.

The tragic seriousness of the Rilke passage is counterbalanced, later in *Cencrastus*, by the farcical ironic humour with which MacDiarmid addresses the problem of art and life in 'Frae Anither Window in Thrums'. The title of this section alludes to the popular success of J. M. Barrie's 1889 novel *A Window in Thrums*, and invokes in more general terms the contrast between the commercially successful sentimentalism of the Kailyard and the Celtic Twilight, and the intellectual elitism and linguistic experimentation of MacDiarmid's poetry in the 1920s. If Jess, the protagonist of Barrie's novel, is confined to her house, viewing the world through the window of the title, MacDiarmid, in this section of *Cencrastus*, is confined and restricted, as a poet, by the economic and personal necessities of life. His response here, however, is not to lament in the fashion of the Rilke translation, but to mock the pettiness of the circumstances that frustrate him. He presents in exaggerated caricature the figure of a newspaper proprietor, with his capitalist delight in material comfort and status symbols and his anti-intellectual rejection of all but that which pays the bills and offers a step up the social ladder:

> Curse his new hoose, his business, his cigar,
> His wireless set, and motor car
> Alsatian, gauntlet gloves, plus fours and wife,
> – A'thing included in his life;
> And, abune a', his herty laughter,
> And – if he has yin – his hereafter. (*CP1*, p. 235)

Alan Bold identifies this figure as James Foreman, MacDiarmid's employer when he worked as a reporter for the *Montrose Review* in the 1920s.[24] In autobiographical terms, it is possible to detect personal resentment here; but the caricature depersonalises the attack and allows the poet to make a mockery of the capitalist anti-intellectualism his former employer is made to embody. The humour of the attack is also its sharpest weapon; the 'herty laughter' of the proprietor inspires all the more contempt because we are already laughing at him. The rhyme of 'laughter' and 'hereafter' trivialises the possibility of the employer's redemption, and emphasises his disregard for the immaterial or transcendent.

MacDiarmid mocks the triviality of the accoutrements – house, business, cigar, radio and car – which, for the man who forms the object of his satire, represent success. In so doing he laughs not only at his boss but also at himself, being, as he is, unable to escape the economic need to support a wife and family and the social requirement to concern himself with exactly those material conveniences that he finds so risible. This self-mockery continues subsequently in 'Hokum' (CP1, pp. 252–4), a comic sequence that concludes 'Frae Anither Window in Thrums'. Here, the autobiographical references are still more explicit; MacDiarmid imagines a plaque in recognition of his achievements in Langholm Academy, where he attended school:

> Losh! They'd ha' put me a brass plate up
> In Langholm Academy,
> And asked me to tak' the chair
> At mony a London Scots spree. (CP1, p. 253)

The reference to Langholm here anticipates the preoccupation with the town of MacDiarmid's childhood that was to dominate his autobiographical writing in the Clann Albann poems of 1931–2. As in the caricature of the employer, however, there is more at play here than personal bitterness or regret. The use of the exclamation, 'Losh!', parodies precisely the language of sanitised sentimentalism and bowdlerised national stereotype that MacDiarmid rejects. Similarly, the line 'I can poke 'em and shock 'em and mock 'em' (CP1, p. 252), at the beginning of the Hokum sequence, presents an anapaestic flippancy and comically excessive assonance that apes the capering lyrics of the Scottish music-hall comedy of Sir Harry Lauder (1870–1950), whom MacDiarmid attacks as another purveyor of saccharine cultural cliché. Despite the autobiographical, self-referential content of these passages, MacDiarmid's use of humour is effective in broadening his concern from personal recrimination to a wider reflection of the conflict between art and life because it invites his audience to participate in his argument. If we share his laughter, we come closer to sharing his frustration.

The irony and bathos of these passages underlines the intrusion of the economic and commercial realities of the material world upon the artistic aspiration to transcendent vision. In contrast, MacDiarmid's response in Cencrastus to Aodhagán Ó Rathaille's 'aisling' (dream vision) lyric, 'The Brightness of Brightness' ('Gile na Gile'), foregrounds in more optimistic fashion the poet's quest for transcendent understanding.[25] MacDiarmid provides a footnote to this section of Cencrastus in which – repeating word-for-word the commentary of Aodh de Blácam in Gaelic Literature Surveyed, which was a major source for MacDiarmid's Gaelic references – he informs the reader that the poet in 'The Brightness of Brightness' 'sees, in the image of an Irish maiden, that idea of which Plato dreamed' (*CP1*, p. 294).[26] The image of female beauty represents both a national and a platonic ideal. As a female muse figure, the 'Brightness of Brightness' in *Cencrastus* is suggestive both of the poet's aspiration to transcendent vision and of his preoccupation with Gaelic identity as a cultural ideal, opposing and counterbalancing the Russian cultural ideal voiced by Dostoevsky and embraced by MacDiarmid in *A Drunk Man*.

The opposing and complementary concepts of the 'Russian Idea' and the 'Gaelic Idea' were explained by MacDiarmid, shortly after the publication of *Cencrastus*, in an essay entitled 'The Caledonian Antisyzygy and the Gaelic Idea', published across two issues of *The Modern Scot*.[27] Dostoevsky's 'Russian Idea', 'in which he pictured Russia as the sick man possessed of devils but who would yet "sit at the feet of Jesus"', is extolled by MacDiarmid as 'a great creative idea – a dynamic myth – and in no way devalued by the difference of the actual happenings in Russia from any Dostoevsky dreamed or desired'.[28] Similarly, the Gaelic Idea is a cultural and creative ideal – an 'intellectual conception' in which free reign is given to a 'national genius which is capable of countless manifestations at absolute variance with each other, yet confined within the limited infinity of the adjective "Scottish"'.[29] MacDiarmid's concept of the Gaelic Idea builds on the image of infinite variety that he established in the symbolism of the serpent Cencrastus. The 'Brightness of Brightness', like the serpent, offers a duality between transcendent escape from worldly hindrance and the infinite multiplicity of life as the object of an alternative, earthbound form of poetic vision.

As a cultural ideal the 'Brightness of Brightness' embodies a concept of racial heritage, bound together and remembered in '*the hair that's plaited / Like the generations o' men*'. At the same time, she is a remote, intangible figure, and her '*noonday face*', like the 'nakit licht' of *A Drunk Man*, seems dangerous and unattainable to a poet who '*daurna look*' (*CP1*, p. 224). And yet, despite the ghostly aloofness of the 'Brightness of Brightness' as the '*Eidolon*' or phantom of the '*fallen race*', this lyric in *Cencrastus* concludes with an image of transcendence in sexuality that links back strongly to *A Drunk Man* and the inspiration of artistic creativity in the Drunk Man's sexual union with his wife:

> *And yet as tho' she didna see*
> *The hopeless boor I was*
> *She's taen me to her white breists there,*
> *Her bricht hair owre us fa's.*
> *She canna blame me gin I fail*
> *To speir my fortune's cause.* (*CP1*, p. 224)

There is an echo here of the '*breists like stars*' in *A Drunk Man* and, as in that poem, the image of the female form implies both a comforting sexuality that ignores the faults and boorishness of the lover and an idealised, transcendent encounter with female beauty. This passage in *Cencrastus* returns us to the Drunk Man's acceptance of the necessary influence of the 'bur o' the world' within poetic vision, but does so within a new context of idealised multiplicity and variety.

When MacDiarmid inserts his early poem 'A Moment in Eternity' into the concluding pages of *Cencrastus*, he places an image of youthful optimism in the midst of the language of frustration and struggle that largely dominates the poem. If both *A Drunk Man* and *Cencrastus* are concerned predominantly with the restrictive intrusion of the world on poetic vision, 'A Moment in Eternity' presents an image of the natural world as a vehicle for transcendent communion with God and the eternal. The poet envisages himself as '*a multitude of leaves*':

> Burgeoning in buds of brightness
> – Freeing like golden breaths
> Upon the cordial air
> A thousand new delights,
> – Translucent leaves
> Green with the goodness of Eternity,
> Golden in the Heavenly light
> – The golden breaths
> Of my eternal life. (CP1, pp. 276–7)

The brightness of the image, and the sensuality of '*golden breaths*', is suggestive in the context of *Cencrastus* of the transcendent image of the 'Brightness of Brightness' as a paragon of natural female beauty. The '*multitude of leaves*' similarly attains a renewed significance when 'A Moment in Eternity' is recast in *Cencrastus*, invoking as it does the multiplicity of worldly knowledge and experience embodied by the eponymous serpent and adopted by MacDiarmid as an alternative form of poetic vision. 'A Moment in Eternity', however, unlike the *Cencrastus* poem itself, depicts a poet in complete unity with the transcendent ideal to which he aspires.

Within the structure of *Cencrastus* 'A Moment in Eternity' functions on several levels. Thematically it connects with images of transcendence and of multiplicity elsewhere in the poem; in autobiographical terms, it takes us back to the youthful optimism of a poet now dogged by the difficulty of the task he has set himself. It does, nevertheless, offer a marked contrast with the main body of the work in *Cencrastus* and, like the Rilke translation, frustrates any desire on the part of the reader to perceive a coherent structural progression in the poem's argument or a unity of self in the poem's autobiographical content.

The depiction of a translucent, transcendent natural world in 'A Moment in Eternity' is also suggestive of the significance of landscape and nature elsewhere in *Cencrastus* as a restorative resource for the poet's reassertion of his struggle. 'Despair seems to touch bottom time and again', the poet tells us in 'North of the Tweed', the eleventh fragment in a sequence of twenty, included shortly before 'A Moment in Eternity':

> But aye Earth opens and reveals fresh depths.
> The pale-wa'd warld is fu' o' licht and life
> Like a glass in which water faintly stirs. (CP1, pp. 269–70)

The reference here to the 'faintly stirring' water recalls the movement of the serpent Cencrastus, and relates to the image, at the beginning of the poem, of Cencrastus as a fish in a pool, hidden under the 'roarin' cataracts o' Life' (CP1, p. 181). The 'licht and life' of the world is suggestive not only of the light and beauty of the 'Brightness of Brightness' but also of the imagery of light and water in the final lyric of *Cencrastus*, 'My *love is to the light of lights*' (CP1, p. 291). Throughout *Cencrastus*, the poet's reference to transcendence in terms of natural images of power and beauty – sun, light, water – invokes an undercurrent of resurgent belief in the possibility of transcendent vision that defuses the frustration and disaffection which characterises much of the poem.

Taken as a whole, *Cencrastus* proffers a duality which corresponds to that of the serpent in the opening stanza. The poem documents the worldly frustration of the poet's aspiration to transcendent vision, but it also presents recurring reminders of the possibility for redemption and recovery that the poet perceives in nature. This anticipates MacDiarmid's return to the landscape and memories of Langholm in the *Clann Albann* poems, and also looks further ahead, to the bleak communion of *Stony Limits* (1934). Following on from the Drunk Man's metaphysical consideration of the limitations of human knowledge, *Cencrastus* struggles with and problematises both the inherent limitations of the poet's vision and the intrusion of external pressures on his writing. The resulting documentation of the struggle between life and art inaugurated an explicitly autobiographical examination of the nature of poetic inspiration and self-sacrifice that was to play a central role in much of MacDiarmid's writing in the 1930s. The multitudinous and varied poetic vision that is embodied by Cencrastus as the movement running through all things represents an ideological shift in MacDiarmid's initial preoccupation with unencumbered transcendence. In this, too, *Cencrastus* looks forward to the collage-structure of *In Memoriam James Joyce* and of MacDiarmid's autobiography, *Lucky Poet*. *To Circumjack Cencrastus* is a problematic text in itself; but it is pivotal in MacDiarmid's oeuvre, both as a development of the metaphysical enquiry of *A Drunk Man*, and as an important stage in the transition to the poetics of autobiography and collage that MacDiarmid was soon to embrace.

CHAPTER FIVE

MacDiarmid, Communism and the Poetry of Commitment

Scott Lyall

The 1930s was a turbulent decade for MacDiarmid. The break-up of his first marriage led to a period of personal instability culminating in his total physical and mental collapse in 1935. His move to the Shetland island of Whalsay two years previously had done nothing to reverse MacDiarmid's growing isolation from mainstream Scottish life. Shortly after his arrival in Whalsay, MacDiarmid wrote to Neil M. Gunn (1891–1973), 'I am rowing about on lonely waters; lying brooding in uninhabited islands; seeing no newspapers and in other ways cutting myself completely away from civilised life.' MacDiarmid was disaffected on the British mainland; in spite of his efforts in Montrose during the 1920s for a Scottish Renaissance, he failed to change Scotland in his own image. In Shetland he is, he tells Gunn, 'gradually finding myself – a new self'.[1]

MacDiarmid's new incarnation was born of necessity. The stripped-to-first-principles philosophy of 'On a Raised Beach' (1934) is his response to personal crisis and Shetland. In this poem he carves out a secular landscape of the spirit, a bleak desert world where 'Great work cannot be combined with surrender to the crowd' (*CP1*, p. 429). Yet for all MacDiarmid's self-willed loneliness in the 1930s his poetry displays a characteristically absolutist commitment to engage politically with the era. MacDiarmid's extremism would see him thrown out of the National Party of Scotland – 'a troupe of gibbering lunatics' – only to join the Communist Party a year later in 1934.[2] This change in his party political affiliations in some measure reflects the developing shift in the language register of his poetry, from Scots through Scots-English to English, and the formal move from lyric poetry to epic. MacDiarmid wrote poetry committed to various ideals that can be broadly characterised as political, predominantly the nationalist revitalisation of Scotland. The 'poetry of commitment' examined and contextualised in this chapter is MacDiarmid's communist poetry, written mainly in the 1930s. However, the poetry MacDiarmid wrote in support of an international revolutionary ideal, uncompromisingly opposed to the poetry of his English and metropolitan contemporaries as it was, remained true to the declarative voice of a Scottish poetic tradition.

MacDiarmid was writing politically socialist verse before the 1930s. The 'Ballad of the Crucified Rose' section (ll. 1119–218) of *A Drunk Man Looks at the Thistle* implicitly laments the failure of the 1926 General Strike. The thistle may be Scotland's national icon yet the thistle of the ballad symbolises the failure of British labour hopes. 'The Dead Liebknecht' from *Penny Wheep* memorialises the German communist Karl Liebknecht (b. 1871), killed with Rosa Luxemburg for his leading role in the 1919 Sparticist Rising:

> His corpse owre a' the city lies
> In ilka square and ilka street
> His spilt bluid floods the vera skies
> And nae hoose but is darkened wi't. (*CP1*, p. 57)

Writing of this poem, published in 1926 when Grieve was based in Montrose, the Marxist critic David Craig states, 'MacDiarmid had nothing to do with revolutionary socialism in those days.'[3] In fact, C. M. Grieve had lectured on Vladimir Lenin (1870–1924) to the Montrose branch of the Independent Labour Party in 1920, only a year after Liebknecht was murdered.[4] Stirred by the 1917 Bolshevik Revolution, the future hymnist of Lenin was already finding sustenance in communism for his poetry and propaganda at least a decade before socially committed poetry became modish in the 1930s.

Poetry and politics collided in the 1930s. Poets responded to the Great Depression, mass unemployment, the 1936 Jarrow March and the fascist threat in Spain and Germany with a new kind of politically committed verse. Stephen Spender (1909–95) sums this up: 'The thirties was the decade in which young writers became involved in politics. The politics of this genera-tion were almost exclusively of the Left.' For Spender, the real roots of social-ism in the 1930s lay in the slaughter of World War One – 1930s poetry 'might be described as a variety of war poetry' – as well as in reaction to the elitism of modernism.[5] Modernist poetry could be difficult and elusive, anti-democratic in both its attitudes to contemporary culture and allusions to the ancient classics of high culture. Poets of the 1930s frequently used language that was plain and immediate, engaged with everyday reality rather than with the myth systems of modernism. W. H. Auden (1907–73) led the way, according to Samuel Hynes, in 'urging a kind of writing that would be affective, imme-diate, and concerned with ideas, moral not aesthetic in its central intention'.[6]

MacDiarmid's socialist poems occupy a marginal zone in accounts of poetry written in the British Isles. Anthologies are particularly significant indicators of prevailing cultural politics. A recent anthology of Scottish poetry fails to include any of MacDiarmid's Marxist poetry.[7] Equally, Robin Skelton's *Poetry of the Thirties*, first published in 1964, does not anthologise MacDiarmid's poetry at all, concentrating as it does on the work of poets born between

1904 and 1916 who, for Skelton, form 'some kind of coherent "poetic genera-tion"'.[8] In Scotland MacDiarmid has been seen mainly as the resuscitator of Scots, central to a Scottish canon and, as such, much of his post-1920s work in Scots-English and English gains less attention. In England, where his Scots work is still mostly ignored, even MacDiarmid's socialist poetry of the 1930s largely eludes critical discussion; in part, this is perhaps because he was peripheral to Skelton's 'poetic generation', led notably by Auden, Spender, Louis MacNeice (1907–63) and Cecil Day Lewis (1904–72) – characterised by the South African poet Roy Campbell (1901–57) as 'MacSpaunday'.

Such critical lacunae are revealing distortions in the narrative of twentieth-century Britain's literary history. Yet for Day Lewis, an Irish poet central to the poetry of the 1930s, MacDiarmid played a seminal role in the period. While for Day Lewis *A Drunk Man* and *To Circumjack Cencrastus* are 'admirable stuff', they remain neglected in England due to their Scots locution. However, MacDiarmid's 'First Hymn to Lenin' 'was followed by a rush of poetry sympathetic to Communism or influenced by it'. 'First Hymn', which was commissioned for Lascelles Abercrombie's (1881–1938) *New English Poems* (1930), is actually written in similarly Scots-inflected English as that of *A Drunk Man* and *Cencrastus*. Day Lewis identifies in those long poems 'a bluntness, a harshness, and a mixture of metaphysical ecstasy and mundane uncouth wildness, which are peculiarly national'.[9] Leaving aside stereotypes of the barbarian Celt, Day Lewis' terms surely also apply to 'First Hymn'. The combination of ideological passion and stanzaic rigour make it one of MacDiarmid's most aesthetically realised socialist works.

> For now in the flower and iron of the truth
> To you we turn; and turn in vain nae mair,
> Ilka fool has folly eneuch for sadness
> But at last we are wise and wi' laughter tear
> The veil of being, and are face to face
>   Wi' the human race. (*CP1*, p. 298)

Much of *First Hymn to Lenin* aims rebellious barbs at Grieve's Langholm birthplace, targeting family and church in particular. The collection's title poem, with its idolisation of Lenin as one of history's 'great men', strikes a powerful, yet discordant opening note, and demonstrates the intracta-ble and elitist nature of MacDiarmid's communism. 'First Hymn' reveals that the 'secret' of Lenin's authority is to be found in the revolutionary's (Nietzschean) will-to-power rather than in adherence to 'the majority will' (*CP1*, p. 298). The poet sounded this anti-democratic tenor in much of his work, while also proposing that the formal practice of his politically socialist verse accessed a democratic tradition in Scots poetry. In spite of Day Lewis' recognition of the importance of 'First Hymn', MacDiarmid believed that his poetry went unacknowledged by the Leftist metropolitan poets of the 1930s, and that the supposed inaccessibility of Scots was merely a pretext for the 'continuance even in these avowedly-Communistic circles of the English Ascendancy attitude and hatred of Scotland' (*LP*, p. 170).

Many of the poets of the 1930s, as Spender in retrospect admitted, 'were ill-equipped to address a working-class audience, and were not serious in their efforts to do so'.[10] MacDiarmid, of a rural working-class background, was scathing of the left-wing credentials of fee-paying-educated poets such as Auden, MacNeice and Spender. In *The Voice of Scotland* from 1939, for instance, he claims of the 'English Literary Left' that it 'is not truly Left at all but a literary racket dependent [. . .] on the "old school tie" business' (*RT3*, p. 31). Referring to Auden, Spender and Michael Roberts (1902–48), poet and editor of the influential anthologies *New Signatures* (1932) and *New Country* (1933), in 'Third Hymn to Lenin' (a Shetland composition not published in full till 1955) MacDiarmid emphasises: 'Unlike the pseudos I am *of* – not *for* – the working class' (*CP2*, p. 900). Yet MacDiarmid remained at core a modernist elitist, for all his repeated boasts throughout the 1930s of his knowledge of Marxism and his organic association with the workers, and he was well aware that his own poetry struggled to connect with the people; indeed, the speaker of 'Second Hymn to Lenin' doubts that poetry has ever truly been a popular form.

> *Are my poems spoken in the factories and fields,*
>   *In the streets o' the toon?*
> *Gin they're no', then I'm failin' to dae*
>   *What I ocht to ha' dune.*
>
> *Gin I canna win through to the man in the street,*
>   *The wife by the hearth,*
> *A' the cleverness on earth 'll no' mak' up*
>   *For the damnable dearth.*
>
> *'Haud on, haud on; what poet's dune that?*
>   *Is Shakespeare read,*
> *Or Dante or Milton or Goethe or Burns?'*
>   *– You heard what I said.* (CP1, p. 323)

MacDiarmid here raises the question, prevalent to the period, of an audience for poetry. Even the high priest of modernism, the decidedly anti-communist T. S. Eliot (1888–1965), grappled with this problem in *The Use of Poetry*, published in 1933 as the social role of literature was coming under closer scrutiny; Eliot had, the previous year, published 'Second Hymn' in *The Criterion*. The poet of 'Second Hymn' wants to speak directly to the workers, but questions poetry's ability to achieve this aim. If the poem is principally an address to Lenin, then through the interjection of italicised passages we also overhear the poet in dialogue with himself. MacDiarmid's adoption of a direct, colloquial style illustrates his aspiration, thwarted perhaps, to communicate more widely with a working-class readership.

In 'Robert Fergusson: Direct Poetry and the Scottish Genius' MacDiarmid says that W. B. Yeats (1865–1939) admired the line *'You heard what I said'* from 'Second Hymn' for the power of its directness. MacDiarmid argues that there is a Scottish poetic tradition of 'direct poetry', 'completely removed from the whole modern English conception of the "poetic"', which can be traced in Scots Gaelic poetry, and which is also to be found in Scots language poets such as Fergusson (1750–74) and Robert Burns (1759–96) – a line of development that MacDiarmid is carrying forward in his own work. For MacDiarmid the 'direct method' is essentially Scottish, even when employed in a line of English verse such as *'You heard what I said'*. He parallels the popular appeal of 'direct poetry' in Scotland with the 'whole national Republican and Radical tradition' that he believed constituted the authentic democratic ethos of the Scottish people, before addressing criticism of political poetry:

> The best corrective to the all-too-common disparagement of political poems is to reconsider first how large a proportion of the best poems in Scots (as in Gaelic) have always been political; and, finally, to reflect on the fact that it has always been substantially the same kind of politics, rebelling against established institutions and received ideas of all kinds and advocating and ingeminating revolutionary measures.[11]

It seems pertinent to interpret this 1952 essay as MacDiarmid's retrospective bid to situate his political poems of the 1930s in their rightful (and for MacDiarmid, distinct) *national* tradition, thus neutering their perceived failure to impact on the English verse of the day. What MacDiarmid does not address in his 'direct poetry' essay that yet seems relevant to his argument, and to his political poetry more generally, is class. Arguably, there are more major writers from a working-class background in the Scottish than in the English tradition. As Hynes notes, 'English literature has been middle-class as long as there has been an English middle class, and the generation of the 'thirties was not different in this respect from its predecessors.'[12] Whereas, as we have seen, the Auden group consisted mainly of the privately schooled and Oxbridge educated, the two most significant poets of the period in Scotland, MacDiarmid and Edwin Muir (1887–1959), went to work early after leaving their local schools, and remained autodidacts who never attended university. The lower-class provenance of many Scottish writers has implications for the national literary tradition in terms of the conceptual and formal frameworks inhabited by their work. What MacDiarmid identifies as the particularly Scottish trait of direct utterance in the poetry of Burns and himself, and even in the work of the university-trained Fergusson, is due as much to their origins in and familiarity with a class that does not fit comfortably into a more genteel English literary tradition. He claims in his introduction to *The Golden Treasury of Scottish Poetry* (1940) that 'poetry in Scots has still an access, not only to a cultured section but to the working classes, in Scotland, that no English poetry has ever had or, to all appearances, can ever have.'[13]

Developing MacDiarmid's argument, one could contend that encoded in English Literature, a discipline that Scottish Literature has found itself subsumed by and satellite to, is a set of class assumptions at odds with the class background and political positions of numerous canonical Scottish writers. The rules of poetry are governed by these class assumptions. The direct utterance technique of MacDiarmid's political poetry, a form that he champions as integral to a Scottish tradition, seeks to break that class code. This might be one explanation for the critical tendency to view MacDiarmid's poetry from the 1930s onwards as a formal failure, or at the very least, to be baffled by the poet's abandonment of the lyric for what G. S. Fraser calls the 'discourse *in poetry*' of his later work, poetry that is 'struggling beyond the limits of art'.[14] Kenneth Buthlay goes further, speculating that much of MacDiarmid's political poetry is 'perhaps the deliberate anti-poetry of a man who has turned (or had to turn) his back on the "mere beauty" of the lyrical'.[15] MacDiarmid was well aware of such criticism, responding in 'The Kind of Poetry I Want' (from *Lucky Poet*): 'Fools regret my poetic change – from my "enchanting early lyrics" – / But I have found in Marxism all that I need' (*CP1*, p. 615). MacDiarmid seems to be claiming here that, rather than simply having lost his lyrical talent and run to revolutionary politics for cover, he has changed the form of his poetry from Scots lyrics to longer discursive work in Scots-English and English in order to accommodate the conceptual demands made by his Marxism. According to the poet,

> It only remains to perfect myself in this new mode.
> This is the poetry I want – all
> I can regard now as poetry at all,
> As poetry of to-day, not of the past,
> A Communist poetry that bases itself
> On the Resolution of the C.C. of the R.C.P.
> In Spring 1925: 'The Party must vigorously oppose
> Thoughtless and contemptuous treatment
> Of the old cultural heritage
> As well as of the literary specialists. . . .

It must likewise combat the tendency
Towards a purely hothouse proletarian literature.' (*CP1*, p. 615)

There is a correspondence, then, between form and content or, as George Orwell (1903–50) put the matter, between literary 'texture' and political 'tendency'.[16] What must not be forgotten, though, is that Grieve adopted the pseudonym 'Hugh MacDiarmid' in 1922 when he first started to write in Scots, but did not drop this name when he turned to communist poetry, written mostly in English, in the 1930s; unlike the example of Scottish novelist James Leslie Mitchell/'Lewis Grassic Gibbon' (1901–35), there is no split in MacDiarmid's creative identity along linguistic lines. This is important when considering the nature of MacDiarmid's communist poetry in the 1930s: poetry in English and English-inflected Scots that yet utilises the declarative, direct voice of a Scots-language tradition in Scottish poetry.

For MacDiarmid, being Scottish and working class and socialist (and male) were virtually synonymous: 'It is, indeed, almost an infallible test of a Scots (or Irish or Welsh) Socialist that he should have not only no use whatever for but a positive objection to Auden, Spender, and the rest, and the English Literary Left' (*LP*, p. 168). In *Lucky Poet*, published in 1943 but written mainly in Shetland, he traces an eccentric line of influence from the English poets Milton, Blake, Charles Doughty and Wilfred Scawen Blunt, through Marx, Lenin and Stalin, 'to that concern to get rid of the English Ascendancy and work for the establishment of Workers' Republics in Scotland, Ireland, Wales and Cornwall, and, indeed, make a sort of Celtic Union of Socialist Soviet Republics in the British Isles' (p. 26).

By the mid to late 1930s MacDiarmid sought Scottish liberation through Celtic communism, a position personified for the poet by the Scottish revolutionary John Maclean, who in 1918 was appointed Scotland's Bolshevik consul. MacDiarmid compares Maclean with Lenin in 'Krassivy, Krassivy' from *Lucky Poet*. In 'John Maclean (1879–1923)', excised from the first edition of *Stony Limits and Other Poems* (1934), Maclean is Christ-like. With its angry, direct, soapbox-prophet style of delivery, 'John Maclean (1879–1923)' demonstrates how easily MacDiarmid's declarative poetry can be confused with class propaganda:

Stand close, stand close, and block out the light
As long as you can, you ministers and lawyers,
Hulking brutes of police, fat bourgeoisie,
Sleek derma for congested guts – its fires
Will leap through yet; already it is clear
Of all Maclean's foes not one was his peer. (*CP1*, p. 486)

In 'Poetry and Propaganda' MacDiarmid accepts the charge of being a propagandist for revolution – 'Propaganda in poetry let humbugs condemn' – declaring 'any utterance that is not pure / Propaganda is impure propaganda for sure!' (*CP1*, p. 558). Lewis Grassic Gibbon, in similar vein, would write to *The Left Review* in 1935, 'I hate capitalism; all my books are explicit or implicit propaganda.'[17] If fascism represents the aestheticisation of politics – and MacDiarmid expressed interest in both Italian Fascism and Nazism, and in the early 1920s advocated a Scottish Fascism[18] – then much of the left-wing writing of the 1930s, including MacDiarmid's communist poems, signals the politicisation of aesthetics. MacDiarmid exemplifies this radicalising of the literary realm in 'Poetry and Propaganda': 'A pretty tribute to the old rural scene / Can mask a base betrayal of mankind' (*CP1*, p. 558). A series of propagandist poems from *Stony Limits* continues to employ the direct method. 'First Objectives' opposes 'All profiteers, monopolists, / And all who claim to own the earth', along with 'censors, police, and teachers who / Instead of just opening out impose' (*CP1*, p. 394). 'The Belly Grip' reverses MacDiarmid's typical elitist stance and promotes instead 'the intelligence and decency / Of the majority' (*CP1*, p. 395). 'Genethliacon for the New World Order' goes further, claiming 'Everyman is the meaning and desire / Of the world' (*CP1*, p. 403). 'Song of the New Economics' is propaganda for the Social Credit scheme of Major C. H. Douglas (1879–1952), whilst 'Etika Preobrazhennavo Erosa' returns to a Marxist position with its assertion that 'Only by the severest intellectual discipline / Can one of the bourgeois intelligentsia win / Up to the level of the proletariat' (*CP1*, p. 407).

MacDiarmid's propaganda poems, with their direct social statements, leave little room for the play of the reader's imagination. Yet, in straining our sense of what poetry should be, one aim of these poems is surely to attack – not only in their subject-matter, but through their style – bourgeois literary expectations. Nevertheless, MacDiarmid never entirely abandoned a concern with traditional aesthetic values, although he did want to combine such values with what he thought of as progressive political commitment. 'Art and the Workers' (1935) wonders why with all their technical proficiency, 'which / Enables them to share imaginatively / In the action of mechanical functions' (*CP2*, p. 1304), the working class should remain so apparently unappreciative of the formal beauty of high art. In his Marxist poetry, for all its propagandist drive, MacDiarmid counters Soviet Russian 'ideas of the Proletkult and socialist realism'.[19] For MacDiarmid, 'no field of criticism makes so many demands on the active imagination as the study of literature in its relations to society', and the ideal critic must censure 'the aesthete who seems to believe that art exists in a vacuum', yet also 'show that art is something more than the "ideological" representation of class forces in society'.[20]

When *First Hymn to Lenin* was published in 1931 MacDiarmid was working in London as a director of the Unicorn Press. The British Security Services opened a file on the poet at this time, concerned that his publishing firm was producing communist propaganda.[21] MacDiarmid was twice expelled from the Communist Party in the 1930s, and as a poet he undoubtedly did not produce agitprop in the service of the Party. However, he retained a wilful idealism in assuming that communism would free humanity's cultural powers when in reality under communism culture would be harnessed to political power. 'First Hymn' relativises the killings committed by the Soviet regime:

> As necessary, and insignificant, as death
> Wi' a' its agonies in the cosmos still
> The Cheka's horrors are in their degree;
> And'll end suner! What maitters 't wha we kill
> To lessen that foulest murder that deprives
>   Maist men o' real lives? (*CP1*, p. 298)

Auden's Spanish Civil War poem, 'Spain', echoes such sanctioning of revolutionary cleansing in the line 'The conscious acceptance of guilt in the necessary murder', which Auden would change to the marginally less brutal 'The conscious acceptance of guilt in the fact of murder'.[22] Unlike Auden and Orwell, MacDiarmid took no part in the Spanish Civil War (1936–9). Spender points out that 'The best books of the war – those by Malraux, Hemingway, Koestler and Orwell – describe the Spanish tragedy from the liberal point of view, and they bear witness against the Communists.'[23] MacDiarmid's Spanish Civil War poem, the sprawling *The Battle Continues*, remained unpublished until 1957. Lacking an informed and disinterested view of the war, the poem fails to acknowledge the authoritarianism of the communists, but instead wastes much of its ammunition in a personal attack on Roy Campbell. Orwell, dismayed by 'Spain', in 'Inside the Whale' (1940) berated Auden for his seeming advocacy of violence from the safety of the study, having earlier disparaged the political poetry of the 1930s as the work of 'the gangster and the pansy'.[24] Notwithstanding Orwell's homophobia, which MacDiarmid, too, could also indulge in when writing on Auden,[25] the poet of *The Battle Continues* and 'First Hymn to Lenin' should not escape criticism for his political attitudinising.

What Iain Crichton Smith (1928–98) calls 'the problem of violence' in MacDiarmid's hymns to Lenin recurs in 'Third Hymn', in which the poet wants Lenin to deal with Glasgow's 'public men' by 'Going through them like a machine-gun through crinkled tissue' (*CP2*, p. 896).[26] Sorley MacLean (1911–96), who visited his fellow poet in Whalsay in 1935, the year *Second Hymn to Lenin* was published, went so far as to claim that MacDiarmid thought 'the bourgeoisie must be liquidated', or at least 'that the ethos of the bourgeoisie must be psychologically or morally destroyed'.[27] Violence is absent from 'Second Hymn', although the poem does celebrate Lenin's 'unparalleled force'. 'Second Hymn' attacks writers – James Joyce, perhaps surprisingly, among them – for being merely 'romantic rebels' who have 'affected nocht but a fringe / O' mankind in ony way'. Yet, in spite of his scepticism of 'Great poets hardly onybody kens o'' (CP1, p. 324), 'Second Hymn' is actually MacDiarmid's defence of poetry's role in a revolutionary society. Only, for this poet, the role of a revolutionary society is to offer the liberty to produce greater poetry. Politics should be about 'Freein' oor poo'ers for greater things'. If that can be provided by the political power of Lenin then the poet is all for communism. That any society is still faced with 'breid-and-butter problems' such as poverty proves that we are in an evolutionary time lag, still at 'the monkey stage' (CP1, p. 325). MacDiarmid was a cultural worker whose real interest lay in the evolution of humanity; he was not an orthodox Marxist-Leninist. However, Neal Ascherson is only partly correct when he says that 'MacDiarmid's intellectual relationship to Marx and Lenin was not a particularly intimate one'.[28] For MacDiarmid, the poet's craft should learn from the Marxist restructuring of society – 'Poetry like politics maun cut / The cackle and pursue real ends' (CP1, p. 324) – and be 'Unremittin', relentless, / Organized to the last degree' (CP1, p. 328). Yet if the political sphere Lenin commands 'comes first' (CP1, p. 323), poetry is a higher power.

Skelton writes of the 1930s, 'there was something religious in the moral fervour of the time'.[29] It is significant that MacDiarmid should write hymns to Lenin. The poet found in communism a contemporary creative mythos to replace Christianity. 'First Hymn' likens Lenin to Christ, who is again mentioned in 'Second Hymn', while 'Third Hymn' is prefaced by passages of Scripture and the 'spirit of Lenin' is invoked: 'Be with me, Lenin, reincarnate in me here.' 'Third Hymn' is set in the Glasgow slums, 'The peak of the capitalist system and the trough of Hell' (CP2, p. 895). MacDiarmid wrote several 'Glasgow' poems, never complimentary to the city or its people. In one, from 1947, he claims, 'Everyone knows that the future belongs to Communism / But they are only anxious the present order / Should last out their time' (CP2, p. 1336). 'In the Slums of Glasgow', from Second Hymn to Lenin, is less dogmatic: 'I have not gained a single definite belief that can be put / In a scientific formula or hardened into a religious creed' (CP1, p. 563). Whereas Marxism sees society's material divisions, the poet of 'In the Slums of Glasgow', with his vision of life's essential oneness, is the seer of spiritual reality:

I have caught a glimpse of the seamless garment
And am blind to all else for evermore.
The immaculate vesture, the innermost shift,

Of high and low, of rich and poor,
The glorious raiment of bridegroom and bride,
   Whoremonger and whore,
I have caught a glimpse of the seamless garment
And have eyes for aught else no more. (*CP1*, p. 562)

'There is nothing quite like this poem in English writing of the period,' Roderick Watson argues in relation to 'In the Slums of Glasgow'; the 'sophisticated irony' of Audenesque poetry is absent here, and Watson points instead to the influence of William Blake (1757–1827).[30] Blake's earnest mix of maverick radicalism and pro-Jesus, anti-Christian mysticism pervades MacDiarmid's work. Crichton Smith notes that both Blake and MacDiarmid started out writing lyrics before moving on to difficult long poems 'based rather insecurely on systems which are fairly private'.[31] MacDiarmid's system is a heterodox communism often premised on a Blakean dialectic of inno-cence and experience – the 'bridegroom and bride, / Whoremonger and whore' of 'In the Slums of Glasgow'; the eagle and the lamb of 'What the Eagle Said'; the 'Divine in human or human in divine' (*CP1*, p. 505) of the anarchic 'Ode to All Rebels' – that will only be resolved in the heaven of a new revolutionary order.

Although its title refers to the tunic Christ wore as he faced crucifix-ion, 'The Seamless Garment' is not an explicitly religious poem. Set in a Langholm cloth mill, the poet speaks to Wullie, 'a cousin of mine', about Lenin, 'The best weaver Earth ever saw', and Rainer Maria Rilke (1875–1926), whose poetry is 'A seamless garment o' music and thought' (*CP1*, pp. 311, 312). However, despite Lenin's exemplary status, nowhere in 'The Seamless Garment' does MacDiarmid call on the workers to unite as a class; rather, he wants the mill hands to rise above the division of labour that ties them to the loom and experience a fuller, more abundant life. Both Rilke and Lenin, master builders in their respective work, strive to see life whole and so create 'a single reality':

Lenin and Rilke baith gied still mair skill,
   Coopers o' Stobo, to a greater concern
Than you devote to claith in the mill.
   Wad it be ill to learn
To keep a bit eye on their looms as weel
And no' be hailly ta'en up wi' your 'tweel'? (*CP1*, pp. 312, 312–13)

Such patronising of the workers comes from the poet's frustrated wish to see human character evolve at the same speed as technological develop-ment: 'Machinery in a week mak's greater advances / Than Man's nature twixt Adam and this' (*CP1*, p. 313). The mystical posture of 'In the Slums of Glasgow' can seem equally elitist, with the God-like poet looking down on 'every squalid lair' (*CP1*, p. 564). MacDiarmid's communist poetry fails to inhabit ordinary lives, yet this may be because he wants no life to be ordinary. The 'single reality' of 'The Seamless Garment' and the 'supreme reality' (*CP1*, pp. 474, 475) envisioned in 'Lament for the Great Music' (from *Stony Limits*) are not the realities of urban working-class existence, but the supra-reality of the mystic.

'The Seamless Garment', with its fusion of Rilke and Lenin, mystic and materialist, poetry and politics, is representative of the aims of MacDiarmid's political poetry in the 1930s. The Marxist dialectic, the thesis and antithesis of fundamental contradiction between the class interests of proletariat and bourgeoisie, finds its synthesis in a revolutionary classless society to end history. The Hegelian dialectic, which Marx inverted, stripping it of its idealism, finds its evolutionary synthesis in history as spirit. As Catherine Kerrigan points out, 'Dialectic requires the principle of faith for its existence. Like traditional religious beliefs, dialectic carries its share of mysticism, which is why in the end MacDiarmid could adapt the concept to his own scheme of thought.'[32] MacDiarmid's poetry of commitment is a creative synthesis of Marxian and Hegelian dialectics, a union of opposites transcending each in a spiritual communism.

Ascherson says that MacDiarmid regarded 'Marxism as a cosmology'.[33] Yet as a science of the universe, MacDiarmid's Marxism is distinctly spiritual. Indeed, for Burns Singer, MacDiarmid's communism is 'a genuine ascetic religion'.[34] 'Song of the Seraphim' (from *Lucky Poet*), with its superior concern for 'the deliverance of the proletariat', sings also of 'a holy poverty / A super-richness which falls to pieces / In its own splendour' (*CP1*, p. 640). In much of MacDiarmid's work there is a search for purity, almost a death-like purity, which is ultimately religious and corresponds to the anti-liberal absolutism of his political positions. This attitude is found in 'On a Raised Beach', but also in 'The Terrible Crystal' (from *A Lap of Honour*, 1967) with its 'Visions of a transcendental country / Stretching out athwart the temporal frontiers' (*CP2*, p. 1095), and in the 'Dìreadh' poems (published together in 1974) – the 'Sheer Communism!' of 'Dìreadh I' is analogous to the poet's vision of rural Scotland in 'Dìreadh III': 'I am possessed by this purity here / As in a welling of stainless water' (*CP2*, pp. 1172, 1187). 'The Terrible Crystal' and 'Dìreadh', written in the 1930s, are fragments of MacDiarmid's unpublished epic *Cornish Heroic Song for Valda Trevlyn*, addressed to his second wife. According to Alan Bold, *Heroic Song* 'was, stylistically at least, intended as an alternative to the Scots lyrics he had written while married to Peggy', the poet's first wife.[35] However, *In Memoriam James Joyce* (1955), written mostly in the 1930s and later redrafted, aligns his late poetry – rational, encyclopaedic, multi-lingual – with 'the epical age of Communism' (*CP2*, p. 740). His

Drunk Man of the 1920s may have pondered life's irrationalism, but from the 1930s onwards MacDiarmid celebrated a divine sobriety symbolised by the transparency of water. Fraser calls him 'a kind of natural theologian' before remarking 'that MacDiarmid though a Marxist is not a humanist, indeed he could be described as an anti-humanist'.[36] This anti-humanism, an aspect of MacDiarmid's extreme Calvinism seen most starkly in 'On a Raised Beach', relates strongly to his communism. While *Second Hymn to Lenin* includes the anti-Christian 'After Two Thousand Years', the collection also contains 'The Covenanters', which celebrates the seventeenth-century Presbyterians who steadfastly opposed the imposition of Episcopal church ordinance in Scotland: 'The waves of their purposefulness go flooding through me. / This religion is simple, naked. Its values stand out / In black and white. It is the wind of God' (*CP1*, p. 551). A 'black and white' value-system implies an illiberal, fanatical, absolutist politics. MacDiarmid seeks God's purity in communism; a theocratic communism that will wash away the stain of capitalist exploitation and bourgeois mediocrity. The 'slum people' of 'The Glass of Pure Water' are not offered a political solution, but are granted instead the hope of spiritual redemption:

> Our duty is to free that water, to make these gestures,
> To help humanity to shed all else,
> All that stands between any life and the sun,
> The quintessence of any life and the sun;
> To still all sound save that talking to God;
> To end all movements save movements like these. (*CP2*, p. 1043)

In a 1967 letter to Iain Crichton Smith, MacDiarmid outlines and defends his communist position:

> I am not really concerned that many people do not think me 'a Communist in any ordinary sense of the word'! They are hopelessly mistaken. So are all those who think Communism is concerned with 'ordinary humanity'. . . . least of all with humanitarianism. They forget that our objective is 'to change human nature'. You are perfectly correct when you say I have no more use for the masses than they have for me. There is scarcely anything that appeals to any considerable body of people that I have anything other than contempt for.[37]

MacDiarmid's communist elitism echoes the totalitarian cult of personality that made heroes of Lenin and Joseph Stalin (1878–1953). MacDiarmid would write poems to Stalin, such as 'Lamh Dearg Aboo' (1945) and 'The Fingers of Baal Contract in the Communist Salute' (1946), which claim to find racial affinities between Stalin's Georgia and Gaeldom. The poet's evolutionary desire 'to change human nature' might almost be mistaken for Stalin's more sinister idea that writers of the revolutionary regime are 'engineers of the human soul'. MacDiarmid visited the Soviet Union in 1950 and the People's Republic of China in 1957: on return, unlike many other Western writers, he saw no reason to renounce communism. He supported the 1956 Soviet repression of popular national revolt in Hungary, and as late as 1975 he defended the violence of 'First Hymn to Lenin', saying, 'Progress demands that recalcitrant or reactionary elements must be swept away.'[38]

In *We*, Yevgeny Zamyatin's (1884–1937) counter-revolutionary satire on Soviet communism, the Numbers are bidden to write 'epic poems' to the 'grandeur of OneState' where lives 'The ancient dream of paradise'.[39] MacDiarmid's religious atheism and his hatred of the middle class kept him loyal to that dream. Yet for all the utter unreasonableness of MacDiarmid's enduring commitment to communist politics, his ultimate commitment remained to the free and direct expression of poetry.

> For I am like Zamyatin. I must be a Bolshevik
> Before the Revolution, but I'll cease to be one quick
> When Communism comes to rule the roost,
> For real literature can exist only where it's produced
> By madmen, hermits, heretics,
> Dreamers, rebels, sceptics,
> – And such a door of utterance has been given to me
> As none may close whosoever they be. ('Talking with Five Thousand People
>   in Edinburgh', CP2, p. 1158)

CHAPTER SIX

MacDiarmid and Ecology

Louisa Gairn

Hugh MacDiarmid is one of the earliest literary figures within the British Isles to write about the science of ecology, and arguably the first Scottish creative writer consciously to apply ideas drawn from ecological theory and practice in his own work. In his autobiography, *Lucky Poet* (1943), he explained that he found it 'necessary' to draw on the Scottish landscape in his work because of the new insights to be gleaned from ecological thought, contending that 'modern ecology has destroyed the delusion which encouraged people to jeer at any suggestion of geographic "control" and human "response" to such control' and that 'to-day physiology and psychology are agreed that there is a relation, a functional relation, between an organism and its environment' (*LP*, p. 310). Embodying his call in *Scottish Scene* (1934) for 'first-hand observation, intimate knowledge and loving particularity' of the natural world as key to the reinvigoration of Scottish cultural life, and influenced by his contact with the Scottish environmental visionary Patrick Geddes as well as his reading of other ecological scientists and thinkers, MacDiarmid's poetry reveals a surprisingly prescient Scottish approach to 'ecopoetics'.[1] This chapter will be based mostly on MacDiarmid's later poetry, focusing in particular on the works he wrote while living in Shetland (1933–42). Most significant among these is 'On a Raised Beach' (1934), a poem which, in its attempt to 'get into this stone world' (*CP1*, p. 426), confronts one of the central questions of ecopoetics: the possibility of reconciling humans and the world of nature through the medium of writing.

MacDiarmid's interest in the emerging science of ecology during the 1930s makes sense in the context of his broader belief in a 'poetry of facts', which he proposed would 'conform with and build on the concrete realities and theories of the universe furnished by science', in line with a Marxist, materialist perspective.[2] But perhaps more importantly, ecology's holistic view as a science of relationships between organism and environment, and, more specifically, Scottish (Geddesian) ecology's multidisciplinary focus on the human world and the world of nature as 'elements of an intelligible and interacting whole', attracted MacDiarmid, who himself was searching for just such a synoptic vision in his later poetry.[3]

Challenging anyone who might complain 'that I should sing / Of philological, literary and musical matters / Rather than of daffodils and nightingales' (*In Memoriam James Joyce*, CP2, p. 749), MacDiarmid sought (not always successfully) to dissociate himself from Romantic views of nature. While, in the 1933 poem 'Whuchulls', he questions anthropocentrism, asking: 'What is oor life that we should prize't abune / Lichen's or slug's [. . .] / Or fancy it ser's "heicher purposes"?', he goes on to argue for the poet's ultimate freedom from moral obligations: 'Poetry isna some / Society for Preservin' Threatened Types, / But strokes a cat or fiddles on its tripes' (CP2, pp. 1089, 1091).[4] However, such ambivalence does not contradict a reading of some of MacDiarmid's work as 'ecopoetics', a form of poetic enquiry which, Jonathan Bate notes, 'is not synonymous with writing that is pragmatically green' but is rather 'a way of reflecting upon what it might mean to dwell with the earth'.[5] In much of his 1930s poetry, in addition to the critical and prose writings contained in works such as *Scottish Scene*, MacDiarmid foregrounds the portrayal and understanding of the natural world as an essential part of the writer's role. The world of nature is frequently adopted in the later work as a metaphor for poetic language, political commitment and national identity. MacDiarmid, though, goes further than that, arguing for the value of nature-writing and study as analogous to poetry. As with the botanist's minute observation of a plant's structure in 'Poetry and Science' (1943), which 'Enriches and makes three-dimensional / His awareness of its complex beauty' (CP1, p. 630), so too can an exquisitely attentive, exhaustive 'poetry of facts' reveal the truth as well as the beauty of reality.

Aspects of this approach can be observed in a lyrical segment from 'Dìreadh I' (first published in *The Voice of Scotland*, December 1938), one of the lengthy Gaelic-influenced poems MacDiarmid was working on during the 1930s. Echoing Charles Darwin's (1809–82) famous example of the 'tangled bank'[6] with its profusion of interrelated plant and animal life in *On the Origin of Species* (1859), MacDiarmid brings the descriptive register of a naturalist's field diary into play alongside the Gaelic 'Dìreadh' ('act of surmounting', CP2, p. 1163) to evoke the biodiversity of a Scottish landscape. Like Scottish languages and culture, the 'neglected peat-hags, not worked / Within living memory' are nevertheless full of life, an ecosystem of pastel-toned sphagnum moss and butterwort 'Waiting with wide-open sticky leaves for their tiny winged prey' (CP2, p. 1171). Thus, in contrast to the inattentive fool 'who cries "Nothing but heather!"', we are offered the perspective of 'another / Sitting there and resting and gazing round', a careful observer who pays close attention to the diversity of the hillside ecosystem, which also functions as a symbol of 'Our multiform, our infinite Scotland' (CP2, pp. 1170–1).

Reflecting on the state of contemporary Scotland with his co-author Lewis Grassic Gibbon in *Scottish Scene*, MacDiarmid argued for the importance of regional and nature writing in fostering Scottish national identity. Although 'germs of promising novelistic regionalism' had begun to emerge, MacDiarmid identified a 'dearth' of nature and travel books demonstrating 'a real knowledge of nature'.[7] However, despite this polemical lament on the lack of authentically Scottish environmental writing, there were already some remarkable exponents of environmental science active in Scotland during the first decades of the twentieth century. T. C. Smout argues that there is a case to be made for a 'special Scottish context for the study of ecology' originating with the botanist, geographer and city planner Patrick Geddes (1854–1932) and continuing in the work of scientific ecologists such as Frank Fraser Darling (1903–79), with whose work MacDiarmid was also familiar. This early twentieth-century Scottish approach to ecology, Smout notes, emphasised human dependence on and responsibility for the environment, and was 'remarkable as seeing man as a prime actor among other animals, instead of searching for a "natural" world uninvaded by man, which was more characteristic of ecology in the south of Britain'.[8]

Geddes's study of environmental science and what would later be termed 'human ecology' led him to establish the Outlook Tower in Edinburgh in 1892. This educational experiment, MacDiarmid explained in an unsigned 1923 article for *The Scottish Nation*, was intended to enable 'the fullest understanding of the place by its people' (*RT1*, p. 131), giving the visitor an overview of his or her relationship to the immediate urban environment, as well as the wider region, nation and ultimately the world as a whole. The tower, as Volker Welter explains, was a kind of 'thinking cell', a species of urban temple or 'secluded [space] for individual meditation and thought'.[9] It also served as a cultural meeting place, featuring an early performance in 1925 of songs from MacDiarmid's first collection *Sangschaw* (1925) by the composer, and MacDiarmid's former schoolteacher at Langholm Academy, Francis George Scott (1880–1958). Together with other environmental education projects such as a proposed (but never realised) national institute of geography, the Outlook Tower reflected Geddes's basic premise of relating the local to the global, and the individual to her or his community and environment, based on ecological principles of interdependence.

MacDiarmid was in contact with Geddes from the mid-1920s until the latter's death in 1932, giving some talks and poetry readings organised by Geddes in Edinburgh, and writing about the Outlook Tower for the Scottish press.[10] He unsuccessfully applied for a role as general editor of Geddes's papers in 1948, claiming in a letter to Geddes's son to 'regard a more complete knowledge of it [Geddes's work] as essential to certain aspects of my own life-work', but he was already acquainted with some of the polymath's key ideas as well as the 'thinking tools' he employed to develop and disseminate them.[11] Geddes's own attempts towards a 'Scots Renascence' (focused on his 1895 periodical *The Evergreen*)[12] may have been linked to the 'Celtic Twilight' and Kailyard MacDiarmid and his peers forcefully rejected, but MacDiarmid would later claim Geddes as one of his key influences in *The Company I've Kept* (1966). Aligning himself especially with Geddes's holistic scientific and ecological interests, MacDiarmid praises him as an unrecognised Scottish genius whose 'constant effort was "to help people to think for themselves, and to think round the whole circle, not in scraps and bits". He knew that watertight compartments are useful only to a sinking ship, and traversed all the boundaries of separate subjects'.[13] The ultimate aim in all this, MacDiarmid suggests, was to foster a 'tremendous change in our conceptual apparatus'. Geddes's generalist synthetic method is, MacDiarmid claims, 'the very practice that has been the theme of all my later poetry and work as a teacher and publicist', and he lists the points of common interest between the two men:

> Form, pattern, configuration, organism, historical filiation, ecological relationship and concepts that work up and down the ladder of the sciences; the aesthetic structure and the social relations are as real as the primary physical qualities that the sciences were once content to isolate.[14]

Looking back at Geddes's work from his 1966 vantage point, MacDiarmid could identify the concepts that best fitted his own quest for a 'synthesis' of knowledge, a quest that had formed part of the motivation for his move from the formal constraints of the lyric to the broader canvas of 'epic' poetry during the 1930s. *In Memoriam James Joyce* (1955), begun during MacDiarmid's Shetland years, names Geddes when calling for 'completeness of thought / A synthesis of all view points' (CP2, p. 801). In his 'Author's Note' to *In Memoriam*, MacDiarmid contends that with the new holistic perspective provided by the sciences 'Our consciousness is beginning to be planetary', a scenario that logically must lead to a '[new] response provoked in the writer in relation to his own language and his own environment'.[15] In order to keep up with the advances in scientific knowledge, the poet must also transform poetry's 'conceptual apparatus'. For MacDiarmid, this meant the all-encompassing world vision announced in 'The Kind of Poetry I Want' (1943; 1961):

> Poetry of such an integration as cannot be effected
> Until a new and conscious organisation of society
> Generates a new view
> Of the world as a whole

As the integration of all the rich parts
Uncovered by the separate disciplines.
That is the poetry that I want. (*CP2*, p. 1025)

Geddes's cross-disciplinary ecological approach, drawing on the Scottish generalist tradition as well as the 'universal geography' then proposed by continental environmental thinkers, while stressing the importance of the individual's memory and power of observation, offered a usefully Scottish model for what Geddes saw as a 'new view / Of the world as a whole'.[16]

Finding the right language to explore and develop this new world view remained crucial. MacDiarmid had argued in his 1923 *Scottish Chapbook* essay 'A Theory of Scots Letters' that the Scots language could '[establish] a blood-bond in a fashion at once infinitely more thrilling and vital and less explicable than those deliberately sought after by writers such as D. H. Lawrence in the medium of English' (*SP*, p. 22). By the 1930s, MacDiarmid remained convinced that language was central to the question of estab-lishing and expressing the bonds between humanity and environment. In *The Islands of Scotland* (1939), returning to themes introduced some years earlier in *Scottish Scene*, he contends that most writers of Scottish travel and natural history books are unable to access the native languages (and hence the psychology) of the places they describe and are thus incapable of con-veying the 'truth' of place: 'the "intellectual climate" in which these books were written made the expression, or (almost wholly) the perception, of the true impossible'.[17] This criticism could equally be applied to MacDiarmid himself, writing increasingly in English and – despite his fascination with the languages and cultures of the Highlands and Islands – lacking profi-ciency in both Gaelic and Norn (the old Shetlandic language). Without recourse to the primordial connection provided by the native language of the place, MacDiarmid suggests that the expression and perception of 'the true' is made possible by an 'observant, vigorous, sympathetic and knowledgeable' outlook.[18]

In pursuit of this ideal, 'Tam o' the Wilds and the Many-Faced Mystery' – published in both *Scottish Scene* and *Stony Limits* (1934), and a poem whose title glances back to Burns's 'Tam o' Shanter' – reveals a lively Scots lan-guage portrait of the Banffshire self-taught naturalist Thomas Edward.[19] Self-educated and, significantly for MacDiarmid, 'a common workin' man' (*CP1*, p. 368), Tam has an all-consuming interest in natural history that alienates him from his peers. His efforts to observe and understand the interconnected lives of the plants and animals that surround him are an example of the ideal synoptic, all-encompassing vision MacDiarmid saw as necessary for a Scottish renaissance. In his depiction of Tam, MacDiarmid is also delineating the characteristics of the ideal poet:

He had the seein' eye frae which naething could hide
And nocht that cam' under his een was forgotten.
Fluently and vividly he could aye efter describe
The forms, and habits o' a' the immense
Maingie o' animals he saw – an incredible tribe! (*CP1*, p. 377)

In the context of *Scottish Scene* and its authors' polemics on Scottish culture and institutions, the poem functions in part as an additional critique of the Scottish educational system. As Robert Crawford suggests, in much of his later work MacDiarmid 'sets himself up as a one-man university', using his poetry of knowledge as 'a challenge to the institutional custodians of learning [to show] that the poet is more intelligent than the headmaster or the don'.[20] 'We're a' owre weel-educated noo I doot / To ha'e ony real knowledge – or love o't – left', MacDiarmid wryly observes: 'Tam's pinkie kent / Faur mair than the fower and a hauf millions o's / Livin' the day' (*CP1*, p. 377). In this he was once again in accord with Geddes, who had critiqued the study of 'dead anatomy' he found in the conventional science classroom, and later tried to reform the way biology and geography were taught in Scottish schools and universities, replacing the 'artificial blindness' of conventional education for what he called the 'synoptic vision' of 'the field-naturalist'.[21] As antidote to ecological ignorance, *Scottish Scene*'s Tam (and by inference, MacDiarmid) demonstrates an encyclopaedic knowledge of Scottish wildlife and landscape similar to the observational practice celebrated in *Dìreadh*. As a laudatory work based on the life of a real person, 'Tam o' the Wilds' can also be read as a kind of praise poem following the Gaelic tradition, and is related to other late-1930s projects such as 'In Talk with Donnchadh Bàn Mac an t'Saoir', which also praises its subject's environmental expertise as a way of speculating on the role of the ideal poet as a tireless observer, describer and synthesiser of knowledge. Throughout these works, however, there is little of the celebratory inclusiveness of Geddes's poet-naturalist, but instead an elitist intellectual heroism and the continuing influence of Nietzsche in MacDiarmid's dismissal of the 'masses'. Like the ideal poet, Tam takes a solitary path which is incomprehensible to society at large, those nameless millions bogged down in 'a solid basis o' dull conventions' (*CP1*, p. 372). This is a quest that continues in 'On a Raised Beach', which also speaks of 'the indifference of the masses of mankind' in contrast to the solitary thinker grappling with the 'hard fact' of reality (*CP1*, p. 430).

Iain Crichton Smith identifies MacDiarmid's stance in these Shetlandic works as one of 'aristocratic loneliness' or 'terrible apartness'. The human 'tenderness' of the early Scots lyrics, he contends, is superior to the abstraction of the later 'poetry of landscape and stones and language'.[22] Edwin Morgan, an admirer of MacDiarmid's work and fellow believer in the potential for poetry to encompass scientific knowledge, also balks at the apparent inhumanity of much of the later poetry. While, he suggests, MacDiarmid's stance makes sense as a conscious reaction against Burnsian and Victorian sentimentality, the result is often difficult to empathise with:

> Hardly ever, in any poem, do you get a sense of a man who is emotionally committed to something other than ideas, words, or landscapes. The beautiful and terrible bonds that are not geological but between individual persons [. . .] are strikingly absent [. . .] He must be the most existential poet ever to have written.[23]

MacDiarmid responded privately to such criticism in typically combative and idiosyncratic mode, welcoming David Daiches's description of him as 'transhuman',[24] and dismissing other critics' interpretations of 'The Watergaw' as being about his father's death.[25] Instead, he explains in a 1975 letter to Edwin Morgan, 'my actual "inhuman" attitude is much more truly expressed in "At my Father's Grave" ',[26] a short poem published in *First Hymn to Lenin* (1931), where 'We look upon each ither noo like hills / Across a valley. I'm nae mair your son' (*CP1*, p. 299). Here, inverting the traditional poetic fallacy of the Romantics, where landscapes are infused with human qualities, death enables us to see the 'thingness', or neutral materiality, of human existence. This existentialism appears ever more forcefully in 'On a Raised Beach', where MacDiarmid identifies himself with the neutrality of the earth itself:

> I am no more indifferent or ill-disposed to life than death is;
> I would fain accept it all completely as the soil does;
> Already I feel all that can perish perishing in me
> As so much has perished and all will yet perish in these stones.
> I must begin with these stones as the world began. (*CP1*, p. 424)

In pursuit of this imperative, 'On a Raised Beach' speaks of the 'Inconceivable discipline, courage, and endurance, / Self-purification and anti-humanity' necessary for the poet to fulfil his proper role (*CP1*, p. 429). Geography and personal circumstances undoubtedly played an important role in forming MacDiarmid's mindset during this period. MacDiarmid's emotional life was in turmoil during his stay in Shetland, and he was living in poverty, aloof yet dependent on hand-outs from the islanders.[27] As a result, Ann Edwards Boutelle suggests, MacDiarmid's poetry 'turns away from the language of vulnerability to the language of impersonal facts, from the world of human beings to the world of stones'.[28] However, the 'terrible apartness' revealed in 'On A Raised Beach' is not merely isolation from other humans, but reveals a more fundamental apartness from the non-human world, a struggle to live authentically, and an ascetic contemplation on the potential for poetry to represent or assist in this struggle. Thus, MacDiarmid argues:

What happens to us
Is irrelevant to the world's geology
But what happens to the world's geology
Is not irrelevant to us.
We must reconcile ourselves to the stones,
Not the stones to us.
Here a man must shed the encumbrances that muffle
Contact with elemental things, the subtleties
That seem inseparable from a humane life, and go apart
Into a simple and sterner, more beautiful and more oppressive world. (*CP1*,
    p. 428)

However, despite this declaration of willpower, Crichton Smith suggests that MacDiarmid's personality remains at the centre of the poem, and detects a 'troubling' trace of animism that undermines the poem's own philosophical argument to 'accept the stones': 'The stone is seen both as itself and as notation and it is in the fluctuations between that the trouble lies.'[29] This was an important issue for Crichton Smith, a poet in the Gaelic tradition who, like Sorley MacLean, critiqued Romanticism's moralising anthropomorphism in contrast to classical Gaelic poetry's descriptive realism and neutrality.[30] However, if MacDiarmid's poem succeeds in imbuing the stones with 'being', at the same time it surely reveals the 'thingness' of the human observer. Daiches suggests that 'On a Raised Beach' 'expresses most concisely an important aspect of [MacDiarmid's] transhumanism [. . .] the poetry of a man who will not draw comforting conclusions from the uncanniness of reality'.[31] This is the same 'uncanniness' identified by ecocritics working in the tradition of Martin Heidegger (1889–1976), what the Scottish eco-anthropologist Tim Ingold refers to as the 'split-level image of human existence': the paradox that humans are both part of nature and observers of it, simultaneously object and subject.[32]

In 'On a Raised Beach' the 'thingness' of physical existence and its temporality (for this poem, as with some of MacDiarmid's other avowedly 'inhuman' contemplations, also enacts the role of an atheistic *memento mori*) finds its objective correlative in 'this stone world'. However, this is not a conventional 'ashes to ashes' message; MacDiarmid is articulating the fundamental problem of ecological thought: the question 'how can we exist both inside the world of nature and outside of it'.[33] This, as Ingold explains, derives partly from Cartesian philosophy, which

takes as its starting point the self-contained subject confronting a domain of isolable objects, [and] assumes that things are initially encountered in their pure occurrentness, or brute facticity. The perceiver has first to make sense of these occurrent entities – to render them intelligible – by categorising them, and assigning to them meanings or functions. Heidegger, however, reverses this order of priority. For a being whose primary condition of existence is that of dwelling in the world, things are initially encountered in their availableness, as already integrated into a set of practices for 'coping' or getting by. To reveal their occurrent properties, things have to be rendered *un*intelligible by stripping away the significance they derive from contexts of ordinary use.[34]

In other words, ecophilosophy makes a distinction between the 'thing-for-us', the natural world as a resource for humans to utilise; and the 'thing-in-itself', stepping away from anthropocentrism to look at the world from a different point of view. Perhaps part of the motivation for MacDiarmid's incantatory use of geological vocabulary – what W. N. Herbert describes as the piling up of a 'philological' raised beach – is to break with his (and our) prior understanding of the stones, effectively to render them unintelligible, mysterious.[35] This recalls the linguistic 'othering' of the planet Earth enacted in 'The Eemis Stane' (1925), where the use of potent yet unfamiliar rural Scots vocabulary – 'how-dumb-deid', 'yowdendrift' – alters the reader's perception of the Earth as much as do the speaker's 'eerie memories' (*CP1*, p. 27). The geological wordplay in 'On a Raised Beach' performs a similar role, searching for an alternative outlook on nature and our place within it which is not accessible to us in our everyday experience of the world. We may think of stones as tools for building, MacDiarmid suggests, but that is not *their* truth: 'There are plenty of ruined buildings in the world but no ruined stones' (*CP1*, p. 425). Neither are they symbols: 'This is no heap of broken images' (*CP1*, p. 427), he remarks, alluding to T. S. Eliot's *The Waste Land* (1922), where a different stony landscape functions as a symbol of modernist alienation. For the reader unacquainted with geological science, the initial phrases of the poem, such as 'Cream-coloured caen-stone, chatoyant pieces, / Celadon and corbeau, bistre and beige' (*CP1*, p. 422), reveal only a sonic beauty. Devoid of their precise meanings, but deployed as what the phenomenologist Gaston Bachelard called 'phenomenological reverberation[s]', the words also represent all that remains unknown about the stones.[36] In the search for answers, MacDiarmid exchanges geological terms for equally obscure Shetlandic vocabulary: 'I try them with the old Norn words', but 'They hvarf [turn, disappear] from me in all directions [. . .] And lay my world in kolgref' – a Shetland expression meaning 'to leave the ground in a rough state' (*CP1*, p. 427).[37] While 'seeking a language in which he indisputably speaks the truth', as Herbert puts it, MacDiarmid is at the same time demonstrating the difficulty, even the impossibility, of that challenge.[38]

In *The Islands of Scotland* MacDiarmid looks to psychoanalytic theory for explanations, suggesting that modern humans suffer from 'a dissociative process that substitutes words for the physiological experience presumed to underlie them', with the result that 'man has lost touch with the hard and fast milieu of actual objects and correspondingly with the biological solidarity of his own organism'.[39] As in his earlier 'Synthetic Scots' period, where he argued for the 'unexhausted evolutionary momentum' of the Scots language as a medium for poetry, MacDiarmid uses this psychoanalytic argument to stress a parallel significance for Gaelic – a language that he was arguably ill-equipped to champion, lacking the native ability and understanding he was able to draw upon in his use of Scots.[40] In 'The Kind of Poetry I Want', Gaelic is figured as 'earth's subtlest speech', analogous to the fluidity of bird calls, which if deployed in poetry could 'put the skids under the whole of modern consciousness' (CP2, p. 1009). However, 'On a Raised Beach' looks beyond national languages to the broader question of what poetry is actually capable of representing, and the qualities the ideal poet should therefore possess – in a way, defining the limits of ecopoetics. Catherine Kerrigan notes that an early draft of the poem included the lines: 'How can language seize the life of a bird / In its buoyancy, volatility, sharp responsiveness . . .'[41] While excised from the final version, that enquiry forms an undertone to the work, and when MacDiarmid says 'I will have nothing interposed / Between my sensitiveness and the barren but beautiful reality' (CP1, p. 431), he highlights that essential paradox of ecopoetics: language is both a barrier and a conduit to our experience of the natural world. As Theodor Adorno says, 'Words tend to bounce off nature as they try to deliver nature's language into the hands of another language foreign to it.'[42]

Thus, the problem of how to 'get into this stone world' remains. 'I look at these stones and know little about them,' MacDiarmid admits:

> But I know their gates are open too,
> Always open, far longer open, than any bird's can be,
> That every one of them has had its gates wide open far longer
> Than all birds put together, let alone humanity,
> Though through them no man can see. (CP1, p. 423)

MacDiarmid was familiar with aspects of Heidegger's philosophy of *Dasein* (human being), explored in *Being and Time* (1927), as is evident from references to the work in *Lucky Poet* and *In Memoriam James Joyce*. In 'Letter to a Young Poet' (1959), MacDiarmid demonstrates this knowledge more fully, observing that 'uncanniness is a fundamental mode of "being-in-the-world"', which means 'the "that" is disclosed to *Dasein*, the "why" is concealed'.[43] *Dasein* is always faced with the problem of being in the world ('thrown' into the world, as Heidegger says) but at the same time separated from it, unable to access the truth of reality, a state of intrinsic 'uncanniness' or 'unhomeliness'.

'On a Raised Beach', with its suggestion that 'We have lost the grounds of our being' (*CP1*, p. 431), and its affirmation of the intrinsic state of exile that is modern life, appears to draw on elements of this philosophy, and indeed anticipates Heidegger's own meditation on stones and dwelling in his lecture 'The Origin of the Work of Art' (published 1950). A stone 'manifests its heaviness', Heidegger says, but 'it denies us any penetration into it'. Even if we split it open, or measure it in some way, it only reflects human properties back towards us – its weight, dimensions, usefulness, but not its essence. Heidegger continues:

> This perhaps very precise determination of the stone remains a number, but the weight's burden has escaped us [. . .] The earth appears openly cleared as itself only when it is perceived and preserved as that which is by nature undisclosable [. . .] The earth is essentially self-secluding.[44]

Heidegger's contention is that art enables us to accept the mystery of the world as mystery, to preserve and celebrate its 'undisclosable' nature. In Heideggerian philosophy, in contrast to the reductive approach of Cartesian science, art builds a temple from the stones. As Greg Garrard explains, in this ecophilosophical line, 'one of the crucial modes of proper letting be or unhindered disclosure of being is poetry; language, especially archaic or oblique poetic language, rightly understood discloses to us the act of disclosure itself'.[45] However, for MacDiarmid, with his avowedly Marxist, materialist perspective, the inherent mystery of reality does not invalidate the human quest to understand it. While 'it is wrong to indulge in these illustrations / Instead of just accepting the stones' (*CP1*, p. 425), the attempt to 'get into this stone world' is nevertheless the modern artist's imperative – 'Bread from stones is my sole and desperate dearth' (*CP1*, p. 423).

The sense of deracination explored in 'On a Raised Beach' was, for MacDiarmid, a cultural and political, as well as an existential condition. In a 1927 article for *The Pictish Review*, he identified the rehabilitation of Gaelic culture as a way to 'repair the fatal breach in continuity which has cut us off from our own roots'.[46] By 1931, writing in *The Modern Scot*, MacDiarmid was proposing a 'Gaelic Idea', 'designed to offset the Russian Idea', and calling for 'a redefinition and extension of our national principle of freedom on the plane of world-affairs, and in an abandonment alike of our monstrous neglect and ignorance of Gaelic'.[47] This Gaelic Idea, also explored in *To Circumjack Cencrastus* (1930), developed and matured during MacDiarmid's time in Shetland, resurfacing with renewed poetic power in *Stony Limits* as 'Lament for the Great Music' (1934). This development was aided by his growing knowledge of Gaelic literature and, from 1934 onwards, his friendship with the younger poet Sorley MacLean (1911–96), a modern Gaelic voice for which the Scottish Renaissance movement had long been seeking. In a 1954 letter to Neil M. Gunn, associating the 'Gaelic Idea' with his other great project, the quest for a poetry of facts, MacDiarmid said he had been 'concerned to dissociate myself from romantic idealisations of Gaelic "spirituality", etc., and a non-scientific attitude to Nature, in accordance with my own Marxist tenets'.[48] Still later, looking back on his career in a conversation with Duncan Glen in 1968, MacDiarmid agrees when Glen says 'you dropped the romantic imagination in the thirties – [. . .] Cartesian dualism had all gone from [. . .] your later work'.[49] For MacDiarmid, Gaelic language and culture, although not part of his own cultural roots, nor indeed the roots of the majority of the Scottish population, nevertheless offered a potent image of a distinct Scottish identity and a point of resistance against English cultural ascendancy. As Scott Lyall notes, the work of Gaelic bards such as Alasdair Mac Mhaighstir Alasdair (c.1695–c.1770) provided MacDiarmid with evidence of a pre-existing heritage which 'undermines the notion that Scottish culture began with its anglicisation'.[50] In its affinity with the epic or 'heroic' mode of poetry he had begun to champion in the 1930s, Gaelic also provided MacDiarmid with a much needed link between his vision of Scottish nationhood and his belief in poetry's ability to synthesise all forms of knowledge, including science.[51]

From the mid-1930s, with MacLean's help, MacDiarmid worked on a translation of one of the finest poems in the Gaelic canon, 'Moladh Beinn Dòbhrainn' or 'The Praise of Ben Dorain' by Donnchadh Bàn Mac an t'Saoir (Duncan Ban Macintyre, 1724–1812), which describes and celebrates the features and wildlife of the mountain Ben Dorain in the West Highlands. As Alan Bold and others have shown, MacLean provided 'literal line-by-line' English prose translations of this and other Gaelic poems, which MacDiarmid then set about transforming into his verse translation published in *The Golden Treasury of Scottish Poetry* (1940).[52] At times somewhat awkwardly prosaic, MacDiarmid's version concludes:

> . . . Though I've told a little of Ben Dorain here,
> Before I could tell all it deserves I would be
> In a delirium with the strange prolixity
> Of the talking called for, I fear. (*CP1*, p. 600)

It was significant for MacDiarmid that Macintyre had concluded 'Ben Dorain' by highlighting this philosophical point about the limits of poetry and of language to express the totality of even one mountain and its wildlife. For MacDiarmid, Gaelic poetics perhaps came closest to a language that 'indisputably speaks the truth' (to reprise Herbert's words). However, as Bold observes, 'if the poetry of the future was to be written in Gaelic then MacDiarmid would be a prophet though not a participant'.[53] MacLean, as a regular correspondent, poetic collaborator and friend who visited him on Whalsay in 1935, was thus a crucial advisor for MacDiarmid. Writing to MacDiarmid that same year, MacLean remarks that while the finished translation of 'Ben Dorain' did not succeed in evoking the rhythm and metre of the original, it 'brought out very well the internal description of physical things in which "Ben Dorain" is so remarkable'.[54] In his essay written during this period, 'Realism in Gaelic Poetry' (1934–6), which resists the mistily romantic Celtic Twilight view of Gaelic culture, MacLean contends that Macintyre's genius consisted in his 'objective naturalist realism': his poetry 'makes no pretension to metaphysical content; actually its realisation of dynamic nature makes its essential philosophic value as far superior to Wordsworth's poetry as it is in pure technique'.[55] Perhaps MacDiarmid had such an approach in mind in his two poetic 'talks' with Duncan Ban Macintyre, 'In Talk with Donnchadh Bàn Mac an t'Saoir' and 'Further Talk with Donnchadh Bàn Mac an t'Saoir', written after working on his verse translation of 'Ben Dorain'. In the first of these, contemplating the limits of writing, MacDiarmid suggests:

> It would be relatively easy to write the history
> Of a pair of nesting dab-chicks or of a day in their life,
> With a continuousness and exhaustiveness that might challenge comparison,
> Without breaks, a seamless garment,
> With the most accomplished and most dangerous works of modern fiction,
> Differing from them only in not pretending to know
> The birds' minds from the inside out, but hoping at best
> To get at their nature from their movements and write their odyssey
> By working from the outside in. (CP2, p. 1100)

For MacDiarmid, scientific enquiry and painstaking field observation were akin to the descriptive power of Gaelic poetics. In pursuit of this idea, both poems incorporate material borrowed from the ecologist Frank Fraser Darling's pioneering ecological study, A Herd of Red Deer (1937). Setting the tone for the first 'talk' is Darling's contention that 'It is very difficult for an active mind stuffed with the matter of "Education" to play its part effectively in stalking wild animals' – another echo of Geddes's belief in the superior value of the field-naturalist over the school teacher (CP2, p. 1098).[56] As in 'Tam o' the Wilds', the persona of the poet-naturalist looms large, this time in the figure of Macintyre himself, and MacDiarmid, having mined Fraser Darling's work for technical information as well as poetic imagery, addresses Macintyre on matters of effective deer stalking, the influence of environmental conditions and aspects of animal biology. Herbert notes that this portrait of Macintyre is 'impersonal' and suggests that it is his 'capacity to store information as much as the cultural value of the information stored that impresses

MacDiarmid'.[57] Perhaps MacDiarmid felt such impersonality was justified or even desirable, given MacLean's view that classical Gaelic poetry was characteristically 'deficient in explicit humanity'.[58] In any case, the 'Talks' form part of MacDiarmid's ongoing quest for a poetry of facts, significant not only as further evidence of his interest in and assimilation of contemporary ecological science, but also because, in the light of his claims for reinvigorated Gaelic culture, they further illuminate the ecophilosophical questions considered in 'On a Raised Beach'.

Cast as a kind of Gaelic 'Pan', Macintyre is capable of expressing 'The speech of one neither man nor animal – or both – / Yet not monster; a being in whom both races meet / On friendly ground'. But this 'being' also stands as a symbol for *poeisis* itself:

> Nature needed, and still needs, this beautiful creature
> Standing betwixt man and animal, sympathising with each,
> Comprehending the speech of either race, and interpreting
> The whole existence of one to the other. (CP2, p. 1099)

In 'On a Raised Beach' MacDiarmid had rejected the need for an interface 'Between my sensitiveness and the barren but beautiful reality' (CP1, p. 431). But while religious belief is discarded, poetry can fulfil this function as the point of connection or translation between humans and the natural world, a liminal 'beautiful creature', positioned 'on the verge of nature' (CP2, p. 1099). It is an idea found elsewhere in Scottish writing – Edwin Morgan, for example, speaks of poetry as 'the brilliant, vibrating interface between the human and the non-human' – and it is the central idea of ecopoetics, what Bate, after Heidegger, describes as 'the song that names the earth'.[59] Addressing Macintyre, MacDiarmid claims that 'only in *your* poetry' do we experience 'the feeling of having reached that state / All watchers of animals desire / Of having dispensed with our physical presence'. 'Or is that it?' he continues; and here perhaps MacDiarmid betrays a fundamental misunderstanding of the Gaelic tradition he claims to be a part of: 'Is not really the bottom of our desire / Not to be ignored but to be accepted?' (CP2, p. 1102). This is surely a romantic response distinct from the Gaelic 'objective naturalist realism' identified by MacLean and the matter-of-fact approach identified by Crichton Smith, for whom 'Ben Dorain' is a 'pagan poem, merciful or merciless', whose author 'would never have dreamed of using the deer as symbols for anything'.[60]

As MacDiarmid noted in 'On a Raised Beach', to recognise the thing-in-itself instead of 'the futile imaginings of men', to fulfil the obligation to 'reconcile ourselves to the stones, / Not the stones to us', is no easy task (CP1, pp. 425, 428). But despite such conflicting impulses, MacDiarmid remains convinced that poetry offers the solution. While, as he says in 'Letter to a Young Poet', 'the "that" is disclosed to *Dasein*, the "why" is concealed',[61] 'In Talk' identifies in Macintyre's work 'that faculty of sheer description / Which not only tells *what* a thing is, but at least / Incidentally goes far towards telling *why*. / – But beyond this how?' (CP2, p. 1099). Here, as in 'The Kind of Poetry I Want', the 'faculty of sheer description', normally the province of the scientist, is claimed as the ideal poet's craft, a possible antidote to deracination and the 'uncanny', groundless state contemplated in 'On a Raised Beach'. While not always successful in his quest for a poetry of facts, MacDiarmid's attempt to bring together Gaelic poetics, Geddesian ecological practice and the philosophy of being can be read as an important Scottish contribution to the discourse of ecopoetics, and a vital link between the polymaths of the nineteenth century, the Scottish Renaissance movement and the radical eco- and geopoetics of our contemporary world.

CHAPTER SEVEN

The Use of Science in Hugh MacDiarmid's Later Poetry

Michael H. Whitworth

Science was present in MacDiarmid's poetry from the start of his career: the phrase about 'the licht that bends', in 'Empty Vessel' (1926), alludes to the general theory of relativity; *A Drunk Man Looks at the Thistle* (1926) explicitly refers to Albert Einstein. However, it was only in the early 1930s that MacDiarmid began to engage more systematically with science and, above all, with scientific languages. Around 1932 or 1933, MacDiarmid began to use *Chambers's Twentieth Century Dictionary* to introduce unfamiliar language into his poetry.[1] The result may be seen in passages such as the opening of 'In the Caledonian Forest' from *Stony Limits and Other Poems* (1934):

> The geo-selenic gimbal that moving makes
> A gerbe now of this tree now of that
> Or glomerates the whole earth in a galanty-show
>   Against the full moon caught
> Suddenly threw a fuscous halation round a druxy dryad
>   Lying among the fumet in this dwale wood
> As brooding on Scotland's indecrassifiable race
>   I wandered again in a hemicranic mood. (*CP1*, p. 391)

In this passage, we could single out as scientific or near-scientific terms such as 'geo-selenic', 'gimbal', 'fuscous', 'halation' and 'hemicranic'. Elsewhere in the collection *Stony Limits*, we find terms such as 'palaeocrystic', 'pellagra', 'paxwax', 'phosphene', 'photopsia', 'thalamus', 'medial nuclei', 'corpora geniculata', 'halophilous', 'cleistogamic', 'gynandromorphic', 'chalones', 'laevorotatory', 'lagophthalmic' and 'lithogenesis'. The list is by no means complete. Moreover, the dictionary was not MacDiarmid's only resource. He also drew on scientific papers, on non-technical scientific books and articles, and on book reviews. He took from them not only isolated terms, but whole phrases and whole passages. Such practices were employed frequently in *Stony Limits*; the incorporation of long prose passages became the main principle of composition for the epic poem that he began to construct in the later 1930s, and which was eventually published as *In Memoriam James Joyce* (1955).

The employment of scientific ideas or language in a poem raises questions of authority. When scientific ideas are removed from the institutional frame-work that guarantees their effectiveness – especially practices of measure-ment and experiment – their validity as science comes to rest increasingly on whether the poet understands them. Should the poet's authority in matters scientific derive from his or her understanding of the science, or might it derive instead from his or her ability to make a compelling poem from sci-entific materials? To ask questions about the poet's understanding of science is to raise reflexive questions about our own terminology: what does it mean to understand science? The terms of the question might be different accord-ing to the context in which it is asked. If we allow that a school-teacher's understanding of science is different from that of an active researcher in the subject, might we allow that a poet's understanding is different again, or might this risk diluting the meaning of 'science' and hence its claim to authority? The practice of engaging with science as a vocabulary and a kind of writing (rather than as a set of ideas) is particularly vulnerable to charges of incomprehension. Anyone can cut and paste.

A poem like 'In the Caledonian Forest' risks alienating readers through its vocabulary, and any poem that engages with science introduces new forms of difficulty for both poet and reader. MacDiarmid had several different motivations. Like many of his modernist contemporaries, he was impatient with the scope of the lyrical tradition he had inherited. His poems of the early 1920s had attempted to renew the Scottish lyric tradition, and his poems of the 1930s attempt to reinvigorate and extend the scope of the English-language lyric poem. He also made criticisms of a wider scope, aimed at the conventions and the forces that limit human potential. In 1923 he identified the problem as being humanism, which was based on 'exclusion, selection, discipline', and contrasted this with science: 'No form of Humanism can ever comprehend totality. But science seeks all, every-where: and literature must follow suit – or cease to survive, save as a dope for inadequate minds.'[2] In the aphorisms of 'Art and the Unknown' (1926), he announces that the function of art is the 'extension of human conscious-ness'.[3] In the early 1930s, he was frequently critical of Basic English and similar schemes for a 'world-language', because they necessitated the limita-tion of consciousness.[4] In 1933, he defended Paul Valéry for what one critic had described as 'indigestible lumps of scientific vocabulary' in his poetry. There was, he argued, no particular merit in everyday language, which he termed 'the jargon of average mentality'; there was no 'special virtue [in] restricting our linguistic medium to a miserable fraction of our expressive resources'. He urged poets 'to extend the general vocabulary' and to make it 'adequate to the enormous range and multitudinous intensive specialisations of contemporary knowledge'.[5]

In the later 1930s MacDiarmid's ambitions, or his rationale for his practice, shifted subtly. In the preface to his autobiography *Lucky Poet*, he describes himself as having insisted on 'a poetry of fact' (*LP*, p. xxxii). In Walt Whitman's words, which MacDiarmid quotes, poetry must 'conform with and build on the concrete realities and theories of the universe furnished by science' (*LP*, pp. xxxii, 187). While such a poetry might legitimately avail itself of the linguistic resources of the sciences, it is also possible to conceive of a poetry that deals with scientific realities and theories in a non-scientific language. If MacDiarmid's 'poetry of fact' was primarily characterised by its incorporation of specialist vocabularies and of near verbatim quotation from scientific writing, it was because these practices had been familiar to the poet since the 1920s and early 1930s, and not because of any necessary connection to Whitman's ideal. The account of 'a poetry of facts' (in the plural) given in the poem 'Poetry and Science' (1943) suggests other motivations. The poem argues that the interconnection of 'all living substance' is a chemical connection, and that consequently 'Without some chemistry one is bound to remain / Forever a dumbfounded savage / In the face of vital reactions' (*CP1*, pp. 630, 631). One implication is that the poet has an educational duty to expand his readers' consciousness, in this case by providing them with 'some chemistry'.

Although Kenneth Buthlay has argued that scientific terminology offered 'a possibility of fresh linguistic sustenance that the English poets themselves had hardly begun to be aware of',[6] MacDiarmid was not the first English-language poet of his generation to draw attention to the importance of scientific ideas, nor was he the first to draw sustenance from scientific language. The well-known essay 'The Metaphysical Poets' (1921) by T. S. Eliot (1888–1965) began a revival of interest in the seventeenth-century metaphysical poets, and the revival was further advanced by an essay now neglected, but of equal importance at the time, 'The Nature of Metaphysical Poetry' (1923), by Herbert Read (1893–1968). MacDiarmid probably read Read's essay in the collection of essays *Reason and Romanticism* (1926).[7] The poetry in Read's *Mutations of the Phoenix* (1923) provided varied examples of what a new metaphysical poetry might look like. Typically, the new metaphysical poets followed the line of John Donne's lyrics and subordinated a scientific idea or ideas to a first-person voice. The interest was in scientific ideas; the invocation of scientific terminology was secondary. Traces of the revival of metaphysical poetry may be found in *Transitional Poem* (1929) and *From Feathers to Iron* (1931) by C. Day Lewis, in *These Our Matins* (1930) and *Poems* (1936) by Michael Roberts, and most prominently in poems by William Empson from the late 1920s. There was, however, another modernist approach to science, and this emphasised science as a distinctive dialect, scientific ideas being secondary. T. S. Eliot's use of 'etherised' in the third line of 'The Love Song of J. Alfred Prufrock' is a case in point: Eliot does not make a conceit out of etherisation, but the intrusion of the term pierces the smooth lyric surface of the poem. MacDiarmid was drawn to this method more than that of the neo-metaphysicals, but, as we shall see, he took it to a distinctive extreme.

MacDiarmid had no formal scientific training, but was fortunate to live in a period when popular science publications were plentiful and were widely reviewed in the 'literary' pages of weekly publications. There were rich quarries for him to mine. Given that scholarly explorations of MacDiarmid's sources are at a relatively early stage, any generalisations must be tentative. The investigation of them is greatly facilitated by the digitisation of texts, but the selective nature of what is digitised means that some kinds of source are more readily discoverable than others, and the present picture may be distorted. Though MacDiarmid often used book reviews, he also drew directly on books. (Of course in some cases he may have drawn on an as-yet unidentified review which quoted extensively from the source.) His sources were varied: although, among books, popular science works predominate (for example J. B. S. Haldane's 1927 collection of essays *The Inequality of Man*, or Gerald Heard's 1935 book based on BBC broadcasts, *Science in the Making*), he occasionally drew on more specialist works, such as Erwin Schrödinger's *Statistical Thermodynamics* (1946). It appears that MacDiarmid's eye was very often caught by lists of technical terminology, and these he found in a wide variety of sources. In *In Memoriam James Joyce* the first part of the account of personality types ('sanguine', 'mercurial', 'somatotonic' and so forth, *CP2*, pp. 843–4) comes from Aldous Huxley's collection of essays *Ends and Means* (1937), while the later part (from 'Pyknic' to 'schizothymes', *CP2*, p. 844) comes from a more technical work, Emanuel Miller's *Types of Mind and Body* (1927). In 'The Kind of Poetry I Want' the names of uranium ores investigated by Marya Sklodowska (better known as Marie Curie) derives not from a technical work, though terms like 'tjujamunite' and 'betafite' (*CP2*, p. 1019) might lead one to believe so, but from a novelised account of Curie's life, Rudolf Brunngraber's *Radium: A Novel*, translated by Eden and Cedar Paul (1937). In all these instances the source was less important than the verbal effects the language allowed MacDiarmid to achieve. MacDiarmid also frequently accessed books indirectly through book reviews and the quotations contained within them. He was particularly indebted to the *Times Literary Supplement*. His account of animal camouflage in 'On a Raised Beach' (*CP1*, pp. 424–5) comes from the *TLS* review of Major R. W. G. Hingston's *The Meaning of Animal Colour and Adornment* (1933), while the account of the 'Paneubiotic Synthesis' in *In Memoriam James Joyce* (*CP2*, p. 787) comes from the review of Edmond Bordeaux Székely's *Cosmos, Man and Society* (1936).[8]

While 'In the Caledonian Forest' demonstrated what could be done using *Chambers's Dictionary*, elsewhere in *Stony Limits* MacDiarmid drew on scientific journal articles. 'Stony Limits', his elegy for Charles Doughty (1843–1926), takes geological terminology from two papers published in the *Geological Magazine* in 1927. Doughty's poetry had been marginalised by critics for its use of archaic word forms and syntactical patterns, but MacDiarmid had recognised in these experiments a precedent for his own work. In his essay 'Charles Doughty and the Need for Heroic Poetry' from *The Modern Scot* (1936) he explicitly linked Doughty's defiance of conventional ideas of poetic diction with 'the urgent and unescapable necessity of the poetic use of the full range of modern scientific terminology' (*SP*, p. 130). To use such terminology in a tribute to Doughty was, in MacDiarmid's eyes, particularly appropriate. The first four stanzas of 'Stony Limits' present, in relatively conventional elegiac terms, an idealised funeral scene ('we bury thee') and the raising of a funeral cairn to 'mark the unfrequented place' (*CP1*, pp. 419, 420). These stanzas also establish the regular pattern of rhymes that runs throughout the poem (ababcdcdee). However, the vocabulary they employ, while wide, contains no unusual technical terms. In the fourth stanza MacDiarmid, in a relatively conventional gesture, questions the right of the mourners to praise Doughty: 'How should we have anything to give you / In death who had nothing in life [. . .]?' (*CP1*, p. 420). This leads to the larger self-questioning of the fifth stanza, and it is in this stanza that the technical vocabulary derived from the *Geological Magazine* first manifests itself:

The poem that would praise you must be
Like the glass of some rock, sleek brown, crowded
With dark incipient crystal growths, we see;
Or a glimpse of Petavius may have endowed it
With the tubular and dumb-bell-shaped inclusions surrounded
    By the broad reaction rims it needs.
I have seen it in dreams and know how it abounded
– Ah! would I could find in me like seeds! –
As the north-easterly garden in the lunation grows,
A spectacle not one man in ten millions knows. (*CP1*, p. 421)

The stanza hints at the poems about poetry that MacDiarmid would later create in 'The Kind of Poetry I Want' (1961), in which an encyclopaedic range of discourses provides the basis for similes about poetry. In 'Stony Limits', however, MacDiarmid draws exclusively on geology. The description of a poem like 'the glass of some rock' derives from an article by the geologist David Balsillie that sought to date volcanic activity in East Fife. Much of the article consists of careful descriptions of the rocks found there; MacDiarmid took several phrases from a description of the typical 'fresh glassy basalt' found at Ruddons Point. The lines under present consideration draw on the following: 'The glass of the rock is bright brown, full of magnetite, and crowded with dark polyzoiform incipient crystal growths.'[9] MacDiarmid makes poetry from some unpromising materials by maintaining the rhyme scheme: 'crowded' forces him to provide 'endowed it' later on, and although the rhyme is a little awkward, the grammar moves the reader on to the next line before the awkwardness has had time to register. He brings a degree of regularity to the rhythm by removing the word 'polyzoiform' from his source text. (The term, extremely rare, is not recorded in the edition of *Chambers* that MacDiarmid used, nor even in the present-day *Oxford English Dictionary*, but apparently derives from 'polyzoism'.) With 'polyzoiform' removed, the plosive 'k' of 'dark' chimes with the 't' of 'incipient' and the 'k' sound of 'crystal'.

Although the phrase 'dark incipient crystal growths' is the first prominent use of technical vocabularies, the fourth stanza's description of Doughty as 'facile as granite [. . .] / A plug suspended in England's false dreams' (*CP1*, p. 420) also suggests a geological formation, and may have been suggested by MacDiarmid's other geological source, an article by E. H. L. Schwarz from the *Geological Magazine*.[10] The article concerns granite structures of volcanic origin: it begins in Scotland, with an example in Glencoe, but draws in examples from a wide range of places, including Germany, Africa and the Moon. It is from Schwartz's article that MacDiarmid draws the name of the lunar crater Petavius, and in the following stanza those of Arzachel and Langrenus. The 'north-easterly garden' is part of the crater Alphonsus, which the turn-of-the-century astronomer William Henry Pickering had suggested contained vegetation, an idea that Schwarz cautiously endorsed and developed.

The extent to which the poem reshapes the scientific texts can only be appreciated if the original articles are read in full. MacDiarmid's art is, at least in part, an art of elimination, of knowing what to remove in order to allow the source materials to achieve their full potential. To give a simple example: for MacDiarmid, the poem in praise of Doughty must be like the glass of 'some rock'. It would have been possible for MacDiarmid to make a roughly metrical line in which the poem must be 'like the fresh glassy basalt of Ruddons Point'; 'Point' would have been easier to rhyme than 'crowded', but such a comparison would have introduced a specificity of reference that would be distracting so early in the building of the conceit.

An examination of the source articles shows that they employ a language that is technical and almost always neutrally descriptive. Although Schwarz allows himself a simile in which the creation of the 'torsion cylinders' is like 'rolling a lump of putty between one's hands', and although Balsillie allows himself to describe one particular feature as 'splendid', these are exceptions to the rule. Though both articles advance theories about the formation of particular geological structures, neither is aiming to develop general geological theories or to effect a paradigm shift in his discipline. While some scientific theories, like Darwin's theory of evolution, have been attractive to literary writers for their fundamental conceptual metaphors, the appeal of these texts to MacDiarmid lay elsewhere. MacDiarmid borrows descriptive phrases from them, but an examination of the source articles reveals the extent of the transformation. MacDiarmid removes the language of impersonal observation (in Schwarz, crossing shear planes 'may be seen'), and removes qualifying phrases that are typical of their cautious generalisations (in Balsillie, for example, crystals 'often' show 'very fine striae'). MacDiarmid also removes explicit numerical indications of scale. Though later in his career he was not shy of including the numerical in his poetry, as we see in 'The Kind of Poetry I Want' in phrases about the 'glow worm's 96 per cent efficiency' and a photograph 'Taken at a speed of 1/75,000 of a second' (CP2, pp. 1016, 1019), in 'Stony Limits' the avoidance of numerical information allows MacDiarmid to merge two very different sources. Though Schwarz and Balsillie are both examining volcanic activity, the scales of the phenomena under examination differ immensely: Balsillie describes microscopic crystal forms, while Schwartz examines granite cylinders with diameters measured in miles and cliffs hundreds of feet high. By splicing together the two sources, and by removing obvious signposts to their incompatibility, MacDiarmid creates phrases that seem plausible to non-specialist readers, but that would furrow the brows of geologists. Such shifts in scale are most prominent in the next stanza. MacDiarmid, conscious of Doughty's Englishness, and that Doughty's travels in North Africa and the Middle East made his best-known landscapes very different from MacDiarmid's own, fashions an imaginary landscape that the two writers might share:

> I belong to a different country than yours
> And none of my travels have been in the same lands
> Save where Arzachel or Langrenus allures
> Such spirits as ours, and the Straight Wall stands,
> But crossing shear planes extruded in long lines of ridges,
> Torsion cylinders, crater rings, and circular seas
> And ultra-basic xenoliths that make men look midges
> Belong to my quarter as well, and with ease
> I too can work in bright green and all the curious interference
> Colours that under crossed nicols have a mottled appearance. (CP1, p. 421)

The 'crossing shear planes', 'torsion cylinders', 'crater rings' are features of Schwarz's lunar landscape, and the phrases all have specific sources in Schwarz's article, but the 'ultra-basic xenoliths' derive from Balsillie's rocks: Balsillie goes on to remark that the xenoliths 'occur in various sizes from mere nut-like pieces to nodules that measure a foot across'.[11] While the difference in scale does not intrinsically prevent the planes, cylinders, rings and xenoliths from belonging together, the poem does nothing to acknowledge their diversity.

MacDiarmid's willingness to conflate diverse discourses risks a loss of scientific accuracy. Edwin Morgan has remarked that '"crossing shear planes" are not "extruded"' and that '"ultra-basic xenoliths that make men look like [sic] midges" (presuming that this refers to size rather than durability) would be exceedingly unlikely since most xenoliths are even smaller than man-size'.[12] In the case of the xenoliths, knowing MacDiarmid's source gives us confidence that he was thinking in terms of durability rather than extension. In the case of the shear-planes, knowing the source enables us to see the source of the error, but does nothing to explain it away. There are two further problems not noted by Morgan. The first is simply an error of transcription: Balsillie describes 'microclines', but in MacDiarmid's poem these becomes 'microlines'. If we assume that this means a very small line, it is entirely compatible with 'cross-hatching', and makes a new kind of sense. The other problem relates to these lines: 'I too can work in bright green and all the curious interference / Colours that under crossed nicols have a mottled appearance'. If we examine the sources, it is clear that the interference colours are attributes of the pyroxenes on one page, and that the activity of viewing a section of stone 'under crossed nicols' comes in a separate part of Balsillie's discussion.[13] It is not clear that the interference colours could be viewed under crossed nicols, nor that they would appear mottled if one could do so. Exigencies of rhyme have forced MacDiarmid to place the phrase 'mottled appearance' in a context where it should not belong.

These errors pose a question of authority. What authorises the poet to appropriate scientific materials? MacDiarmid's own answer might have been that the end justified the means: that the need to expand our expressive and cognitive resources gave him the right to borrow as he pleased. But can such acts of appropriation be justified if they diminish the accuracy of the concepts? If scientific terminology acquires precision only as part of the institutional framework of science, then all literary appropriations will result in some imprecision, but MacDiarmid's errors are very specific. If we equate authority with a formal education in science, it is relatively easy to criticise most poets for their lack of authority, with a few rare exceptions like William Empson, who had degrees in both mathematics and English literature. If we set the bar slightly lower, we might require proof that the poet had read relevant popular science writing. MacDiarmid's plagiaristic strategy means that we can demonstrate with unusual certainty which texts he had read, but we are left uncertain as to how well and in what way he understood them. In any case, it may be that the poet's authority to appropriate derives from elsewhere: the authority comes not from the poet's scientific understanding, or at least not only, but from his or her ability to shape scientific materials into a convincing poem. The regular stanzaic form of a poem like 'Stony Limits' might persuade us, sometimes against our better judgement, that MacDiarmid is in control of his materials.

A more developed objection to MacDiarmid's use of scientific discourse was advanced by Veronica Forrest-Thomson.[14] Forrest-Thomson argues that science is a *system* of thought. It is not enough to understand isolated terms: the poet must understand the relevant semantic field. Metaphor, it follows, is not an isolated trope, but the whole action of transporting discourse from one domain to another. In transporting scientific terms from their original domain, the poet is 'mythologising' science: science becomes 'a formal system of suggestive fictions, the relations of which may be exploited without reference to their factual content for the purpose of poetic metaphor'.[15] Forrest-Thomson refers to the process of mythologisation as the 'thinking through'[16] of the original system: the phrase suggests both that the poet must 'think through' the system in the sense of contemplation and comprehension, and that, having done so, he or she will be able to make it a medium for new thought, thinking *through* it just as one might see through a lens. When a system of thought is properly thought through, the poem will be able to 'create a new structure of meaning which will integrate the diverse significances of the words it uses'.[17] Conversely, a failure to 'think through' the alien concepts will result in a 'stylistic failure' in the poem. Forrest-Thomson notes that MacDiarmid's approach was quite different. Though she concedes that 'On a Raised Beach' assimilates scientific knowledge to the extent that it creates a poetic metaphor, in general she believes that MacDiarmid's guiding principle was 'the avoidance of metaphorical transformation in the use of scientific terms'.[18] She singles out for criticism 'The Kind of Poetry I Want': it is, she says, 'simply a statement of prose popularization and of the emotional attitude we are intended to adopt towards it'.[19] It is not clear whether by 'prose popularization' Forrest-Thomson means that MacDiarmid is creating popularised versions of technical scientific works, or that he is incorporating popular scientific texts, but, either way, she implies that 'The Kind of Poetry I Want' incorporates without assimilating; it transcribes scientific texts, but does not think through scientific discourse. Similar criticisms might easily be levelled at *In Memoriam James Joyce*: ultimately each of the many kinds of knowledge referred to in the poem signifies something that we should greet with an emotional attitude of excitement and receptivity. In both poems, one piece of knowledge is effectively interchangeable with another: this is clearest in 'The Kind of Poetry I Want' and its use of repeated formulae at the start of each paragraph ('A poetry like . . .', 'A poetry that . . .').

However, Forrest-Thomson's view of the proper use of science is often highly prescriptive, and it fails to comprehend MacDiarmid's achievement. In her emphasis on the unity of the poem and its ability to integrate 'diverse significances', Forrest-Thomson subscribes to an essentially New Critical idea of the poem as unified object. Moreover her insistence that 'mythologised' scientific ideas become purely systems of formal relations echoes the New Critical idea that the poem, the 'verbal icon', achieves a quasi-religious transcendence of everyday referentiality. One might ask whether it is really so easy to remove all referential function from scientific language, or whether, in fact, the real might awkwardly reassert itself. And one might further speculate that the tension between scientific terms understood in their referential function and in their formal relations to other terms might have the potential to produce arresting aesthetic effects. MacDiarmid's achievement is to create striking poems from scientific materials while allowing the scientific text a degree of autonomy, whether this is in the retention of a prose-like rhythm, or the creation of awkward rhymes.

The poem 'Stony Limits' borrows distinctive words and phrases from geological discourse, but by 1934 MacDiarmid was plagiarising whole sentences and paragraphs. The most sustained example of plagiarism in *Stony Limits*, 'Etika Preobrazhennavo Erosa', uses non-scientific sources, but a more tentative experiment in the incorporation of science is to be found in the fourth paragraph of 'On a Raised Beach' (beginning 'Actual physical conflict or psychological warfare . . .'), which, as noted earlier, borrows extensively from a *Times Literary Supplement* review.[20] In the 'On a Raised Beach' passage (*CP1*, pp. 424–5), as in 'Stony Limits', MacDiarmid asserts control of the prose materials by incorporating them into a loosely rhyming structure. Typically, the first word in each rhyming pair derives from the prose source, while the second is MacDiarmid's addition. 'Etika' and 'On a Raised Beach' were early experiments in a method that MacDiarmid employed to a much greater extent in the composition of *In Memoriam James Joyce*. The appropriation of isolated words became less important than the appropriation of whole passages, although these passages are very often marked by their unusual lexis. In the later phase of his career, MacDiarmid also used borrowed passages of scientific material to construct shorter lyric poems: 'To a Friend and Fellow-Poet', a poem written in 1937, provides a good specimen case.[21]

In considering MacDiarmid's adaptation of his prose sources, it is as illuminating to note the unused passages and phrases as to highlight what he selected. 'To a Friend and Fellow-Poet' presents an astonishing analogy between the reproductive processes of a parasite, the female guinea worm, and the creative processes of a poet. The reproductive cycle requires the guinea worm to turn her entire body into a womb, to her eventual destruction. The underlying analogical framework, in which literary creation resembles biological reproduction, is an age-old one: for example, in the first sonnet of *Astrophil and Stella* (1591), Sir Philip Sidney is 'great with child to speak'. The traditional analogy enables the transfer of biological discourse into the new linguistic domain with relative economy. All MacDiarmid need do is frame the poem with the initial declaration of analogy ('It is with the poet as with a guinea worm'), and with the concluding three lines:

> Is it not precisely thus we poets deliver our store,
> Our whole being the instrument of our suicidal art,
> And by the skin of our teeth flype ourselves into fame? (CP2, pp. 1057–8)

Though the broad analogy between biological reproduction and artistic creativity is long-established, the reproductive biology of the guinea worm is so far removed from that of humans that the analogy is dramatically altered; Sir Philip Sidney could never have anticipated this poem. The account of the guinea worm is not MacDiarmid's. It is drawn from a description by the physician and parasitologist Sir Patrick Manson (1844–1922) in his *Lectures on Tropical Diseases* (1905); it is possible that MacDiarmid drew on a long excerpt given in a 1927 biography of Manson. Manson's own account shares with MacDiarmid's a dual perspective on the worm: it moves rapidly and unexpectedly between an anthropomorphic perspective and one that is more detached and technical. The passage as excerpted in 1927 begins by stating that 'The female guinea-worm has a good knowledge of anatomy, for when at maturity she moves down to the leg, without wounding the blood-vessels or nerves, and rarely strays into the joints.'[22] Manson's use of 'knowledge' is somewhat ironic, given that the worm's actions are apparently entirely instinctual; later, Manson presents the extrusion of the embryos from her body in mechanistic terms of stimulus and response. The idea that the worm possesses anatomical 'knowledge' offers a point of identification for Manson's clinical audience, though not one that they would have taken too seriously. It also implicitly poses questions about the nature of knowledge and what it means to possess it, and we might speculate that the opening phrase, though unused by MacDiarmid, pricked his curiosity.

MacDiarmid's selection from Manson tends to present the guinea worm in a more detached tone; above all, it removes nearly all reference to the human host of the worm and to the idea that a human clinician might be studying it. At times, however, MacDiarmid's revisions increase the anthropomorphic element. Take, for example, the opening sentence, minus the parenthetical interpolation:

> It is with the poet as with a guinea worm
> Who, to accommodate her teeming progeny
> Sacrifices nearly every organ of her body, and becomes [. . .]

Almost wholly given over to her motherly task,
Little more than one long tube close-packed with young. (CP2, p. 1057)

The relevant sentences in Manson run thus:

> If, at the time of her appearance at the surface of the body, you manage to procure an uninjured guinea-worm and dissect her, you will find that from head to tail she is little more than one long tube packed with young. To accommodate the millions of long-tailed embryos nearly every organ of her body has been more or less sacrificed. Although thus devoting herself practically entirely to reproduction, the guinea-worm is nevertheless at this stage in a grave obstetrical dilemma.[23]

In Manson's text the parasitologist's knowledge of the worm is produced through an experimental intervention; in MacDiarmid's, the parasitologist becomes invisible, and we are given unmediated knowledge of the parasite. Only occasionally in MacDiarmid's poem do vestiges of Manson's original address to his audience survive, in phrases such as 'You see her dauntless head protrude' (CP2, p. 1057), and even in these cases, the original scenario, in which the audience was asked to imagine itself performing the observations, has been completely removed. Other phrases are paraphrased by MacDiarmid, and inevitably altered in the process. The conversion of 'millions of long-tailed embryos' to 'her teeming progeny' reduces the species-specific quality of the phrase; indeed given that 'teeming' often occurs in discussions of human over-population, the rephrasing introduces a note entirely absent from the prose source. The verb 'sacrifice' belongs to the original text, but MacDiarmid replaces Manson's passive voice with the active, making the worm more willingly the agent of her own destruction. What is perhaps surprising is that while Manson spoke of the worm being devoted 'practically entirely to reproduction', in MacDiarmid the technical and detached phrase is rendered as 'Almost wholly given over to her motherly task'. In this instance, contrary to his more general tendency, MacDiarmid has rewritten the source text in such a way as to strengthen the anthropomorphism.

MacDiarmid's removal of human agency in the production of scientific knowledge is most apparent in the passage describing the emergence of the 'beautiful, delicate, and pellucid tube' (CP2, p. 1057) from the mouth of the worm. Reading MacDiarmid's poem, it is easy to forget that the worm itself partly emerges from the body of a human host. In Manson's account, both the doctor and the patient are fully present. Although Manson speaks of the doctor paying daily visits to the worm and not the patient, and of protecting it from injury, we may take these remarks as intentionally ironic when addressed to an audience that understands the Hippocratic oath. The doctor who pays regular visits will 'very likely [. . .] witness a display of obstetric surgery not to be beaten even in the most advanced clinics':

> Sooner or later, on one of your daily visits, on removing the dressing you will find that the worm herself has partly emerged from her hole, half an inch or even more of her head protruding. Now repeat the douching and watch the head carefully. Presently a beautiful and pellucid tube is slowly projected from her mouth to the extent of three-quarters of an inch or thereabouts.[24]

MacDiarmid's text removes the patient and the daily visit, and allows the reader a narrower focus and an almost exclusive concentration on the worm; it loses the lighter, urbane tone of Manson's lecture. Moreover, MacDiarmid removes some of Manson's anthropomorphic tropes. In Manson's text, the worm is presented first as an intelligent agent attempting to overcome a 'difficulty' (rather than as a lower life-form following an instinctive process); later, and more elaborately, it is presented as an obstetric surgeon displaying great ingenuity. In both cases the anthropomorphism is so implausible as to be ironic: it reminds us of the distance between worm and man. Although MacDiarmid inserts an epithet which tends towards anthropomorphism – the worm becomes 'dauntless' – his anthropomorphisms do not have the self-aware, ironic tone of Manson's.

The core of the poem focuses closely on the worm, turning to another frame of reference only twice, when a quite distinct voice exclaims 'and that stimulus / O Poets! but cold water!', and then when a voice glosses the worm's emptiness by reference to 'Alexander Blok's utter emptiness after creating a poem!' (CP2, pp. 1057, 1058). In this regard, although the poem pursues an extended analogy between worm and artist, it is far removed from the tradition of metaphysical poetry derived from John Donne, in which the poet's voice more frequently intervenes to amplify the analogy or to dampen unwanted resonances and vibrations. Here, with the crucial exception of the framing lines and the two interventions just mentioned, MacDiarmid presents the guinea worm in itself. This places a particularly great burden on the final three lines, where the framing analogy is reasserted. Two details call for particular attention. The word 'flype' stands out: by virtue of being dialect it presents a completely different frame of reference from that of the Standard English used in the body of the poem, perhaps to suggest a sudden outburst of passion on the part of a speaker who has for much of the poem adopted a coldly clinical tone in speaking of a grotesque biological process. The phrase 'precisely thus' also stands out. Although the self-sacrifice of the guinea-worm offers a broad analogy for poetic self-sacrifice, especially in the fact of her exposing her interior to the outside world, the extent of technical detail in the description far exceeds the needs of the analogy. There is, for example, no obvious equivalent in the life of the poet for the 'little circular sore', or for the entire 'musculocutaneous coat' (CP2, p. 1057) becoming a substitute uterus and, even if there were, the poem has done nothing up to this point to indicate what they might be. While 'precisely' might prompt us to ask what the analogies could be (could the 'pellucid tube' be a pen, for example?), it also serves to remind us of the distance between the precise description that forms the body of the poem and the vaguer and emotionally charged uses to which the framing discourse would like to put that description. Although in some poems MacDiarmid might legitimately be accused of not having adequately digested the scientific discourse that he employs (of not having 'thought through' it, in Veronica Forrest-Thomson's terms), in 'To a Friend and Fellow-Poet' the incompleteness of the appropriation of science serves its own purposes: it reminds us of the partial autonomy of scientific discourse from other kinds of discourse, and also of the autonomy of the natural world which that discourse describes. There is something about the guinea worm that remains beyond appropriation. If the gestural term 'thus' opens up a space within the poem between the frame and the content, and thereby between the tenor and the vehicle of the metaphor, it does so with good reason.

Though MacDiarmid was not alone among poets of the 1920s and 1930s in engaging with scientific language, he did so on an unparalleled scale, and in a mode entirely different from poets like Read, Roberts and Empson. His poems relish scientific language and create unprecedented verbal textures and imaginative landscapes. His plagiaristic approach leaves him open to the criticism that he did not understand the materials he was working with, and that he was happy to be associated with the authority of science without doing the work necessary to understand it, and the work necessary to shape it into poetic material. But his willingness to present materials that are not fully tamed, not fully 'thought through', has a value all of its own. MacDiarmid's incorporations of science verbally dramatise the strangeness of science, and thereby dramatise the strangeness of the non-human world to which scientific language refers.

CHAPTER EIGHT

Hugh MacDiarmid's (Un)making of the Modern Scottish Nation

Carla Sassi

Hugh MacDiarmid's work as a poet, journalist, essayist, critic and political activist, as well as his contentious persona, are all indelibly and inextricably bound to his life-long, controversial engagement with inter/nationalism. Expelled from the National Party of Scotland in 1933, in part because of his increasing communist affiliation, and in 1936 from the Communist Party of Great Britain because of his 'nationalist deviationism', MacDiarmid personifies, possibly like no other writer, the conflict between two over-arching ideologies, opposed yet co-existing throughout the post/modern age. His long life, critically spanning the early decades of modernism to the eve of the digital revolution, as well as his position within a stateless nation which was both agent and arguably object of British colonialism, make him a pivotal figure not just within the Scottish literary canon but also – as the present chapter purports to demonstrate – within the emerging map of global modernisms, one in which Europe and the United States are important, but not exclusive, sites of cultural production. Such a reconfigured vision of Modernist Studies, advocated in recent years by postcolonial and feminist theorists and redefining modernism as a transnational movement deeply related to the world expansion of nineteenth-century empires, with simultaneously local and global affiliations,[1] will provide the privileged theoretical framework for the present investigation. Seen under this decentred, planetary perspective, in fact, MacDiarmid's engagement with both nationalism and internationalism does not seem any longer either contradictory or eccentric, as it has often been labelled, but rather it can be reassessed as a valuably complex and nuanced expression of modernism's unease with eighteenth- and nineteenth-century concepts of the nation and the modernist quest for new paradigms of trans/national spaces. His re-vision of the Scottish nation, as we shall see, can be seen as a pioneering attempt to transcend not only nineteenth-century constructions of Scottishness, but also to question powerfully the discourse of the nation-state through two distinct and yet deeply related strategies: an 'autoethnographic' account of Scotland and an embodied sense of belonging in the Scottish landscape.

It is worthwhile pointing out, as an opening remark, that even canonically defined Anglo-American modernism is grounded on a tense dialectic between globalism and localism. It is well known, for example, that Ezra Pound, W. B. Yeats, T. S. Eliot, James Joyce and Virginia Woolf actively promoted cosmopolitanism as an existential as well as an aesthetic practice, and that they also all engaged at different levels with nationalism: Pound was drawn by fascist cultural nationalism; Yeats and Joyce supported, in different ways, Irish nationalism; Eliot theorised the centrality and continuity of national traditions; and Woolf subtly articulated ideas of Englishness in her fiction. Beyond Anglo-American modernism, the downright collusion of modernist poetics with explicitly nationalist agendas was hardly an exception. In Poland, for example, as in Hungary, 'the national style, reconciling modern art with a local vernacular would now express the state's modernity as well as its national tradition.'[2] Similarly, in the United States, the Harlem Renaissance promoted racial self-assertion and self-definition in the face of normative white supremacy – the particularity of blackness in this case aimed at unsettling notions of white 'universality'.

If, then, a complex dialectic between globalism and localism in itself can be regarded as a significant feature of modernist discourse, irrespective of whether we define modernism traditionally or not, it is also evident that such dialectic takes on a different structure, depending on the political or cultural context in which it is uttered. If a generalisation may be attempted, in fact, in high modernist writers such as Pound, Yeats, Eliot, Joyce and Woolf, such tension remains circumscribed within a binary logic that defines global-local interdependence in hegemonic terms (with the latter term subordinated to the former), thus generating a specific logic and order of reality. These writers, as Caren Kaplan has observed, 'foster the collective imagining of a condition where national identity matters only in its distance from a present space and time [. . .] in such a modernist formation "dislocation" is confused with "detachment", signaling [sic] a perceived "freedom from ideology"'.[3] As such, high modernist cosmopolitanism adopts a stance of superiority over the national and the local, which are meaningful only insofar as they are perceived as an integral part of a wider and 'universal' context; it privileges a view from without, so to speak, rather than from within, as implied in Eliot's famous commendation of uprootedness as leading to a more 'authentic' identity: 'it is the final perfection, the consummation of an American to become [. . .] a European – something which no born European [. . .] can become'.[4] It is worthwhile observing that the binary logic fostered by Anglo-American modernists survives throughout the twentieth into the twenty-first century. As Barbara Abou-El-Haj has pointed out, we are indeed still struggling with such a logic, as

our ambitions to do equal justice to global and local is limited at the outset by
our failure to generate a comparative language beyond the set of tidy binaries
which reproduce the global regime in the very attempt to eviscerate it: center/
periphery, western/non-western, developed/developing, etc.[5]

In different contexts – (post)colonial, or where ethnic minorities or threatened nationhood are involved – the uniqueness of the local is instead bound to
undermine the normalised discourse of cosmopolitanism. This chapter contends that MacDiarmid, while partaking in the same tension foregrounded in
the writings of his Anglo-American colleagues, often distinctively subverted
their binary conceptualisations of the global/local by either inverting their
hegemonic relation or by fostering simultaneously a globalised vision of the
local and a localised approach to the global. 'True internationalism, and true
nationalism go hand in hand,' he claimed defiantly as early as 1929, challenging the then Labour prime minister Ramsay MacDonald 'to mark the definitive re-emergence of Scotland as a distinctive entity among the nations of the
world' and 'to find a means of overcoming this cursed Metropolitanism, and
the soulless Cosmopolitanism to which it in turn is tributary'.[6] Fluctuating
restlessly between the discourse of the nation and the internationalist vision
of socialism – and a misfit in both ideological realms – MacDiarmid was by
no means the only writer in early twentieth-century Scotland to undertake
a re-vision of the global/local binary. Lewis Grassic Gibbon and Catherine
Carswell, for example, undertook similar experimental paths, and at times
with equally challenging outcomes, and yet the very width and complexity
of MacDiarmid's work, as well as its development across such a considerable
span of time, makes it uniquely compelling and meaningful. He may not have
succeeded in generating that 'comparative language' necessary 'to do equal
justice to global and local' called for by Abou-El-Haj, but, as we shall see, his
work may indeed be considered as a 'systematically unsystematic' pioneering
contribution towards it.

It is possibly appropriate to start our investigation with a quotation
from Norman MacCaig (1910–96), poet, fellow Scot and a great friend
of MacDiarmid, who on the day of MacDiarmid's funeral suggested 'two
minutes of pandemonium' as a suitable way to celebrate the memory of
the departed writer.[7] MacDiarmid's work is notoriously run through by
contradictions, unsolved tensions, as well as being characterised by an
'archive fever' – an irrepressible desire to hoard details, information and
quotations from the most diverse writers and sources. MacDiarmid often
had to defend himself against critics who pointed out the formlessness and
aimlessness of his writing style: 'the way in which I bespatter all my writings
with innumerable quotations from the most heterogeneous writers of all
times and countries is one of the most frequent points of complaint against

me', he lamented in the 'Introductory' section to *Lucky Poet* (p. 27), yet
he never really amended his style. On the contrary, he revelled in it and
consciously defended it. MacDiarmid's formidable body of writing indeed
often defies ideas of 'order' – be it formal, structural or ideological. This
feature can be assimilated only in part to high modernist experimental
dis-order. While high modernist code-transgressing is also code-productive,
in fact, there is something entropic in MacDiarmid's work which resists
re-encoding, something that is constantly shifting and thus yields itself to
conflicting interpretations which cancel each other out. It would of course
be a mistake to try either to pigeon-hole such 'unthought' residue into
mainstream ideologies or aesthetic practices, or, even worse, to dismiss it
as irrelevant. Unresolved 'contradictions' here are a dynamic site of production of meaning – with meaning understood as being in a constant
state of process and construction. To adapt MacCaig's phrase to our critical
concerns, MacDiarmid's work articulates a productive 'pandemonium' – not
an indistinguished chaos, but the powerful and unfathomable anti-order of
Milton's demonic city, a utopia of fluidity and instability. His contradictions generate a promise, a disruptive promise that cannot be fulfilled in
the sharp patterns of (social) order at all – a promise that can only exist
and have power as long as it is not brought to terms that try to define and
fix it. It is within this anti-order perspective that MacDiarmid's re-vision
of the Scottish nation must be evaluated: (un)wittingly his militantly 'contradictory' stance reveals in fact the fluidity and complexity of (national)
identity constructions. Notwithstanding his obsessive investigation of the
meaning of Scotland, MacDiarmid never fully lined up with conventional
nationalism, often articulating openly and vigorously negative statements
against nationalist ideologies, as in the 1972 'Author's Note' to *Lucky Poet*,
for example, where he emphatically claimed: 'I am a Communist, a Scottish
separatist, and republican – and I do not believe I have any idea in common
with ninety-nine per cent of these so-called Scottish Nationalists' (*LP*,
p. xvi). We can never take any statement at face value with MacDiarmid,
and yet it is worthwhile observing how here, as in many other cases,
by defining himself through the combination of 'conflicting' terms, he
unsettles their original meaning, questioning their semantic boundaries.
Probably MacDiarmid's most quoted lines, from *A Drunk Man Looks at the
Thistle* (1926) and inscribed on his gravestone, suggest a similarly turbulent
transgression of set boundaries:

  I'll ha'e nae hauf-way hoose, but aye be whaur
  Extremes meet – it's the only way I ken
  To dodge the curst conceit o' bein' richt
  That damns the vast majority o' men. (*CP1*, p. 87, ll. 141–4)

This might indeed be taken as MacDiarmid's anti-order manifesto – that 'pandemonium effect' acutely evoked by MacCaig.

Much of MacDiarmid's radical approach to the idea of the nation was, however, lost to subsequent generations of Scottish writers, who identified him as a 'national genius' – the 'Prophet', as Helen Cruickshank (1886–1975) affectionately nicknamed him,[8] the guiding light for a twentieth-century literary expression of Scottishness. Alexander Scott's (1920–89) words in *The MacDiarmid Makars* (1972) are eloquent in this respect:

> If emulation is the compliment which talent pays to genius, Hugh MacDiarmid has been one of the most complimented writers in the history of Scottish poetry, for the fifty years since he began to publish verse in Scots in *The Scottish Chapbook* of October 1922 have witnessed the emergence of generation after generation of poets, fired by his example, who have attempted in their turn to adapt the ancient native Scots tradition in order to try to express the highest reaches of spiritual and intellectual awareness and the deepest levels of emotional and physical experience in terms appropriate to the twentieth century.[9]

Scott's rhetoric will strike the contemporary reader as consistently and traditionally nationalist. Furthermore, Scott questionably portrays the Scottish Renaissance as centred on a single, charismatic figure, rather than as the polyphonic movement that it was in reality,[10] going so far as to include Cruickshank among the writers inspired by MacDiarmid when actually she had started writing in Scots before him. This passage is in fact quite emblematic of MacDiarmid's reception in Scotland between the 1960s and the 1980s, and gives an idea of how much his 'dis-orderly' re-vision of the Scottish nation was often tamed into appearing to represent a more traditionalist political perspective.

If it is very difficult, or downright impossible, to trace an organic theorisation in MacDiarmid's writings, we may however identify the lines along which MacDiarmid developed what we will term here his '(anti)nationalism' – not as an indication that he rejected localism for globalism, but rather as a recognition of his attempt to transcend the crippling local-global binary. In what follows we will elucidate the two principal imaginative clusters – autobiographical and geographical/topographical – around which he (un)made the Scottish nation and challenged the discourse of the nation-state.

If there is an organising principle in MacDiarmid's work, this is no doubt a pervasive autobiographical impulse, one antithetical to Eliot's extremist pull to depersonalisation. It can be detected in *A Drunk Man*, his most famous work and arguably his finest and most sustained piece, which provides an in-depth investigation of 'this root-hewn Scottis soul' (*CP1*, p. 95, l. 395) and is written in the first person. The Drunk Man acts as a projection of MacDiarmid's persona, in his literary and political engagement as well as in his vitriolic yet humorous and ironic style of argumentation. Here, the modernist technique of montage achieves a precarious unity in the single (yet not monolithic) voice of the narrator, a set-up akin to that deployed in another seminal work, *Lucky Poet* (1943), which similarly assembles personal memories, descriptions of places, excerpts and quotations from several writers, political statements, clips of Scotland's cultural and natural history, weaving them into an unpredictably shifting vision. *Lucky Poet* is indeed a stunning tour de force, connecting inextricably the writer's life-world to a radical re-vision of Scottishness, in a way that both parallels and complements *A Drunk Man*. Beside these two works, most of MacDiarmid's work, both poems and essays, revolves around the autobiographical self. Many of his writings stage an intrusive 'I' which takes control of the narrative to give opinions, narcissistically to celebrate himself, to chastise and elevate, to select and exclude. Writing for MacDiarmid may be described as a rebellious act of self-definition, often shifting into a histrionic performance, as in 'The Outlaw', a short poem published posthumously:

> I am the outlawed conscience of Scotland,
> The voice that must not be heard,
> The bane of all time-servers and trimmers,
> Helot-usurpers of the true aristocracy of awareness.[11]

The 'I' or a shadow 'I' haunts *The Raucle Tongue*, for example, a collection in three volumes of MacDiarmid's 'hitherto unpublished prose' that contains several anonymous articles and reviews by MacDiarmid on his own work. The lyrical 'I' that speaks out in his major poetic works (beside *A Drunk Man*, also *To Circumjack Cencrastus* and *In Memoriam James Joyce*) surfaces in many of his poems, as does the obsessively inextricable link between poet and nation:

> Ah, this is my ambition indeed:
> To rise up among all the insipid, unsalted, rabbity, endlessly hopping people
> And sing a great song of our Alba bheadarrach
> – An exuberant, fustigating, truculent, polysyllabic
> Generous, eccentric, and incomparably learned song.[12]

The 'inward gaze' that underlies so much of MacDiarmid's work may be taken as (and no doubt is) a distinctive modernist trait – witness Joyce's organisation of *Ulysses* (1922) around the rhythms and workings of the mind of a central character; this autobiographical self-projection can indeed be compared to the Drunk Man's monologic and encyclopaedic account of his world-view. We know that MacDiarmid greatly admired the Irish writer and that *Ulysses* in particular had kindled his enthusiasm. And yet Joyce's autobiographism differs in many ways from MacDiarmid's by being less explicit and invasive, less antagonistic and dis-orderly. Furthermore, what emerges in MacDiarmid's writings is a decentred identity, which can never be fully apprehended or determined, an identity seen as constituted out of discontinuous fragments, and emerging in the play of difference between self and other, each defined by its 'constitutive outside' – the 'other' being principally England, or the British Empire, or who or whatever (region, individual, writer) he saw as antagonistic.

MacDiarmid's autobiographism seems, in fact, to be balanced between canonical modernist practices and postcolonial autobiographical expressions – an association, the latter, not entirely out of place, given the status of political subordination and dire cultural marginalisation that characterised Scotland in the first half of the twentieth century. Within this theoretical field, the notion of 'autoethnography' in particular may indeed help us make sense of MacDiarmid's complex autobiographical impulse. The term was first used by Marie Louise Pratt to indicate the (post)colonies' appropriation of the genre of autobiography 'to represent themselves in ways that *engage with the colonizer's own terms*',[13] and has been further developed by Deborah Reed-Danahay, who has observed how such a theory

> reflects a changing conception of both the self and society in the late twentieth century [and . . .] synthesizes both a postmodern ethnography, in which the realist conventions and objective observer position of standard ethnography have been called into question, and a postmodern autobiography, in which the notion of a coherent, individual self has been similarly called into question.[14]

Seen from this angle, the revolutionary potential of MacDiarmid's autobiographism in relation to a redefinition of the Scottish nation becomes evident: his work represents indeed an attempt to bridge the gap between public and private by balancing the autobiographical impulse (the inward gaze) with the ethnographic impulse (the outward gaze). As with postcolonial autoethnography, it transcends self-referentiality 'by engaging with cultural forms that are directly involved in the creation of culture. The issue becomes not so much distance, objectivity, and neutrality as closeness, subjectivity, and personal engagement'.[15]

It may be of interest in this context to remember how other writers of the Scottish Renaissance resorted to similar forms of self-writing to recreate Scottishness after over two centuries of cultural marginalisation within Britain. Edwin Muir (1887–1959) in his *Scottish Journey* (1935), but also in *An Autobiography* (1954) and in the autobiographical novel *Poor Tom* (1932), filters the history and culture of his country through the complex prism of his personal experience; Catherine Carswell (1879–1946) also engages in issues of Scottishness in both her autobiographical novels, *Open the Door!* (1920)

and *The Camomile* (1922), as well as in her unfinished autobiography, *Lying Awake*;[16] Lewis Grassic Gibbon (1901–35) partly projects his life experience onto a female character, Chris, in his monumental trilogy *A Scots Quair*,[17] a work whose title announces explicitly the author's ambitious (anti)nationalist project. Even Gibbon and MacDiarmid's joint project, *Scottish Scene* (1934), a selection of essays intended to deal with aspects of Scotland's past and present life and culture, is in fact firmly structured around the idiosyncratic perspective and style of the two individual authors. It seems clear, then, that for all these writers, in a way not dissimilar to what happens in postcolonial countries, rewriting the nation does not entail so much distance, objectivity and neutrality, as closeness, subjectivity and personal engagement. They all opt for an approach that emphasises the relational patterns, dialogue and performance of autoethnography over the monologic, autonomous dimension of traditional historiographical practice. In a way, then, they do not simply react against the source of political and cultural marginalisation, but they also try to forge radically new formally and ideologically adequate tools, to deconstruct and reconstruct what was indeed, at many, if not all levels, a 'colonised' nation. Of the writers listed above, however, MacDiarmid is the only one who shows a certain degree of consciousness of the import of such 'subjective' revolution; his militantly autobiographical style may indeed be regarded as evidence of such an awareness.

MacDiarmid's most celebrated and enduring act of national re-creation – the reinvention of the Scots language, along with his stunning reappropriation of the English language in poems like 'On a Raised Beach' (1934) and *In Memoriam James Joyce* (1955) – might indeed be taken, at least in part, as one such autoethnographic act. In defiance of canonical Western ideals of language purity and fixedness, as well as of the high modernist metropolitan tradition, he idiosyncratically created in *A Drunk Man* a hybrid vernacular, a language constituted of words from different historical and geographical areas of Scotland, a live and dynamic tool, which both shapes and adapts to the poet's expressive needs. Similarly, the 'world English' deployed by MacDiarmid in 'On a Raised Beach' and *In Memoriam James Joyce* questions the authority of monologism by revealing the stratification of language and by 'using the world to talk about language'.[18] Here MacDiarmid seems indeed to anticipate Mikhail Bakhtin's theorisation in *The Dialogical Imagination*, wherein what ensures the vitality of language, allowing it to regenerate continuously, is the encounter between the variety of languages spoken in a fixed area (polyglossia) and the characteristic internal stratification of each national language (heteroglossia).[19] According to Bakhtin, these two movements – centralising and decentralising – contribute in equal measure to destabilise the myth of national language. MacDiarmid's 'pluralistic' linguistic re-vision, in its most radical implications (despite the occasional traditionalist cliché), foregrounds a Scottish nation caught in a dynamic web of changing and interconnecting languages, where no hierarchy between varieties is possible, and where the very notion of 'national' language (in the current sense of standard and/or standardised) is ruled out. Even in this particular aspect, MacDiarmid's revolutionary re-vision of Scottish nationhood is centred on his persona as well as on his personal perspective: it is in fact by asserting his own individual right to shape subjectively Scottishness, that he is able to launch a formidable attack on both anglocentrism and on conventional constructions of the nation, grounded on the notions of a depersonalised tradition and of an external, objective authority.

Deeply connected with the autobiographical and autoethnographic impulse, there is at least a second major strain of thought in MacDiarmid's work that implies a radically (anti)nationalist agenda: a reimagination of the (Scottish) nation as a kaleidoscopically biodiverse, and yet still distinctively 'national', physical environment; indeed, as Louisa Gairn points out, 'MacDiarmid invokes Scottish biodiversity as a national metaphor.'[20] In *Lucky Poet* MacDiarmid expounds his *ante litteram* ecocritical approach in several passages, such as here for instance:

> I have acquired the knowledge of many sciences in relation to Scotland – particularly geology, botany, and ornithology – and use them freely in my work; I have lived in almost every part of Scotland, traversed every foot of by far the greater part of the whole country and all its islands [. . .] I have always unlimited material to draw upon, all of it dyed through and through with lived experience. (*LP*, p. 254)

The nexus between self and landscape has been widely explored theoretically in the past decade, with scholars highlighting how the experience of being in a place is always mediated by the embodied corporeal self. As Edward Casey has suggested, 'In the presence of place, there can be no subject other than a corporeal subject capable of possessing habitus, undertaking habitation, and bearing the idiolocality of place itself'; there is a 'concrete self of the hearth, not a disembodied occupant of the cosmos'.[21] It is one such concrete 'self of the hearth' that voices MacDiarmid's identification with the Scottish land in a poem included in *Lucky Poet*:

> It requires great love of it deeply to read
> The configuration of a land,
> Gradually grow conscious of fine shadings,
> Of great meaning in slight symbols [. . .]
> So I have gathered unto myself
> All the loose ends of Scotland,
> And by naming them and accepting them,

Loving them and identifying myself with them,
Attempt to express the whole. (*LP*, p. 324)[22]

Space starts from the perceiver in many of MacDiarmid's writings; in the
'Dìreadh' poems, for example, as Gairn points out, 'we witness MacDiarmid
in the act of performing [. . .] a survey, a "synoptic" view of Scotland [. . .]
"Dìreadh", MacDiarmid notes, is "a Gaelic word meaning 'the act of surmounting"'' (*LP*, p. 255), suggesting that 'these poems attempt to give birds'-
eye views – or rather, eagles'-eye views – of the whole of Scotland, each from
a different vantage point'.[23]

It is important to stress here that by dealing with the Scottish landscape
MacDiarmid was setting himself against a powerful conventional representation of the Scottish nation. Landscape, as it is constructed in literary
texts and in visual art, has been the privileged discursive space wherein the
Scottish national 'imagined community' has been constituted since at least
the eighteenth century. From the powerful literary figurations of Scotland
as the archetypal land of romance disseminated by influential works like
James Macpherson's 'Ossian' poems or Sir Walter Scott's novels,[24] to
many twentieth-century writers' reappropriations and subversions of such
romantic figurations (from Grassic Gibbon's *A Scots Quair* to Irvine Welsh's
Trainspotting (1993) and its cinematic adaptation), geographical symbolism
has taken a central role in the (re)construction of nationhood in modern
Scottish literature. The importance of landscape in MacDiarmid's work can
hardly be overestimated: he delves into its description with sensuous zest
and dissecting precision, often resorting to scientific jargon to do justice to
the innumerable shapes and colours of rocks, animals and plants that distinguish the different microcosmic Scotlands that he visits and/or settles into.
In the memorable opening of 'On a Raised Beach', for instance, a stunning
catalogue of the seemingly-infinite varieties of rocks take on a (poetic) life
of their own, transmuting from inert matter into a dynamic feast of (bio)
diversity:

All is lithogenesis – or lochia,
Carpolite fruit of the forbidden tree,
Stones blacker than any in the Caaba,
Cream-coloured caen-stone, chatoyant pieces,
Celadon and corbeau, bistre and beige,
Glaucous, hoar, enfouldered, cyathiform,
Making mere faculae of the sun and moon. (*CP1*, p. 422)

In a passage from *Lucky Poet* MacDiarmid presents us with a similar, if less
starkly essential, catalogue of the natural features of his native region, the
Scottish Borders:

My earliest impressions are of an almost tropical luxuriance of Nature – of great forests, of honey-scented heather hills, and moorlands [. . .] and of a multitude of rivers, each with its distinct music and each catering in the most exciting way for hosts of the most stimulating and wholesome pleasures a fellow can know in the heyday of his youth – ducking, guddling, girning, angling, spearing eels, and building islands in midstream and playing at Robinson Crusoe. (*LP*, p. 219)

Here the landscape is simultaneously presented as distinctively Scottish (as suggested by terms like 'guddling' and 'girning'), as 'universal' (scaled down to its basic components – 'forests', 'hills', 'rivers') and as 'exotic', referring to something other than itself. Once more, MacDiarmid's outlook is pluralistic. His nationalist project of retrieving a suppressed authentic geographical symbolism is undermined by the 'universal' value of the individual components of the landscapes described. Each of the above descriptions, then, functions both centripetally and centrifugally, thus creating a complex dialogic tension between the local and the global. Such tense dialectic becomes significantly explicit at the end of Chapter 5 of *Lucky Poet*, 'On Seeing Scotland Whole', where MacDiarmid's vision stretches to accommodate what he sees as the astrophysicist Sir Arthur Eddington's 'impression of a world of diverse particularity which has quality other than obedience to physical law' (*LP*, p. 308), and where the poet's narrow focus on Scotland expands to become 'vitally interested in every local *chauvinisme*' (*LP*, p. 309). Meaningfully, MacDiarmid quotes the historian and political scientist Harold Laski's idea that 'Universities have reformed too many minds by confining them within a space too narrow for a vision of the horizon to be possible. The discoveries are made at the boundaries of subjects and not at their centres' (*LP*, pp. 308–9). This stands almost as a 'glocalisation' manifesto, with MacDiarmid defending at the same time a global perspective and a decentred, local one. And yet, quite clearly, his bias is with 'local *chauvinisme*' – the uniqueness of the local – as the privileged starting point for a revision of the discourse of cosmopolitanism.

MacDiarmid often wrote from and about the topographical margins of Scotland. Langholm, Montrose and Whalsay became the privileged perspective from which the nation was reimagined not as unitary, but as fragmentary; not as grounded on the renown of its historical cities and sites, but expressed in the remoteness and apparent anonymity of some among the least known Scottish provinces. Robert Crawford has aptly commented on MacDiarmid's 'particular location in small-town Scotland' where,

without at all renouncing international concerns, he matured in various areas of his work through an interaction with the minutely local [and] in so doing, he can be seen as developing an exemplary aesthetic of the local-international that is [. . .] bound up with participation in the events of a small community.[25]

In so doing, we may add, MacDiarmid went a long way not just (as he openly intended) to deromanticise and deanglicise the Scottish nation, but also to decentre it as the monolithic subject of history, by demonstrating that the 'nation' is not an essentialised unity but a highly contested zone, fragmented in regions and overlapping with other similarly complex geopolitical realities. For example, in *In Memoriam James Joyce* he resorts to the metaphor of house building to promote local diversity against metropolitan homogenisation:

> if English stone for Scottish buildings
> Is proposed [. . .]
> Ask why the excellent Earnock and Auchinlee freestones
> From Blantyre and Cleland respectively,
> The red sandstones of Ballochmyle,
> Locharbriggs or Corsehill,
> The fine-grained honey-gold Leoch stone fron Dundee,
> Whitsome Newton from the Borders
> Or Braehead stone from Fauldhouse
> Should not be preferred. (CP2, pp. 796–7)

Further on he switches to a global vision, though one equally rooted in locality and diversity:

> We must respond maximally
> To the whole world we can,
> Even as in building houses you can have
> Gurjun, Mengkulang, and East African camphorwood
> For ceiling joists; external door frames
> Made from Chumprak, Afrormosia, or Berlinia,
> Draining boards of Merawan or Thingan. (CP2, p. 798)

This works as an eloquent example of how, by uncovering the geographical and historical pluralism of the Scottish nation and by suggesting the simultaneous existence of uneven and different national territories, MacDiarmid indeed gestured towards the possibility of a local *and* global citizenship.

Finally, within MacDiarmid's geographical and topographical re-vision of the Scottish nation, one of the most radical features concerns his discussion of Scotland's 'islandness'. MacDiarmid became interested in islands through his 'exile' in Shetland, a region to which he never felt he belonged but that nonetheless became the privileged geographical perspective from which he reimagined his country. Indeed, as Scott Lyall has observed,

> On the island archipelago of Shetland [. . .] MacDiarmid discovers the essentially fragmented nature of all national cultures, isolated in the sea of their own historical identity yet linked to other cultures by the very fluidity of that sea [. . .] His experience of the islands allows a clearer view of Scotland. On seeing Scotland whole, MacDiarmid discovers that there are many Scotlands, each different and difficult of combination.[26]

Shetland is not only Scotland's northernmost and most remote region, but it is possibly its most contested one, given its complex history of 'colonisation' by the Norse, the Scots and finally by the United Kingdom. In *The Islands of Scotland* (1939) MacDiarmid significantly places Shetland at the centre of his investigation: reverting what would have been the standard sequence, replicated by history books or geographical accounts, he starts his scholarly and literary journey from Shetland, moving on to Orkney and concluding with what has been traditionally perceived as the more quintessentially Scottish Hebrides. 'The Shetlands are at the furthest remove from the general conceptions bound up in the term of "Scottish"' he explains, and takes up the challenge to draw a different map of Scotland, one where the Shetland Islands would acquire a new centrality.[27] Even though apparently quite conventional in its layout – that of a vade-mecum to the Scottish archipelago, with photographs and detailed descriptions – *The Islands of Scotland* contains some extraordinarily visionary passages. MacDiarmid celebrates the islands' bio- and cultural diversity ('It pleases my patriotism [. . .] and flatters my Scotist love for minute distinctions, that Scotland has so many islands') and, more generally, their islandness – their being microcosms isolated from and yet connected to one another.[28] In the closing paragraph of the book, MacDiarmid provides us with a striking figuration of the global connectedness that islandness implies – a prefiguration, indeed, of Edouard Glissant's 'archipelagic thinking':

> There are invisible bridges from every one of the Scottish islands, I think, that cross as far as the mind of man can go and reach across whatever space lies between us and anything that has ever been or ever will be apprehensible by the minds of men, – bridges to even greater ends, I think, than Mr. Henry Beston was thinking of when, in his foreword to Professor Herbert Faulkner West's *The Nature Writers*, he said that good writing on Nature is 'a bridge of the soul's health over an abyss'.[29]

In recent years, Glissant has focused on the (liminal) centrality of the archipelago in both understanding the Caribbean and the world ('the entire world is becoming an archipelago'), and in representing the complex, ambivalent and chaotic relations among distant regions in the (post)imperial age.[30] MacDiarmid, in a not too dissimilar way, rejects the traditional notion of islands as 'insular' (that is, as peripheral, secluded and isolated worlds) and sees them as connected and connecting within local archipelagos and within the world.

By confronting the notions of culture and nation from the 'edge of the world', by navigating through global and local connections and disconnections, by mediating daily, through his personal and individual experience, the conflicting demands of localism and globalism, by reimagining the nation in regional and global terms, MacDiarmid goes a long way to alert us to the dangers of ideological closure, to destabilise the discourse of the nation and to prefigure postmodern theorisations of glocalism. All this makes MacDiarmid relevant not merely as a paradigmatic modern Scottish intellectual but indeed also as an imaginative thinker of global significance.

CHAPTER NINE

Hugh MacDiarmid: The Impossible Persona

David Goldie

One of the most consistent themes in MacDiarmid criticism, dating back almost to its beginning, is that of the misunderstanding and disregard to which MacDiarmid and his writing have been subjected. The adjective 'neglected', whether implied or explicitly stated, has been a frequent presence in critical discussion of his work, often being employed as the condition for a necessary reassessment or rehabilitation.[1] This dialectic of neglect and vindication is one that MacDiarmid himself did much to promote almost from the start of his career and sprang largely from his sense of injustice at being denied his proper place by a combination of English metropolitan prejudice and the small-mindedness of the Scottish cultural and public spheres.

MacDiarmid was and is widely perceived to be a 'difficult' writer, and this may go some way to explaining his agonistic relationship both with his contemporaries and posterity. His difficulty is manifested in a number of ways. Firstly, it is the formal difficulty of an experimental modernist who challenges the norms of poetic diction and structure. Then it is the difficulty of a writer engaged in a bold attempt to construct a new Scots literary language, one who is, moreover, not afraid to outrage conventional opinion, whether in politics (*Three Hymns to Lenin*, for example) or sexuality ('Tarras', 'Harry Semen'). And then there is the difficulty of his compositional practice – his habit of making poems and essays by stringing together fragments drawn opportunistically, and often without attribution, from dictionaries, poems, critical essays and novels.[2] Above all, perhaps, sits the problem of MacDiarmid himself: that is to say, the difficulty a reader faces in engaging sympathetically with a persona which at times appears to have been constructed wilfully out of paradox for the purposes of confrontation and provocation; a persona designed less as a consoling, authoritative individuality and more as a catalysing reagent for the generation of a poetry that can be by turns beautiful and cumbersome and opinions that are incisive, awkward, heterodox and frequently self-contradictory. This is a figure, after all, who could variously call for a Scottish form of fascism in the early 1920s and then renew his support for Soviet communism after the suppression of the

1956 Hungarian uprising;[3] who would famously deride fellow Scottish writer Alexander Trocchi (1925–84) as 'cosmopolitan scum';[4] who would denigrate traditional Scottish folk poetry as 'songs which reflect the educational limitations, the narrow lives, the poor literary abilities, of a peasantry we have happily outgrown';[5] and talk openly of 'the moronic character of most of our people'.[6] It is to this difficult and complex persona, 'Hugh MacDiarmid', as it is variously manifested in the poetry and, particularly, explicated in the critical and autobiographical books, *Scottish Eccentrics* (1936) and *Lucky Poet* (1943), that this chapter is addressed.

Hugh MacDiarmid came into being in 1922: the year, as is often noted, in which James Joyce's *Ulysses* was first published in book form, in which T. S. Eliot's *The Waste Land* first appeared, and which saw the first publication of Virginia Woolf's first novel in her mature modernist style, *Jacob's Room*. When C. M. Grieve invented this new persona he was a thirty-year old writer with a small but growing reputation for accomplished minor verse in English and a strongly-expressed aversion to the tentative current attempts to revive vernacular poetry in Scotland.[7] He would later claim that his 'earliest literary efforts were all in Scots' (*LP*, p. 17), but this appears to have no evidential backing and has as a consequence gained little credence among critics.[8] The switch to Scots dialect with the publication of 'The Watergaw', and to an unambiguously Scottish persona – the dropping of a surname, Grieve, which spoke of the debatable land of the English-Scottish border, for another, MacDiarmid, that conjured a more straightforward Celtic-Highland glamour – changed things irrevocably. In particular, it allowed Grieve the freedom to reinvent himself as someone whose purposes were no longer aligned with the metropolitan literary culture; an individual who now boldly rejected many of the values in which British literary culture was centred. In decentring himself in this way – literally rendering himself eccentric to the dominant culture – MacDiarmid allowed himself not only an enabling freedom from literary, cultural and political constraint but also the possibility of eventually recentring his political and cultural practice in a reconstituted sense of Scottishness. The manifest oddness and apparent self-contradiction of Hugh MacDiarmid, then, might be said to be, in the first instance, a kind of strategic eccentricity deliberately designed to outrage conventional opinion; an eccentricity designed in particular to discompose and dislocate British literature with a view to the recomposition and relocation of a new independent literature north of the Border. In order to do this fully MacDiarmid found it necessary to be not just a 'difficult' character but an 'impossible' one. This, at least, is what he told Neil M. Gunn in a letter of 22 June 1933 when he wrote that 'if I am not already literally an impossible person I intend to become one' (*L*, p. 252).

This sense of strategic eccentricity can be found running through much of the work of MacDiarmid's first decade. It can be seen in the formal and thematic structure of A Drunk Man Looks at the Thistle (1926) which destabilises the authority of its speaker by having him fuddled with drink, and disorients its frame of reference with its rapid alternations between low vernacular speculation and high philosophical and literary allusion. It is a wilfully unstable poem that uses its formal and linguistic innovations as a way of estranging its religious and nationalist arguments, prompting the conventional reader to thought by jolting his or her expectations. It is the poem, too, in which MacDiarmid outlines his position of principled self-contradiction, having his speaker commit himself, in a phrase that would come to define MacDiarmid, to 'aye be whaur / Extremes meet' (CP1, p. 87, ll. 141–2).[9]

This sense of a powerful internal contradiction had preceded the persona of MacDiarmid, having been seen in Grieve's earlier work. In his midtwenties, in a letter of 20 August 1916 sent from Macedonia where he was serving during World War One, he had written to George Ogilvie describing 'the many contrasting personalities in me', admitting that 'my thoughts are thus forever like a man moving through the ever-increasing and various confusion of an enormous higgledy-piggledy lumber room' (L, pp. 10, 11). His early writing attests to that multiplicity and want of singular focus, as can be seen in the formal and thematic diversity of his first collection Annals of the Five Senses (1923). The opening prose fragment in that collection, 'Cerebral', is often taken as a thinly-veiled autobiographical portrait, and is notable for the way its speaker epitomises the struggles an aspiring artist and thinker has with the contradictions of his own personality: 'he would watch with painful realism the break-up of his mental life. Every one of his separate egos became violently anarchical, creating an unthinkable Babel. Disunity and internecine hostility tore him into shreds.'[10]

As Hugh MacDiarmid, Grieve was able to find a persona through which that 'unthinkable Babel' might be purposively articulated, and in which he might find a productive outward expression for what had previously been a self-destructive and inward-looking 'internecine hostility'. This is the quality of productive contradiction that critics as diverse as David Daiches and Christopher Whyte have admired in MacDiarmid. Daiches reads a 'Whitmanesque largeness' in MacDiarmid as a consequence of his willingness to embrace his extremes, arguing that 'self-contradiction is for him a mode of poetic awareness'.[11] Whyte suggests that in a work such as the 'entertaining and enormously playful' In Memoriam James Joyce MacDiarmid offers a fundamental challenge to 'the notion of writing as expressing a subjectivity, a pre-existent body of experience or emotions'. For Whyte, MacDiarmid's playful deconstruction of his own internal coherence as author destabilises readings that are 'underpinned by a coherent psychological reality, associated with the biographical figure', with the result that 'concepts such as originality, subjectivity and intellectual property collapse in the maelstrom of MacDiarmid's compilation'.[12]

This sense of a productive eccentricity, a willed refusal to revolve in a regularly-ordered manner around a stable centre, was immediately apparent in practice in MacDiarmid's various interventions in Scottish culture and politics. In theoretical terms, one of its more forceful and sustained expressions can be found in *Scottish Eccentrics*. This book offers what would appear to be an appropriately random collection of essays on notable as well as less noted Scottish eccentrics, from the religious enthusiast Elspeth Buchan to the *Ossian* fabricator James Macpherson, from Lord Monboddo to William McGonagall. In one way the book is a straightforward defence of eccentricity, a plea for the importance of valuing individuals who choose to dance to a different tune. One such is Sir Thomas Urquhart, a Royalist in the Civil War period out of step with his time and incapable of being understood by his enemies, 'since "only a mind like his own could trace the maze of its windings and turnings, and fathom the depths of its eccentricity. In his thoughts 'truth is constantly becoming interfused with fiction, possibility with certainty, and the hyperbolical extravagance of his style only keeps even pace with the prolific shootings of his imagination"'' (*SE*, p. 27).[13]

Some readers might note a certain similarity between this description and MacDiarmid's own persona, a resemblance that perhaps intensifies as MacDiarmid continues in his description of a figure who 'reminds us of Don Quixote', who makes 'frequent allusions to struggles with pecuniary difficulties, as well as in his use of magniloquent language', and who has a 'lively fancy, a strain of genuine erudition beneath his pedantry, and some sparks of insanity' in his 'fantastical character' (*SE*, p. 27). Whether or not there is a degree of self-justification going on here and in the book's other essays, MacDiarmid is clearly making a bold argument about the need to understand rather than simply condemn what appears to the conventional mind to be irrationality and self-contradiction. He is, in this way, not being simply capricious but is following in the footsteps of irrationalist philosophers such as Leo Shestov, a thinker to whom he often alluded and whom he would name as his 'master' (*LP*, p. 402), who had advanced the view 'that truth lives by contradictions' by posing the provocative question of 'whether contradictions are not the condition of truthfulness in one's conception of the world'.[14]

But there is also a second purpose to the book, a specifically nationalist one, which becomes fully explicit in its concluding chapter. In that essay, 'The Caledonian Antisyzygy', which MacDiarmid had intended to be the introduction, he puts forward a bold argument that the condition of eccentricity is not accidental to his subjects but is rather fundamental to their national make-up, so that in their actions they are doing little more than articulating in exaggerated form the self-contradictions of post-Union

Scotland.[15] In this view, 'the eccentric actually becomes the typical and the wildest irregularities combine to manifest the essence of our national spirit and historic function' (*SE*, p. 286). As the essay's title suggests, MacDiarmid is drawing on an argument first articulated by G. Gregory Smith in 1919 and which has become enshrined in Scottish literary and cultural criticism since: that of an essential schizoid Scottish personality divided between extremes of realism and fantasy, canniness and uncanniness, civility and savagery, sacredness and profanity.[16]

Scottish Eccentrics is a profoundly eccentric book in itself, then, but it is a manifestation of an eccentricity with a purpose, an example of what has been described earlier as a strategic eccentricity. In it MacDiarmid is not only making a case for a modernist strategy of cultural and literary estrangement but also showing how this can be tied to an argument about Scottish national culture. Grieve was perhaps never quite manipulative or cool-headed enough to maintain a cynical distance between himself and the character he had created, and it is arguable that they were more or less identical in temperament and attitude from the start, but for a time in the 1920s and early 1930s it seemed that he was able to deploy MacDiarmid's eccentricities productively in the cause of developing a vital new Scottish poetic and cultural practice. For a while the poetry and the cultural politics seemed, as idiosyncratic and offbeat as they were, to complement and feed off one another.

By the time MacDiarmid came to publish his autobiographical 'self-study' *Lucky Poet* in 1943, however, that balance appeared to have been lost. The eccentricities in that book are as profound as in the earlier work but they are arguably much harsher and less winning. MacDiarmid had undergone a number of severe personal and professional setbacks in the fifteen years before the book appeared, among them job disappointments, marital break-up and family estrangement, problems with alcoholism and sexually transmitted disease, exile in Whalsay, difficulties in seeing eye-to-eye with a number of political parties, literary feuds and a cultural climate in Scotland that was not always as welcoming to him as he would have liked. A number of these problems had developed before *Scottish Eccentrics*, but had not found expression in that work. In the more confessional mode of *Lucky Poet*, a work produced, moreover, in the stress of wartime, they are more explicitly present as the sources of a splenetic anger and a defensive arrogance that go far beyond the idiosyncrasies found in the earlier work. *Lucky Poet* celebrates similar types of refractoriness and self-contradiction as are found in *Scottish Eccentrics*, with MacDiarmid characterising the book in a later 'Author's Note' by drawing on what Bold tells us was a favourite quotation from Walt Whitman's 'Song of Myself': 'Do I contradict myself? / Very well then I contradict myself, / (I am large, I contain multitudes)'.[17] But the sense that this is a productive rather than merely destructive contradiction has arguably disappeared. One reason for this, perhaps, derives from the way MacDiarmid's persona had developed from mere eccentricity, which implies a recognition of decentredness from normative behaviours and values, towards a megalomania that believes itself the rightful centre of normative value.

One of *Lucky Poet*'s epigraphs is from Søren Kierkegaard and states that 'the literary and social and political situation requires an exceptional individual – the question is whether there is anyone in this realm who is fitted for this task except me' (*LP*, p. vi). The extent to which MacDiarmid takes this seriously quickly becomes apparent in the book, which is characterised by a *folie de grandeur* that can be entertaining and provocative if read as rhetorical hyperbole but more than a little troubling if taken as a statement of fact. Here, for example is MacDiarmid talking of the extent of his erudition and sensitivity:

> For twenty years I have read everything about Scotland I could lay my hands on, developing as a consequence a faculty which seems to attract to me instantaneously all the available information on points no matter how obscure or technical from sources no matter how far scattered, and at the same time 'grangerizes' any such issue that is in my mind with a simultaneous recollection of all manner of connected (or, no matter how remotely, connectable) matters drawn from the whole field of my tremendous reading, and at once establishes a compenetrant complexity of relationships and ideas for their literary and political utilization. (*LP*, p. 254)

MacDiarmid had never been, as David Norbrook has put it, a stranger to the 'immodesty topos', but even by his own standards this sounds delusional, as though he really has irrevocably crossed the threshold from difficulty to impossibility.[18] More immediately alarming is the effect that such attitudes actually have on the literary and political utilisations that MacDiarmid talks of here, and the impact they have on his larger reputation. *Lucky Poet* helps cement the impression that many commentators have formed of MacDiarmid's exasperating impossibility in these fields.

Politically, MacDiarmid's self-contradictions are well documented, but it is important to note the way he effectively marginalised himself from meaningful politics by the kinds of attitude manifested in *Lucky Poet*. John MacCormick, the effective leader of Scottish nationalism in the late 1940s, wrote in his *The Flag in the Wind* that MacDiarmid 'has been politically one of the greatest handicaps with which any nationalist movement could have been burdened', citing 'his love of bitter controversy, his extravagant and self-assertive criticism of the English, and his woolly thinking'.[19] More recent political commentary has concurred: Colin Kidd arguing, for example, that MacDiarmid's influence has been a particularly malign one and that 'his bequest to Scotland was an uncompromising and Manichean nationalism'.[20]

MacDiarmid had always been a somewhat authoritarian socialist and nationalist, one who argued for the necessity of an elite to guide the intellectual and political development of the masses and had drawn accordingly on models as diverse as V. I. Lenin and the American historian and social theorist James Harvey Robinson.[21] In *Lucky Poet* such elitism at times shades into what looks like a more open hostility to his compatriots. In spite of his insistence at various points that it is with a middle class perverted by English values that his quarrel lies, and that the only thing he cares about 'is what the masses of the people think and believe and like and dislike' (*LP*, p. 97) it is sometimes difficult from the way he hectors and ridicules those masses to distinguish political argument from more straightforward misanthropy and disdain. 'Modern Scotland is a disease in which almost everything has turned into mud', MacDiarmid writes, and what it 'needs above all else is a stiff dose of [. . .] well-bred arrogance' (*LP*, p. 236). By means of aggressive argument and some semi-farcical mathematics, MacDiarmid asserts that across the English-speaking world there are only five 'reasonably civilized' people for 'each 100,000 souls' (*LP*, p. 103). The consequence is that he does not feel bound to the values of the general mass of people who, in this view, have been vitiated by British imperialism and popular culture, but rather stands high above them, heaping murderous contempt on their failures to recognise the eternal truths of art and the leadership qualities of the great artist who moves among them:

> There can be no end to war, to mutual mass-extermination, so long as most people remain such morons. Their condition – their attitude to life – is in fact a species of cancer, entirely similar to the way in which cancer cells develop in the body of the host, by the failure of his own tissues to abandon their embryonic form and assume adult status and responsibility. That exactly describes the content of the lives of all but an infinitesimal minority of mankind – that infinitesimal minority, constant through all history, who have built up our entire human heritage of arts and sciences, not only without any help or understanding but in the teeth of extreme indifference and often active opposition from the vast majority who, if that minority were killed out, would speedily lose and be utterly helpless to do anything to replace all the gains of civilization. (*LP*, pp. 406–7)

Something that becomes horribly apparent in *Lucky Poet*, something that had perhaps never been fully formed or expressed so insistently in his earlier writing, is that MacDiarmid does not see himself so much as a fellow sufferer with his fellows in the condition of modernity as a divinely-appointed physician destined to cure them with his draconian surgery. Friedrich Nietzsche said much the same thing in *Ecce Homo* (1888), a similarly self-aggrandising work of autobiographical criticism, but Nietzsche was already beginning the slide into clinical insanity by this time and, besides, had left a legacy one part of which MacDiarmid was currently experiencing in the form of a Nazi war: both elements which should perhaps have given MacDiarmid pause in taking him as a model. And while Nietzsche might be excused writing chapters such as 'Why I am so Clever', 'Why I Write Such Excellent Books' and 'Why I am a Destiny' on the grounds of his substantial lifetime recognition and success, MacDiarmid is writing in a context in which for all his bluster of being recognised as the best Scottish poet since Burns he realises he is 'a sort of Ishmael' (LP, p. 234), an outcast of the nation he seeks to shape, his books unread and his poetry undervalued. The consequence is that what had seemed like a canny eccentricity or at least an excusable oddity in the character of MacDiarmid, appears in Lucky Poet to harden into something more bitter and potentially, at times, more sinister.

If these attitudes were restricted to the political arena then they might be separable from MacDiarmid the poet and thus be rendered irrelevant to his literary reputation. But Lucky Poet shows the way such attitudes work directly into both the content and the form of the poetry. When he writes verses on Glasgow, for example, MacDiarmid uses similar images of infestation and eradication, pathology and cure, that he employs in his political and cultural discourse, commenting that

> I have likened these people in my Glasgow poem to those insects which are repelled rather than attracted if an electric light is substituted for an old-fashioned kerosene lamp, and speculated on consulting Helsmoortel as to what the effect on their mentalities might be if irradiation methods were applied to their genital organs. (LP, p. 105)

And again, when he talks of his ideals for poetry – of the type of poetry he has been working on in wartime but which would not receive publication until the 1950s as, for example, In Memoriam James Joyce (1955) and his Spanish Civil War poem The Battle Continues (1957) – a similar emphasis seems to haunt both its form and its subject matter. MacDiarmid talks of having a

> dream of creating a poetry which will operate on mankind as one obituarist of James Joyce said of Joyce's novels – that 'even the strongest of his characters seems dwarfed by the great apparatus of learning that he brings to bear on them. They are almost like atoms being smashed by a 250-ton cyclotron'. This, indeed, is what I would like to see people, not characters in books but all their readers, subjected to; I dream of a literary equipment which may bring immense erudition to bear on the general unsanity of mankind, on the appalling mindlessness of almost everybody, like the insulin and metrazol 'shock' treatments, or Dr Lother Kalinowsky's later utilization of electricity, for dementia præcox. (LP, pp. 407–8)

This is, in its quasi-scientific language and its insistence on deploying vast amounts of knowledge as a kind of blunt clinical instrument to effect violent behavioural change in its subjects, an effective if rather chilling outline of the mode of much of MacDiarmid's later poetry.

MacDiarmid was perfectly capable of producing great poetry that was at variance with his critical and political ideas as well as his personal circumstances, as a poem such as 'On a Raised Beach', written during the harshest years of his Shetland exile, shows. But it is arguable that as the ideas expressed in *Lucky Poet* take hold of his poetry the less rewarding it becomes, and the less he can break free of them to create a poetry like that exemplified in 'The Terrible Crystal' that is capable of 'fusing the discordant qualities of experience, / Of mixing moods, and holding together opposites' (CP2, p. 1095). His work instead tends increasingly toward discordance without fusion, towards intemperance and an inordinate, sometimes incoherent, prolixity – work, in other words, that grows and grows in the warmth of its author's sense of his infallibility to the point where it leaves simply no room for the common reader. In *The Company I've Kept* (1966) MacDiarmid would suggest that the reason his poetry had developed in the way it had was precisely because of his need to make it affront the expectation and baffle the comprehension of what he described as the 'bastard democracy'. In this view the massive sprawl of his writing and the hyper-inflation of his persona, summed up in his call 'for GIANTISM in the arts', are part of his master plan for an 'expansion of creative genius to a point where all the little people simply can't comprehend it and are excluded automatically'.[22]

None of this can, on its own, entirely destabilise the poetry. By allowing his persona to swell to a size that made his political and cultural pronouncements absurd and sometimes monstrous, MacDiarmid could never extinguish the technical skill and the flashes of insight and beauty that mark his best poetry. But he certainly made them much harder to find, and made even critics who wanted to praise him feel they had to qualify their remarks to account for his excesses. C. H. Sisson was one: a poet and critic who valued MacDiarmid as an inspiration to his own development but who remained troubled by MacDiarmid's poetic and personal indiscipline:

> For the oeuvre is a vast, untidy, often cantankerous affair and the author not just a man who wrote poems but an off-beat politician of the most injudicious kind, occasionally violent in language and apparently unable to resist the pleasure of making small noisy impacts on a world he had neither the patience nor the practical sense – nor perhaps really the will – to act on more effectively.[23]

Seamus Heaney is another admirer who acknowledges that 'anyone who wishes to praise his work has to admit straightaway that there is an un-get-roundable connection between the prodigality of his gifts and the prodigiousness of his blather'. For Heaney, 'the task for everybody confronted with the immense bulk of his collected verse is to make a firm distinction between the true poetry and what we might call the habitual printout'. This, however, is a distinction Heaney is prepared to work on, and he finds especially in the early work in Scots enough to justify MacDiarmid's status as a significant poet, even though he admits that MacDiarmid's later poetry, with its 'skewed rhythms, egregious diction, encyclopedic quotation, sheer monotony [. . .] certainly gave his detractors plenty to work with'.[24]

Richard Aldington noted something very like this quality in criticism of D. H. Lawrence: the sense that praise of Lawrence never came unqualified and that any ascription of literary genius to him was always followed by a 'but'.[25] It is arguable whether the work of MacDiarmid and Lawrence can really be fruitfully compared but in this regard at least it is against Lawrence and the likes of Ezra Pound that he should be measured. Like them he is an eccentric, a member of the awkward squad, a modernist gadfly: valuable for his boldness in confronting convention and capable of some very fine writing, but the practitioner of an aesthetic so contentiously singular and ego-driven that it can never be fully subscribed to nor productively followed. The reasons why no-one would really think seriously about placing Lawrence at the centre of the English literary tradition or Pound the American tradition are exactly those that make it difficult to give MacDiarmid the place he felt was his at the centre of a revivified Scottish tradition. Pound and Lawrence were both in their own ways 'impossible people' in the terms MacDiarmid had characterised himself to Gunn, but they lacked MacDiarmid's sense of a larger commitment to nation. The concerns of both were eccentric to their compatriots, but the loss of that common centre appeared to cause them few qualms. Their impossible personae were consistent with their status as exiles and their rightist politics.

The consequences of MacDiarmid's eccentricity were quite different. How could a figure who had strategically embraced 'impossibility', self-centredness and volatility as the constituent elements of his public persona occupy the centre of a culture and speak with the normative voice that is demanded by the discourses of democratic leftism and nationalism, what he called 'that particular Scottish democratic spirit' (LP, p. 207), which he ostensibly – if, as we have seen, only rather intermittently – espoused? Instead, we find an individual who in Lucky Poet states it is 'part of my job to keep up perpetually a sort of Berserker rage' (LP, p. 79), and who would later describe his role as being 'to erupt like a volcano, emitting not only flame, but a lot of rubbish'.[26] MacDiarmid was being unduly hard on himself here, and perhaps even being a little wry, yet there is something arresting and appropriate in these images. A volcano is a visible manifestation of tectonic activity, of the kind of immense seismic pressure that forges new continents and makes diamonds from organic detritus. It is magnificent and elemental, but it is also a nuisance and a threat to the people who try to make their daily living in its shadow. A berserker, too, is impressively elemental but a figure whom one might not be inclined to invite into one's home, whether in the pages of a book or not.

MacDiarmid's attempt to make himself a remorselessly inhuman figure in his criticism and later poetry, to be as Iain Crichton Smith put it, a 'cold eagle, a man in love with stones',[27] might be seen as an impressive assault on the values of what MacDiarmid saw as 'the emptiness and insignificance of sentimental humanism' (LP, p. 78). But it perhaps came at a personal cost. There is much evidence, especially in his later life, that Christopher Grieve was a very different, much kinder man than Hugh MacDiarmid: a generous mentor to young poets and a man keen to build the bridges with family and friends that he had earlier burned in the fires of his MacDiarmidian mania. The sense in which there was a more vulnerable person lurking behind MacDiarmid had not been lost on Valda Trevlyn, Grieve's second wife, even from the beginning of their relationship. She would tell Alan Bold after Grieve's death of a different, gentler kind of eccentricity to which she was attracted in his character and which proved decisive in committing herself to him:

> I didn't really believe in the business of 'Hugh MacDiarmid' or any of that: this business of being a Scottish poet was all baloney. What really decided me was when I was standing in the Tottenham Court Road. Christopher had gone down to the lavatory and had gone into the women's. I thought, 'Oh, my God, I can't leave him.' A silly way to decide anything.[28]

Had MacDiarmid opened himself up a little more to the very human fallibility present here, been more alert and sympathetic to the frailties and vulnerabilities not only of others but of himself, he might have become a more rounded, less remorselessly fractious figure and would almost certainly have enjoyed a more settled life. He might have felt less temptation to use his poetry as a bludgeon rather than a foil, and as a consequence have required less of the special pleading that those who value his work often feel they need to apply in its defence. If he really wanted to be the saviour of his national culture he might have tried a little harder to get his readers to nod their heads rather than scratch them. Hugh MacDiarmid had only himself to blame for being an impossible person but C. M. Grieve should, perhaps, have known a little better.

CHAPTER TEN

Transatlantic MacDiarmid

Jeffrey Skoblow

What does MacDiarmid look like from across the Atlantic? And what did MacDiarmid see when he looked this way? These are the two main questions this chapter will address, at least in a preliminary way, and specifically from an American (I should say US) perspective. Canadian reflections on these matters might well be very different, with Canada's very different history, both colonial and postcolonial, as backdrop, with different politics and cultural narratives, and with a more pronounced sense, perhaps, of Scottish heritage north of the border. Central and South American MacDiarmid, to the extent that he exists at all in those terms, would be another story (or stories) yet again.

The main thing MacDiarmid sees when he looks this way, it seems, is Walt Whitman (1819–92). Relatively little attention is paid to any other American figure, at least in terms of MacDiarmid's own written testimony: there are some extended meditations on Gertrude Stein, and frequent although generally fairly fleeting references to T. S. Eliot and Ezra Pound scattered through MacDiarmid's correspondence and essays, with an occasional mention of other figures (Wallace Stevens, William Carlos Williams, Marianne Moore) – but these are about the extent of it. (Not that it should be otherwise, necessarily.) The references are for the most part positive – although there is the 'deplorable' example of T. S. Eliot with regard to 'how devitalising and injurious religion can be to a poet';[1] and – a blind spot – MacDiarmid does not like Williams, apparently does not hear the good doctor's vernacular, or recognise the vernacular enterprise as akin to his own. Pound and Eliot (up to and including *The Waste Land*) clearly are fundamental figures for him: references to *The Waste Land* figure prominently in *A Drunk Man Looks at the Thistle*, for instance; Pound's early Imagist work is crucial to the development of MacDiarmid's own early lyrics; and Eliot and Pound both clearly show the way to a conception of the fragmentary modern epic, a central and kindred project for all three poets, as an act of cultural reclamation. (Eliot, for his part, published MacDiarmid in his influential literary journal, *The Criterion*.) These two figures are routinely referred to as giants of contemporary poetry and recognised as modernist elder brethren, but MacDiarmid regards them in any case as 'supra-national, belonging neither to England nor America',[2] that is, hardly transatlantic figures at all; and Stein and Stevens he prizes in similar terms, as modernists who (thus) represent among other things a rejection of nationality in general, not to mention more specifically the rejection of – the shedding of all apparent trappings and traces of – America's prevailingly puerile and heinously commercial national culture, personified for MacDiarmid in the figure of 'a man called Grubb', as he presents matters in 'On American Literature' (fairly early, 1924, signed C. M. Grieve).[3] What is important about American writers who are important to MacDiarmid, it seems, is in part that they are not American in any but the most circumstantial sense. (Indeed, in looking to Pound, Eliot and Stein, self-exiles all, he looks more to London and Paris than across the ocean.) America for the most part would seem to be virtually invisible to him – a cultural abomination on the far horizon, but not the centre of any real concern of his. Again, not that it should be otherwise.

Whitman, however, is a different matter; Whitman is not only present, he is central. (This complicates matters, since it would seem to make America itself central – since imagining Whitman without America is like trying to imagine MacDiarmid without Scotland.) Citations from and references to Whitman run throughout MacDiarmid's work, and he explicitly acknowledges or claims on more than one occasion that the American occupies a foundational place in the construction of his own project. 'I haven't been much influenced by any other poet,' he says in a late interview from 1977, 'but Whitman is one who probably did influence me – when I was younger [. . .] I'm very interested in Whitman, more so than I've been in any subsequent American.'[4] Similarly, in a 1972 letter to Alan Bold he writes: 'I wouldn't think I was given directions by any other English-Language poets other than those you mention (Doughty, Pound, Milton, Blake) save only – and very influentially – Walt Whitman.'[5] This influence extends, moreover, beyond MacDiarmid's individual case: in an early essay on Byron he notes of the lord: 'With Walt Whitman he has been, and remains, perhaps the profoundest influence on subsequent and contemporary poetry in every country in Europe.'[6] (MacDiarmid, like Whitman, was not one to shrink from big claims.) Although MacDiarmid nowhere elaborates very expansively on the nature of this influence and centrality, in his own case at least certain points of connection are made quite explicit, and others can perhaps be deduced.

Whitman, of course, is a foundational figure in American literature and an important world figure, following Burns and Wordsworth (to put complex matters in blunt terms) the next great hero of the vernacular revolution in poetry, in Whitman's case linked to the invention of a new kind of nation/ people and new kinds of poetic forms, as he saw it, writing in New York (mostly) over the latter half of the nineteenth century. It is not hard to see why MacDiarmid would be drawn to him as a model or forerunner, teacher or kindred spirit. Whitman's free verse makes a radical break with poetic traditions, and claims the voice of a 'natural' self (personified in 'Song of Myself') that is at once personal and universal, distinctively American and transnational. His *Leaves of Grass*, issued first in 1855, and subsequently many times, in emended and expanded and rearranged editions over the remainder of his career until his death in 1892, is among other things a kind of proto-type of the fragmentary modern epic, and a model of organic form as well, to which MacDiarmid would have been drawn (though nowhere does he comment on this explicitly with regard to Whitman). This epic form for Whitman is, moreover, fully identified with the vernacular, more like Dante in this regard than like Pound or Eliot, who of course both engage the vernacular with vigour but in the context of a wider range of more exclusive registers, including, for instance, foreign languages. The melding of the self and the nation in one discourse, the identification of poetry with national identity – poetry's claim to speak a national (and universal) tongue – and the radical representation of the self's 'barbaric yawp' (in Whitman's famous term, from 'Song of Myself'): all this would appeal to MacDiarmid, and indeed apply to him as well. But in fact of all this, in connection with Whitman, we hear next to nothing from MacDiarmid himself.

The most sustained representation of what Whitman means to MacDiarmid comes in *Lucky Poet*. At the closing peroration of his prefatory 'Author's Note' (dated March, 1941, Island of Whalsay, Shetland Islands), he writes:

> The programme for poetry I advocate is, in Walt Whitman's words: 'To conform with and build on the concrete realities and theories of the universe furnished by science, and henceforth the only irrefragable basis for anything, verse included'; and like Whitman, I cry: 'Think of the petty environage and limited area of the poets of the past, no matter how great their genius. Think of the absence and ignorance in all cases hitherto of the multitudinousness, vitality, and the unprecedented stimulants of today. It almost seems as if a poetry with cosmic and dynamic features of magnitude and limitlessness suitable to the human soul were never possible before. It is certain that a poetry of absolute faith and equality for the use of the democratic masses never was.' (*LP*, p. xxxii)[7]

Whitman is talking about a number of things here which MacDiarmid appropriates to his own discussion in this 'Author's Note', in which he seeks (among other things) to situate himself 'as a Scottish poet' in relation to 'what Mr. T. S. Eliot has called "the living whole of all the poetry that has ever been written"' (*LP*, p. xxxii). The key point here for MacDiarmid is his own affinity with Whitman's 'insistence upon a poetry of fact' (with supporting citations, in MacDiarmid's case, from the Russian theorist Plekhanov, lending a presumed scientific, or even better, Scientific Socialist, heft to his claims – but this matter of 'concrete realities and theories of the universe furnished by science' (note how silently 'theories' insinuates itself into the company of facts and realities) blends almost indistinguishably into both a spiritual endeavour (involving 'cosmic [. . .] features', 'the human soul' in its 'magnitude and limitlessness', and 'absolute faith') and a political imperative as well, 'for the use of the democratic masses'. Whitman in effect for MacDiarmid here represents the fusion of these concerns in one vernacular poetic voice: a radically democratic politics, a universal spiritual dignity regardless of creed, and faith in science, which is to say progress; the claims of the rational against oppressive traditions and injustice, the claim of the modern, in other words, of (implicitly) the vernacular as modern, not a throwback (as some might regard Scots verse to be in the twentieth century, as MacDiarmid is fully aware in 1941, fifteen years after A *Drunk Man* when he himself is writing mainly in English) but the leading edge of the future instead.

These fused notes of the scientific, the spiritual and the political sound throughout *Lucky Poet* whenever Whitman's name comes up. Again climactically positioned at the end of the long chapter 'The Kind of Poetry I Want', where the prose gives way and the argument is carried forward in verse, we find this conjoining, in Whitman's name, of poetry and science:

'In the beauty of poems', as Whitman said,
'Are henceforth the tuft and final applause of science.
. . . Facts are showered over with light,
The daylight is lit with more volatile light,
The poets of the cosmos advance
Through all interpositions and coverings
And turmoils and stratagems
To first principles. . . . Beyond all precedent
Poetry will have to do with actual facts.' (*LP*, p. 189)[8]

Poetry here is to be not only dedicated to facts, but to their redemption (as it were) as well, their confirmation and adornment. This follows a passage from Whitman quoted a page earlier (the same passage quoted in the 'Author's Note' discussed above, with minor changes to Whitman's text) on 'the concrete realities and theories of the universe furnished by science', as well as on 'the petty environage [. . .] of the poets of past or present Europe', the 'cosmic and dynamic features of [. . .] the human soul' and 'the democratic masses' (*LP*, pp. 187–8). Following his quotation here of Whitman's reflection on 'the democratic masses' and the unprecedented possibilities afforded by modern American experiments in 'magnitude and limitlessness' and 'equality', MacDiarmid says: 'That is why I insist on the necessity of world consciousness', and he goes on:

> Whitman has perfectly expressed my standpoint when he says: 'Whatever may have been the case in years gone by, the true use for the imaginative faculty of modern times is to give ultimate vivification to facts, to science, and to common lives, endowing them with glows and glories and final illustriousness which belong to every real thing, and to real things only. Without that ultimate vivification – which the poet or other artist alone can give – reality would seem incomplete, and science, democracy, and life itself, finally in vain.' (*LP*, p. 188)[9]

Poetry for Whitman, for MacDiarmid here again, serves and glorifies fact and 'common lives', but also is what ultimately redeems it all (fact and life and politics and culture) for human use and pleasure, a spiritual and political dedication 'to first principles'.

We should note that for Whitman here 'the poets of past or present Europe' are set apart, explicitly enough, from the poets of America – who have, in Whitman's view, certain cultural advantages when it comes to imagining 'multitudinousness, vitality, and [. . .] unprecedented stimulants' – the nation of many nations, which expresses, at least in principle, a radical democracy (*LP*, p. 188).[10] This reference to Europe is the part MacDiarmid elides from Whitman's text in his preface, changing it to 'the poets of the past' (*LP*, p. xxxii), leaving Europe and nationality in general out of it, showing himself to be (among other things) the modernist Whitman of course was not. But he lets the reference stand in the context of 'The Kind of Poetry I Want' (*LP*, p. 188), showing himself to be the nationalist he inescapably after all was as well.

These Whitmanic 'first principles' and 'common lives' of MacDiarmid's vision are factors in other invocations and quotations of Whitman elsewhere in *Lucky Poet*. In the chapter 'On Seeing Scotland Whole', in a paragraph that includes references to Jacob Boehme, St Augustine, Dr Thomas Arnold, Lytton Strachey, Wordsworth, Mr Joseph Wood Krutch and Ruth Pitter as well as Whitman, with quotations from several of these figures, MacDiarmid (whose own comments close this passage) discusses the assertion that, in the words of Joseph Wood Krutch,

> what shocked Dr Arnold was the absence in brutes of that 'sense of moral evil' to which he attached so much importance. They could sin without suffering even the pangs of conscience by way of retribution. But is not that exactly the fact which moved Whitman to such envious admiration for the animals, who did not make him sick 'discussing their duty to God'? 'Not one,' he said, 'is respectable or unhappy over the whole earth.' My vote certainly goes to

Whitman, and to Augustine in respect of the worms, if not of the Angels. (*LP*, p. 269)[11]

In his identification with 'the animals', MacDiarmid's Whitman here is the voice of a commonality indeed, or beyond that, even (beyond, that is, the political), a voice of the elemental. He stands pointedly as alternative/in resistance to the commonalities and elemental claims of the Church, alternative to metaphysics of every kind, from respectabilities to deities, 'their dignities and a' that'.[12] The elemental, as appropriated by MacDiarmid through Whitman's claims, is a quality he would seem to seek in his own claims, whether spiritual, scientific, political or poetic.

In a similar vein, Whitman comes up again when MacDiarmid discusses Havelock Ellis 'writing on the ulterior significance of psycho-analysis'. He quotes Ellis on:

> the fact that Man [. . .] remains a mass of primitively fundamental, even unconscious, human impulses, woven in and out of each other, as equals, no longer divided into some that may be shown, being respectable, and others that must be concealed, suppressed, or aspersed with contempt, as though they had no right to existence. (*LP*, p. 92)

Here we find the political as well as the elemental – the elaboration of 'fundamental [. . .] impulses' into systems of social order (and disorder). MacDiarmid's quotation from Ellis continues:

> So the way is opened for a new vision [. . .] That is still some way ahead. The psychoanalysts are not themselves the people who can bring it. But glimpses were caught of it – as by Whitman – before they even existed. (*LP*, p. 92)

This passage is another one that MacDiarmid offers as the expression of his own affinity (though here Whitman is twice removed, appropriated first by Ellis and then by MacDiarmid in an enveloping embrace): 'For, like the late Havelock Ellis [. . .] I see in it [i.e. in psychoanalysis] a "hand that is pointed towards an approaching new horizon of the human spirit"', but not that horizon itself. Science in this instance is judged '"too pedestrian, too prosaic, too (as they used to say before 'matter' was recognized as a poetic fiction) materialistic"' – it is for the poets and prophets, perhaps, to vivify what the modern science of mind reveals. In any case – and still quoting Ellis – the hand of science here points 'towards the direction in which poets and prophets will raise the curtain that covers the new horizon'. Whitman, in effect, in this context, is the proof of this claim: the poet-prophet of 'a new vision' of elemental Man (*LP*, p. 92).

What is interesting to notice here also is perhaps a bit of Oedipal exchange between MacDiarmid and Whitman. When Ellis says that the hand of science (merely) points the way, the new vision itself to be achieved only by poets and prophets (a point essentially the same as Whitman's own, quoted above, with regard to vivification), he goes on as if to correct himself, to say of the psychoanalysts that 'they are doing more' than merely pointing the way, 'they are actually laying the foundations of the structure on which the poets and prophets will stand' (LP, p. 92). Some great poets/fathers, like Whitman, have glimpsed this 'new horizon' through the force of their genius. But now, presumably, with science (even the science of the mind, unimaginable in Whitman's pre-Freudian day) extending its reach, MacDiarmid as poet/son will get more than 'glimpses'; he will stand on the very structure that science has built beyond Whitman's materialist dreams. (Needless to say, this is not Ellis' claim, but MacDiarmid's implication by quotation.) Through no fault and to no credit of his own – like Oedipus indeed in that regard – MacDiarmid finds himself at a socio-historical moment propitious for the completion and surpassing of Whitman's work.

Again it is interesting to note in this connection that the matter of the vernacular does not come up in connection with Whitman in any but the most indirect manner – a general reference to 'common lives', for instance. When one thinks of Whitman in the context of his possible centrality to MacDiarmid, it is Whitman as revolutionary hero of the vernacular that necessarily first springs to mind – that, and perhaps their shared concern for Nation, and for the role of poetry, specifically, in the development of their nations. But nowhere is this mentioned in Lucky Poet – itself an Oedipal omission perhaps? Instead we get Whitman the advocate of science and the envious admirer of animals – an oddly canted portrait of him, and of the relationship between these two poets, on the face of it, for what it leaves out. Nowhere else in MacDiarmid's work is the subject of Whitman's importance as a vernacular writer/model/brother-in-arms broached, either, except when it is implicit, as when he quotes a critic saying 'Whitman intended, more than any poet had ever done, to represent common humanity' – but 'represent' covers a multitude of sins, and there is no reference whatsoever here specifically to Whitman's language.[13]

Gertrude Stein (1874–1946) is an interesting figure in this regard in that she is American, like Whitman, but contemporary (not to mention in some sense European) like MacDiarmid. As it turns out, he effectively turns her *into* Whitman. 'Gertrude Stein's work in general, represent[s] a wholesome dissatisfaction with all the innumerable divergencies of literature which *go nowhere* so far as the mass of mankind is concerned' (this from a piece dated February 1926).[14] This seems an odd claim to make with regard to Stein, whose artful impenetrability partakes of vernacular elements, for sure, but seems to represent in the end a most refined and elite, high-culture discourse. For MacDiarmid, Stein's work could be regarded as

> spadework, pioneering, towards a dynamic literature – a literature that will do what literature has never done in the past, act directly on general conscious-ness, circumvent all those elements which have hitherto protected the inertia, the refusal to think, to experience, of the masses and restricted literature to direct effect upon a negligible fringe.[15]

The description in fact fits Whitman far better than it fits Stein, whose work has apparently not spoken to the masses with the directness and clarity that MacDiarmid claims for it. Again, too, it is not Stein's vernacular or national interests, but her modernist enterprise that draws MacDiarmid's attention. Even disguised as Stein, as it were, Whitman's concerns with language and nation-building remain hidden or at least unvoiced, even as they remain central concerns to him as to Stein, and as to MacDiarmid.

For all these curious wrinkles around the edges of MacDiarmid's presen-tation of Whitman, it is nevertheless easy enough to see how MacDiarmid would be pleased to imagine himself a kind of Whitman for Scotland – a constructive foundational voice of the new nation's creation, a pioneer of its vernacular poetry and a champion of principles beyond mere Nation, such as democracy, multiplicity, internationality or communism – a voice, a 'barbaric yawp' of postcolonial independence and global recognition. But the cultural and national conditions of Whitman's nineteenth-century American world and of MacDiarmid's twentieth-century Scottish world, of course, differ considerably. Whitman has the advantage in this regard of working in the context of a new nation, a programmatic entity (rather than an organic, historical-cultural entity of long standing) based at least in theory on a few principles of equality and openness – to which he can give poetic form. MacDiarmid, on the other hand, has a long established and not pro-grammatic but, arguably, organic entity with a complex political history (i.e., Scotland) to which *he* wants to give voice: an act not of self-creation exactly as much as reawakening – more Scottish Jeremiah than American Adam. And, of course, MacDiarmid is working crucially in a synthetic language, whereas Whitman represents (par excellence) an organic one, a kind of cul-mination, as noted earlier, of the great modern/Romantic levelling projects of Burns or Wordsworth, the vernacular unbound. These are luxuries, as it were, afforded to Whitman in his time and place, to which MacDiarmid has no (or limited) access. (This point too may play into the suggestion of Oedipal struggle made above, though I would not want to make too much of that, or lean too heavily upon the claim, which is quite secondary in my mind to the poetic and political points of connection between the two poets, the vernacular and radical democratic impulses to which they both give voice/shape.)

Of course, what MacDiarmid sees when he looks over here to the United States is not simply a matter of whom he refers to or quotes most frequently, and how he does so; it is also a function of how he looks from over here. That is, my reading of MacDiarmid's Whitman is no doubt skewed by my own extra-national perspective on MacDiarmid, as well as by my own native sense of Walt (which is probably closer to Burns than to MacDiarmid). I see the world from within an American (indeed, in large measure, Whitmanic) frame of reference, to some necessary extent, just as MacDiarmid does from within his Scottish frame; even when imagining a more universal, international frame of reference, one's vision is always reflected through the prism of perspective, American or Scottish as the case may be, among other variables. And not (of course) to say that these are hard lines or borders in the mind, just that differences are inevitable and fairly pervasive. For instance, from my transatlantic perspective, MacDiarmid appears a figure drawn repeatedly, indeed consistently, to totalising systems of one kind or another – the Scottish pre-eminent among them, of course, but also communism, or a kind of fundamentalist geology as in 'On a Raised Beach', or nature itself, as in the citations from Whitman above – conceptual frameworks that promise a comprehensive explanatory or justificatory power, single principles to which to hold, causes to champion. (Whitman is given to such tendencies as well.) In the end, however, the Scottish for MacDiarmid is master signifier; in the end all others have to be reconciled with that one. (*Lucky Poet* appears at the moment when MacDiarmid has rejoined the Scottish National Party after having been expelled from the Communist Party of Great Britain for 'nationalist deviation' more than once, having been expelled in the first place from the National Party of Scotland for being a communist.)[16] The privileging of the national, and of cultural identification, must have some impact on Scottish (or for that matter British) readers' experience, must call forth some complex of receptive or deflective responses, simply not available to other readers not included in that national or cultural circle. Whitman avoids this situation, to the extent that he does, by claiming – being, as it were, authorised to claim – the American as a universal entity, available to all, at once a nation and all nations, a culture of others. From a transatlantic perspective, however, Scottishness is not necessarily privileged among the various totalising systems to which MacDiarmid was attached.

As Americans, of course, we have our own encounters and obsessions with forms of totalisation (Whitman's democracy among them), our own totalising narratives and our own ongoing arguments about what America means, and what it means to be American. In this context, 'Scottish' is not an identity but an analogue, perhaps, or a kind of metaphor – something to take interest in, respond deeply to, understand and even identify with, but not to identify oneself *as*, not a master signifier. This has certainly been borne out in my experience of teaching MacDiarmid to American students, and perhaps this encounter in the pedagogical domain (rather than the critical or scholarly) is as good a way as any, and more democratic than most, to show how MacDiarmid and the Scottish might characteristically be framed in a contemporary context, from a transatlantic perspective.

Keeping in mind that what MacDiarmid looks like from over here in the United States depends in part on how 'here' is defined, when I read MacDiarmid I read him in the context of Scottish traditions and/or of his modernist peers (while also in the context, or against the backdrop of my own American perspective, experience, assumptions); when I teach MacDiarmid the context tends to be postcolonial. It need not only be so, of course – it could well be modernist – but it is in some sense naturally so, even though MacDiarmid is not living a 'post'-colonial situation in the strictest sense; I take 'postcolonial' as shorthand for a full spectrum of colonial and postcolonial struggle, a capacious enough category to include Scotland. Where the context is postcolonial (as in more strictly Scottish contexts for that matter), questions of centrality and marginality are ever-present, often central and always vexed; and MacDiarmid seems positioned at the far margin even of that relatively marginal territory; for my students, a harder border to cross in some ways than the Yoruba-inflected English of Amos Tutuola or the radical astringencies and tortured opacities of late Samuel Beckett ('Worstward Ho', for instance), though these are deeply alienating texts for my students (though, as such, exciting texts as well). These authors are MacDiarmid's company in the seminar on Global English, which I have taught for several years in different forms, but always as a type of advanced study, a graduate seminar or one for undergraduates in their final year as a kind of culminating course; in other words a matter, relatively speaking, of literature and 'poetry for connoisseurs in abnormal cerebration – mental gymnastics of a remote order' (as MacDiarmid characterises the work of Wallace Stevens in one admiring review).[17] In addition to Tutuola and Beckett, the only slightly less alarming V. S. Naipaul, Les Murray, Arundhati Roy, Michael Ondaatje or Margaret Atwood would typically round out the setting, which moves among many centres, from Scotland to Nigeria to Trinidad to Australia to India to Ireland to Canada by way of Sri Lanka. If MacDiarmid's Whitman is not exactly the Whitman an American expects to see, an American MacDiarmid is clearly a MacDiarmid recontextualised as well: 'the Scottish' here not a synonym for 'the nation' but a subset of 'global English' (although he is not exactly that, either) or 'the postcolonial'.

My own selection of texts for the seminar plays a role as well in framing MacDiarmid for my students, of course. We read a handful of the earliest lyrics from *Sangschaw* and *Penny Wheep*, along with 'Gairmscoile', and a smattering of later pieces, including 'On a Raised Beach'. (I have tried reading *A Drunk Man Looks at the Thistle* with a class, but it was too much too soon, I imagine.) Among this group, the surest footing on the question of Scottish identity comes with 'Gairmscoile', and students do engage with the poem in those terms, certainly, although other questions framed by the poem – notions of the primordial and of dark contentions deep within us – make equal and more primary claims on the group's attention. (I base my own claim here not only on my memory of seminar discussion, but also on the commentary and discussion of students in an online extension of the seminar, a freewheeling zone where students set their own agenda for discussion, from which I will be quoting.) Other poems, like 'The Bonnie Broukit Bairn', for example, lend themselves to metaphorical engagements with the question of the Scottish, but for the most part suggest other lines of inquiry. Along with 'The Bonnie Broukit Bairn', 'The Dying Earth', 'The Eemis Stane' and 'The Innumerable Christ', not to mention 'On a Raised Beach', tend instead towards a focus on cosmic perspectives that cast questions of the political or the national distinctly in the shade; certainly for an American reader, these cosmic matters are a more prominent dimension of the poems than any political or cultural allegory they might carry.

One of the features of the postcolonial framework is a sense of having one's roots and history cut off, so that one has to fight to construct an identity without access to certain crucial cultural tools – one's own language, for instance, instead of the language of one's conquerors and overlords. MacDiarmid's situation certainly fits the bill. The Scots language and Scottish culture were central to his upbringing, and obviously to his whole career, but just as obviously this career was one of struggle on behalf of this language and this culture, based on an awareness that Scots was a threatened tongue and Scotland itself a threatened entity. (A Scottish Renaissance presupposes a kind of Scottish death.) Though he himself would have been more comfortable in Scots than many of his contemporaries, and believed himself to be more broadly and deeply knowledgeable about Scottish culture, he too is confronted with the general problem: the fading of the language (thus its need to be synthesised) and of the culture more broadly. We Americans respond to the concept of the threatened native land in our own complicated ways, given our history; we respond as well to the notion of constructing, even fighting to construct, an identity in the absence of abiding traditions of a shared community, this yearning for a root, although America itself is that strange historical monstrosity, at once postcolonial and imperial from the beginning. One student seeking to account for the Scottish condition, and in particular MacDiarmid's impulse to preserve, protect, restore and resynthesise, invokes 'Said's theories of an exile': 'MacDiarmid can be seen as an exile because he is not connected to his roots: the Scottish language and culture. He's in a world he doesn't wish to be in: an English dominated Scotland'.[18] Obviously MacDiarmid is not literally an exile (but he can be seen as one); and, arguably, he is more connected to his roots than most, as noted above. Still, just as clearly, the language and the culture are not available to him in the way, and to the degree, they would be in a 'normalised' (i.e. non-postcolonial) political situation. The student notes, however, as several other students do, that MacDiarmid's 'escape' from this postcolonial condition of cultural extremity, or his method of coping with it, is in creating texts that live 'on a cosmic, personal [and] national level' simultaneously, in effect negating the primacy of the political. The postcolonial context tends to turn questions of nationality inside out, so that the concept of nation is marked by its own absences, contradictions and confusions.

Nor is the postcolonial perhaps the only unexpected context for MacDiarmid from a transatlantic perspective. 'Nature seems to be his religion,' another student notes, 'his supreme being in his manifesto, "On a Raised Beach".'[19] In the context of these students' training in British and American literature, this is a poem read against a Romantic backdrop, a poem seeking refuge and transcendence in nature – a deeply (though not, of course, exclusively) American trope – and MacDiarmid among his modernist peers (Eliot, say, or Joyce) is distinguished, perhaps, by this touch. The Romantic (i.e. transcendental) vision of 'Nature' makes him more familiar to my students, in a sense, than the other modernists, as if in compensation for the manifold estrangements of his language. Though not of course a Romantic by any usual measure – quite the reverse he would appear – from this distance in time and angle in space MacDiarmid's commitment to Nature as bedrock and guide makes him available at least to a different set of associations. His style is not Romantic, that is, but, typically, more jaggedly and (in 'On a Raised Beach') scientifically modern; nevertheless, in his search for (or insistence on) a secular transcendental, and in his interrogation of Nature as a possible solution to the problem of secular alienation, he at least inherits and renovates fundamental Romantic assumptions. But whether modernist, Romantic (or post-Romantic), colonial or postcolonial, MacDiarmid's transatlantic profile takes form within a global rather than national frame of reference.

None of this is necessarily different, of course, from what a Scottish reader of MacDiarmid might see; certainly all of these angles on his work are available to a Scottish reader as to any other. In the end a transatlantic perspective and a Scottish one may be closer than they first appear. In either case we find a MacDiarmid caught between two paradoxical imperatives: to raise and transcend the flag of Scotland. In his expressions of affinity for Whitman we see his interest in an escape (if only partial and provisional) from the Nation, not to mention the Scottish nation, while recognising at the same time, in

'Gairmscoile' for instance, his fundamental commitment to Scotland and the Scots language, his essential claim that (in the words of another student) 'what is at stake in the silencing of language is the possibility of destroying a world'.[20] (Holding onto a world and escaping from it at the same time: a contradiction Tutuola, Naipaul and Beckett address continuously.) Ultimately 'the transatlantic' may be, as 'the nation' is for MacDiarmid, at once a fundamental orientation and something of not much account, something of a fiction, which otherwise obscures more broadly universal points of connection between human beings. But maybe that's just my Whitman talking.

CHAPTER ELEVEN

MacDiarmid's Ambitions, Legacy and Reputation

Margery Palmer McCulloch

Emigrating from North Britain

In contrast to modernist poets such as T. S. Eliot and Ezra Pound, but
to a significant extent like W. B. Yeats, MacDiarmid's ambitions for his
poetry, and his legacy and reputation, are intimately linked to his relationship with his country. From the first his objectives were both national and
international, and in the initial stage of his project, he looked to Yeats and
the earlier Irish literary revival for encouragement and models, believing
(despite his stated wish to encourage all three of Scotland's languages), that
at this point any modern and ambitious attempt to revive Scottish writing
would have to use the English language as the Irish had done. He argued in
the *Aberdeen Free Press* in December 1921, for example, that 'Synge, Yeats,
and other great Irish writers found no difficulty in expressing themselves
in an English which they yet made distinctively Irish' (*L*, p. 751); and in
the *Dunfermline Press* of August 1922, a few weeks before the launch of his
Scottish Chapbook, he again looked to the Irish for support, emphasising
that a Scottish literary revival using English 'would be no more English in
spirit than the literature of the Irish Literary Revival, most of which was
written in English, was English in spirit'.[1] What MacDiarmid recognised
in these comparisons he made with the Irish context – and what remained
significant even after he had replaced the Irish Revival's English language
and leading writer Yeats with his own literary refashioning of Scots and the
modernist Joyce – was the decolonising nature of his project. For what was
intended was not the kind of Scottish cultural revival that had occurred in
the post-Union years of the eighteenth century in the poetry of Ramsay,
Fergusson and Burns, or the late nineteenth-, early twentieth-century 'renascence' envisaged by Patrick Geddes and the writers of the 'Celtic Twilight'
(neither of which had an explicitly political dimension). This modern – and
modernist – movement, taking place in the aftermath of World War One,
was one that sought to emigrate from the country's existing provincial
status as 'North Britain' and recover a self-determining position in relation

to a revitalised Scottish culture, and in the longer term, in relation to the country's political status.

This need for what would be recognised in today's transnational cultural and political discourse as a decolonising or postcolonialist agenda is something that has not always been acknowledged in Scottish scholarly accounts of MacDiarmid and the revival movement that developed around him. Yet, after the 1707 political union with England, the Scots and their culture were subjected to what Derek Walcott has called 'a sound colonial education'[2] (by some participants acquired only too willingly); a conditioning increased from the nineteenth century onwards by the growth and syndication of the newspaper industry, and by the headquarters of significant publishing firms and new media such as broadcasting being situated in London. Historical studies such as Linda Colley's *Britons* and T. M. Devine's *The Scottish Nation* have argued that by the end of the eighteenth century the Union had already brought a new prosperity to Lowland Scotland, accompanied by opportunities for Scots to enter the administrative elite of the new Britain. Yet even in these early days, this successful commercial and administrative forging of Great Britain could be seen to have its downside for the junior partner. Cultural commentaries on the period are awash with stories of the unseemly haste with which the Edinburgh literati and upper and growing middle classes attempted to acquire the appropriate *English* accent. In his preface to *Edinburgh Essays on Scots Literature*, published in 1933 during the interwar literary revival initiated by MacDiarmid, H. J. C. Grierson (1866–1960) quotes from a speech given at a Walter Scott dinner by the president of Magdalen College, Oxford, who commented on this phenomenon:

> 'It is an extraordinary thing,' said the President, 'and a remarkable testimony to the force of convention, to see a man like Hume [. . .] or like Robertson [. . .] writing anxiously about trifling solecisms of our Northern idiom, smuggling one to the other their little lists of Scotticisms, and, in short, hoarding and brooding over these tiny matters with the passion and almost the idiocy of collectors of postage stamps [. . .] Hume corrects Beattie's Scotticisms, and Beattie Hume's; Malone corrects Boswell's.'

Grierson adds: 'And as my edition of *Scott's Letters* shows, Lockhart silently corrected Scott's lapses of this kind.'[3]

Grierson also comments in his preface that he himself has been 'with other of my colleagues, often accused of not giving sufficient attention to Scottish Literature', although when he occupied the Chair of English at Aberdeen University he 'lectured regularly on the Scottish poets of the fifteenth and sixteenth centuries so far as it was possible to do so usefully when texts were not available for my students – and on the revival of Scottish Literature in the eighteenth century, that revival which culminated in the work of Burns and Walter Scott'. When he moved to Edinburgh University, not even this (largely antiquarian in 1930s terms) teaching was possible. In Edinburgh, 'Scottish Literature was not a definitely prescribed portion of the work of the Chair, which had been a Chair of Rhetoric and *Belles Lettres*, but had been converted into a Chair of Rhetoric and *English Literature*' in the time of Hugh Blair. Despite his admiration for Blair and a successor such as David Masson, Grierson concludes that 'the tradition that an important function of such a Chair of Rhetoric was to teach young Scots how to write good English long endured. The intricacies of "shall" and "will", never mastered by Sir Walter, have been wrestled with by successive generations of Scottish students'.[4] In such circumstances, it would be difficult to disagree with the speaker in MacDiarmid's *To Circumjack Cencrastus* (1930) who thinks he has come to the wrong educational establishment: '"I'm beggin' your pardon / A mistake has been made. / It was SCOTS Universities / I was seekin'," I said' (CP1, p. 204).

In addition to the situation in the universities described by Grierson, Devine quotes the educational historian Robert Anderson to the effect that 'as far as its curriculum and organization went, a Scottish elementary school in the 1900s was much more like its English counterpart than a Scottish university was like an English one'.[5] As with Edwin Muir, MacDiarmid's 'university' was that provided by Orage's cosmopolitan *New Age*, but his secondary schooling, especially in the literary area, conformed to the English model, with favourite teaching material consisting of Palgrave's *Golden Treasury*, and in particular its selections from Shakespeare, Milton, Shelley and Tennyson (with Burns as a representative Scottish voice). The influence of English literature, and especially of the English Romantics, was therefore early embedded in his imagination, as we can see in his subsequent poetry alongside its modernist features.[6] On the other hand, however much he might have appreciated the qualities of these English writers, and even in certain circumstances have been influenced by aspects of their work, by the 1920s MacDiarmid was in no doubt that if Scottish culture was to be truly revitalised, then this must be done on its own self-determining terms and not through a continuing acceptance of its provincial status and the attempt to accommodate itself to a dominant, but ultimately alien, English tradition.

Awareness of such a historical context is important for a proper understanding of the motivation behind the programme of the interwar literary revival led by MacDiarmid and, therefore, for any assessment of its achievement in its own time and its legacy for the future. For this was not a belated nineteenth-century Romantic nationalist revival, as suggested by Tom Nairn in *The Break-Up of Britain* (1977). It was a modern movement, influenced by recent political and cultural events in Europe and the British Isles, and wishing to 'make things new' in Scotland, culturally and politically, on that modern basis. And for the future poet MacDiarmid, ambitious to become himself a significant modern writer, one of the first areas for necessary trans-formation was the existing retrogressive Scottish literary tradition and its literary icons, Burns and Scott, memorably characterised by Edwin Muir (1887–1959) as 'sham bards of a sham nation'.[7] If a new phase of Scottish culture was to be created, then not only the Kailyard followers of Burns and Scott in poetry and fiction had to be swept away, but these literary idols themselves had to be toppled from their pedestals.

MacDiarmid's relationship with Burns was always an equivocal one. Before the launch of *The Scottish Chapbook* in August 1922, he had quarrelled vio-lently with the Vernacular Circle of the London Burns Club in relation to its proposals to revitalise and encourage the use of the Scots language through writing and speaking competitions in schools, claiming that 'any attempt to create a Doric "boom" just now – or even to maintain the existing vernacu-lar cult in anything like its present tendencies – would be a gross disservice to Scottish life and letters'.[8] Similarly, in many periodical articles as well as through the protagonist in his long poem *A Drunk Man Looks at the Thistle* (1926), he attacked the Burns Cult and its clubs where 'No' wan in fifty kens a wurd Burns wrote / But misapplied is a'body's property' (*CP1*, p. 84, ll. 41–2). However, Burns himself was viewed differently by MacDiarmid at this point, being compared with Christ by his Drunk Man, and with Milton in the lines 'Rabbie, wad'st thou wert here – the warld hath need, / And Scotland mair sae, o' the likes o' thee!' (*CP1*, p. 85, ll. 61–2), with their implicit allu-sion to Wordsworth's appeal in time of trouble to his seventeenth-century poet hero, John Milton.[9] *A Drunk Man* is full of such explicit and implicit references to MacDiarmid's 'elder Brother in the muse', and it was with Burns's 'Tam o' Shanter' that he told George Ogilvie he hoped his long poem would be compared.[10] His slogan 'Not Burns – Dunbar', from his 1927 book *Albyn*,[11] was not either an attack on Burns himself or a call for Scottish poets to return to the language and formal methodology of the sixteenth-century Dunbar as a model, but a recognition that what Scottish poetry needed at the present time was a return to the spirit of confidence in the remaking of poetry in Scots in that earlier period (a time when Gavin Douglas had the daring to translate Virgil's *Aeneid* into Scots) as opposed to the continuing tendency in the early twentieth century to reproduce feeble imitations of Burns's poetry. *Albyn* is notable, among other things, for MacDiarmid's acknowledgement at this later point in the 1920s that the literary revival he had instituted had not yet achieved the goals set by its optimistic inaugural programme, and it is noticeable that negative comments about Burns himself become more often woven into his customary critical comments about the Burns Cult around this time. Writing in the *Radio Times* in January 1930, for example, he com-ments that 'the Burns sentiment is one of the principal opponents of the new movement in Scottish arts and affairs' and that Burns himself 'has nothing

to contribute to the crucial problems of today and tomorrow': a view that
brought Catherine Carswell (1879–1946) into the controversy on the side
of Burns, and ultimately into a closer relationship with the revival movement and a friendship with MacDiarmid.[12] Yet MacDiarmid's recognition
elsewhere in his article that 'it is not good for any country to be so long and
completely dominated by a single writer as Scotland has been dominated by
Burns' is a valid one. It was illustrated forcibly when Carswell herself was subjected to much abuse in the Letters pages of the *Daily Record* in the autumn
of 1930 when pre-publication extracts from her biography of Burns appeared
to challenge the iconic image of the man held by readers. 'Womanhood
Degraded', one headline proclaimed over a letter from a Jean Armour of Ayr;
while Mr J. Stewart Seggie, president of the Edinburgh Ninety Burns Club,
protested that the book 'will be killed at the Burns festivals in January', an
unfortunate metaphor which anticipated the actual bullet sent to Carswell in
a letter.[13] Perhaps it was indeed time to move on to other influences.

Walter Scott, who was the subject of a number of scholarly and bio-
graphical studies in the interwar period, also offered a subject for challenge
to the modern reformers. In contrast to his numerous references to Burns,
MacDiarmid has very little to say in print about Scott in the early 1920s.
However by 1926 and his *Contemporary Scottish Studies*, he is regarding any
revival of interest in Scott equally as unacceptable as the continuing Burns
Cult, although for different reasons. While Burns 'belongs mainly to Scots
Literature', he sees Scott as belonging to the 'central traditions of English
literature', and his supporters as 'all either English or Anglo-Scottish lit-
terateurs'. He finds that 'the movement to reinstate Scott in critical esteem
and popular regard must therefore be regarded as one designed to conserve
and reinforce certain elements in English culture, while taking it for granted
that Scotland and England have identical cultural interests'.[14] This suggestion of a common culture was of course entirely contrary to the objectives of
the still infant revival movement, and could be seen, equally with the stul-
tifying Burns Cult, as a threat to its development. By the time of the Scott
Centenary in 1932, MacDiarmid was insisting that Scott 'had no profound
and progressive sense of his country'.[15] This complaint was restated in Neil
Gunn's comments in his 1936 review of Edwin Muir's *Scott and Scotland*. For
Gunn (1891–1973), Scott's failure as a novelist was that a new social order
could not grow organically from his historical narratives:

It is not that the history was untrue or was inadequate subject matter for his
genius; it was that it no longer enriched or influenced a living national tradition
[. . .] it was story-telling or romance set in a void; it was seen backwards as in the
round of some time spyglass and had interpretive bearing neither upon a present
nor a future.[16]

Burns and Scott were the two outstanding targets in this attempt to change
the direction of Scottish writing, but there were many revisionary articles in
newspapers and periodicals of the time, putting forward the new ideas and
attacking the conservatism and/or negative achievement of the old. The
poet and journalist Lewis Spence (1874–1955) wrote that MacDiarmid had
created 'a veritable *kulturkampf* in Scottish literary circles, a tumult in which
his ideas have been greeted with the most savage condemnation mingled
with praise almost extravagant'.[17] Therefore, despite the many difficulties
faced by MacDiarmid and the writers who joined him when he advertised for
supporters for his *Scottish Chapbook* venture, there is an exhilarating optimism
fuelling these controversial and often condemnatory writings of the 1920s.

On the other hand, as discussed in earlier chapters, the 1930s was on the
whole a difficult decade for MacDiarmid. He spent the period from 1933 until
1942 on the small Shetland island of Whalsay, with reduced access to reading
material and, with no magazine under his editorship until he started the *Voice
of Scotland* in 1938, fewer opportunities for publication. He did, however,
write a considerable amount of new poetry during this time. On mainland
Scotland itself, concern over the economic condition of the country and the
threat posed by political developments on the continent of Europe increasingly took precedence over cultural renewal. However, perhaps the most
serious happening so far as the literary revival and its legacy were concerned
was the rift between MacDiarmid and Edwin Muir as a result of Muir's comments in his book *Scott and Scotland* (1936) that 'a Scottish writer who wishes
to achieve some approximation to completeness has no choice except to
absorb the English tradition'. His comments on the state of Scots-language
poetry were particularly offensive to MacDiarmid:

> In an organic literature poetry is always influencing prose, and prose poetry; and
> their interaction energizes them both. Scottish poetry exists in a vacuum; it
> neither acts on the rest of literature nor reacts to it; and consequently it has
> shrunk to the level of anonymous folk-song. Hugh MacDiarmid has recently
> tried to revive it by impregnating it with all the contemporary influences of
> Europe one after another, and thus galvanize it into life by a series of violent
> shocks. In carrying out this experiment he has written some remarkable poetry;
> but he has left Scottish verse very much where it was before. [. . .] Scots poetry
> can only be revived, that is to say, when Scotsmen begin to think *naturally* in
> Scots. The curse of Scottish literature is the lack of a whole language, which
> finally means the lack of a whole mind.[18]

Muir had always admired T. S. Eliot's criticism, and the influence of Eliot's
'Tradition and the Individual Talent' (1919) and his review of Gregory
Smith's *Scottish Literature: Tradition and Influence* – also published in 1919
and titled pejoratively 'Was there a Scottish Literature?' – is clear in Muir's

Scott and Scotland argument, as is Eliot's 'dissociation of sensibility' argument from his essay 'The Metaphysical Poets' (1921). As an Orcadian, Muir was not himself at home with Lowland Scots, and used it on only a very few occasions in his early poetry. In the 1930s he was still finding it difficult to achieve poetic maturity in English (and the influence of Eliot the poet is strong in his *Variations on a Time Theme* of 1934). His own artistic insecurity may therefore have played some part in his negativity towards poetry in Scots. MacDiarmid never forgave Muir for his comments and took every opportunity he could to attack him and belittle his work, despite Muir's response in a series of articles published in 1938 in the Glasgow *Bulletin* (in which both poets took part) that his wish had been principally to 'clarify a problem [. . .] that I had often discussed in the most friendly way with Mr Grieve'. He pointed out that 'Mr Grieve himself began by writing in English; he still does so both in verse and in articles proving that Scots is the only language for a true Scotsman.' And Muir ends by repeating that his comments were made in the hope of starting a discussion.[19]

The Legacy of MacDiarmid and the Interwar Revival

This *Scott and Scotland* dispute was not relevant in its own time since even by 1936 the project to recover a distinctive, outward-looking, indigenous literature freed from both the provincial and parochial effects of its previous North British status had had considerable success. There was already a wide range of confident writing by male and female writers in poetry and in prose fiction using both Scots and Scottish English in a variety of fresh, creative ways. And although the Gaelic revival had been slower to emerge, Somhairle MacGill-eain (Sorley MacLean, 1911–96) was beginning to transform traditional Gaelic verse in the early 1930s and his *Dàin do Eimhir* (*Poems to Eimhir*), which developed out of his responses to the Spanish Civil War, would be published in 1943 to stand alongside MacDiarmid's early 1920s modernist transformation of poetry in Scots. As Muir commented, MacDiarmid himself was writing mostly in English in the mid-1930s, with no sign of a return to provincial status in that writing. In the context of the writing of the time, the question of whether Scots or English should be the language of literature in Scotland had already been answered by the actuality and variety of contemporary creative practice. It is therefore unfortunate that this personalised dispute between two major poets of the early part of the century should have been kept alive in Scottish criticism for so long, perhaps aided by its seeming illustration of Gregory Smith's Caledonian antisyzygy 'theory' of Scottish literature, with an emphasis on the two extremes within Scottish writing – a polarity into which Muir and MacDiarmid's dispute fitted only too easily. Such a static view of language ignores the distinction between literary language and everyday speech (Saussure's idea of *langue* and *parole*, which is very relevant to any discussion of MacDiarmid's literary 'Synthetic Scots'), and ignores also the evolutionary nature of language through time. Tom Leonard's development of a demotic urban poetic diction might seem to have few connections with MacDiarmid's Synthetic Scots (although both are in their different ways 'langue' as opposed to 'parole'), but it was MacDiarmid's linguistic experimentation that led the way to a future flexibility in poetic language that made Leonard's medium possible. MacDiarmid's legacy, and that of the writers who wrote alongside him, has been to open up the road to a new self-determining creative writing situation where writers feel free to use whatever language they have inherited or choose to adopt. Despite his polemical insistence on Scots in his quarrel with Muir, MacDiarmid's language legacy has been to show that good writing from Scotland can be carried through in any language that works for the writer; and that writing out of your own place and experience is no barrier to engaging also with intellectual stimuli and aesthetic influences that come from outside. For Alasdair Gray, Muir's *Scott and Scotland* 'predicament' was 'a huge failure of nerve, a cowardice in the face of our best examples'. And for Gray, 'MacDiarmid was one such example':

> He spoke of all the things he believed, using all the language he could master; local and historical, scientific-technical, political-polemical [. . .] MacDiarmid had to make poetry from the dialectics of his self-contradictory intelligence. But that intelligence, that poetry, is still big enough for us to have worthwhile adventures inside.[20]

Scottish creative writing, over the decades from MacDiarmid to the present time, and through a series of outstanding writers in poetry, prose and drama unimaginable in the pre-World War One period, has had just such 'adventures'.

Arguably, however, it is not yet certain that the legacy demonstrated by the transformation in Scotland's creative writing situation has been replicated in the country's educational system, where, at the time of writing (2010), there is still no obligation in the school context to introduce Scottish texts, contemporary or historical, into the teaching syllabus, and include them in the examining process. Nor is it necessary for student teachers of the language and literature subject called 'English' to have professional qualifications in Scottish literature. It is difficult to imagine educational ministries in the USA or Canada, or in European countries – including England, Ireland and Wales as well as continental European nations such as France, Germany, and Italy – refusing to make sure that their national literature is officially represented in the school curriculum and that their teachers have professional knowledge of it. Such a situation may also have some relevance in relation to the university system. Glasgow University is still the only university in Scotland which has a specific department of Scottish Literature, with an established Chair in the subject; and David Robb's recent biography of the poet and academic Alexander Scott (1920–89), who was head of department until 1983 before the Chair was established in 1995, demonstrates just what a struggle it was to give the subject an accepted place in the university curriculum. In the Scottish universities apart from Glasgow, Scottish literature is mostly taught in a department of English Literature, or English Studies, and the decision to offer Scottish topics, as well as what Scottish topics to offer, would appear to some extent to depend upon the availability and research interests of staff at any given time. Scottish literature generally has not yet developed an identity as a discrete academic discipline as has, for example, Irish literature (from both north and south of the island), which has successfully marketed itself internationally as an independent study. Yet, as Professor Ian Duncan of the University of California at Berkeley comments: 'It seems bizarre to me that the study of Scottish literature should require a defence in Scotland in this day and age, although I know from experience that the case needs to be made elsewhere.'[21] Such a defence is particularly needed in the area of Scottish modernist studies, and it is unfortunate that there would not yet appear to be, in the Scottish universities or in universities outwith Scotland, a specific or comparative study of a Scottish modernism within British and anglophone modernisms, just as it is seldom that one finds the name of MacDiarmid listed in the indexes of books about modernism; and the names of other Scottish modernist writers almost never at all. Yet without incorporation into such wider studies, MacDiarmid, Muir and other innovative writers of the twentieth-century Scottish interwar revival will remain to a significant extent the prisoners of their national context, with the full extent of their literary achievement and their legacy underestimated. National identity is certainly a significant element in MacDiarmid's inspiration and his poetry, but philosophical and intellectual themes and formal aesthetics, influenced by his awareness of the cosmopolitan culture of his own time, are more important in his poetry than a nationalist agenda. And to understand this, we must read him in the context of his contemporaneous literary peers.

MacDiarmid's Reputation

In his own time, MacDiarmid became something of a legend within Scotland, with James Caird commenting in a valedictory tribute in 1978: 'For my generation, MacDiarmid *was* Scottish Literature.'[22] Yet it was not until 1962 that a *Collected Poems* was published, and this came not from a Scottish or British publisher, but from Macmillan of New York. The year 1962 also saw the publication of *Hugh MacDiarmid: A Festschrift*, edited by K. D. Duval and Sydney Goodsir Smith, the first collection of scholarly essays on his life and work, and this was followed in 1964 by Kenneth Buthlay's *Hugh MacDiarmid*, the first book-length study of his poetry, and Duncan Glen's *Hugh MacDiarmid and the Scottish Renaissance*: a biographical and contextual study of the man and the movement he inspired. This steady growth of scholarly material, mostly from Scottish sources, continued in the later 1960s and during the 1970s, culminating in 1978 in the publication of his *Complete Poems* in two volumes, edited by W. R. Aitken and MacDiarmid's son Michael Grieve. The period from 1978 to the mid-1990s was important for the more wide-ranging nature of critical writing on MacDiarmid's poetry, building on the reprinting of primary sources and critical work of the previous years. As the first *Collected Poems* had come from America, so a number of significant studies in this new period came from American scholars such as Nancy Gish, M. L. Rosenthal, Harvey Oxenhorn and John Baglow. Buthlay's critical study had set MacDiarmid's poetry firmly in the modernist period and this perspective, with its implicit emphasis on an international context, is characteristic of the new critical work from the post-1978 period. Edwin Morgan's review article on the *Complete Poems*, published in *Comparative Criticism* in 1981, expresses well this collective awareness that what we are dealing with here is a significant *modern* poet. For Morgan, the *Complete Poems* enables readers 'to begin to understand, for the first time now that all the poems are gathered together, the unity of his work [. . .] the overall effect seems to me to be clear, that he is one of the great modern poets'.[23]

So what has happened in the new millennium when Modern Language Association (MLA) bibliographical listings for the years 2000–9 for MacDiarmid show a total of thirty-four results against 746 for Eliot, 473 for Pound and 249 for Yeats, and when a check in the indexes of books on modernist writing seldom elicits MacDiarmid's name; when, as Patrick Crotty has commented, there seems little prospect of summer schools being run for the study of MacDiarmid, as they are for Yeats in Ireland, and when Michael Schmidt of the Carcanet 2000 reprint project finds that MacDiarmid's reputation 'is on the skids among poets and some critics in Scotland', and that he is less read now in Scotland than he was?[24] It could be argued that the problem of MacDiarmid's reputation, in Scotland at least, has its roots in the continuing refusal of the Scottish educational institutions to accept that Scotland has a literature that should be given formal recognition and equal status with English. And given this absence of contemporary teaching and research in the home market, it is perhaps not surprising that awareness of his work is not travelling quickly or far. Yet in the immediate decades before his death he did have a reputation abroad, travelling and reading his poetry in Soviet Bloc countries, and in China, as well as in Canada and the USA. Many overseas poets, visiting Britain, made their way to his cottage at Brownsbank, including the Russian Yevgeny Yevtushenko in 1962, and a considerable number of his poems were translated into European languages including Russian, German, Norwegian, Hungarian, Italian, Spanish and French, as well as Hebrew, Persian and Chinese. Some were even translated into Esperanto.[25]

There are, however, encouraging signs amid what appears to be the current decline. It is noticeable that in the admittedly poor MLA listings, much of the MacDiarmid material is coming from overseas scholars, especially from the USA, and that his poetry is being discussed by these scholars alongside new research into modernism itself, thus bringing the Scottish dimension into interaction with transnational experience. There are also a few books and articles listed by young Scottish and English scholars, taking up under-explored areas of his work. In addition, Scottish and American scholars, working together, have succeeded in establishing Scottish subject panels in the annual MLA conferences, with Scottish book displays organised by the Association for Scottish Literary Studies proving particularly successful. MacDiarmid's magazines are discussed in a chapter on Scottish periodicals in the *Oxford Critical and Cultural History of Modernist Magazines, Volume 1: Britain and Ireland, 1880–1955* (2009) and a chapter on Scottish Modernism is included in the *Handbook of Modernisms* (2010), also from Oxford University Press.[26] Information from conference contacts suggests that there is an increasing awareness among anglophone and continental European scholars that MacDiarmid is a writer who should be on their modernist programmes, although they feel they lack the knowledge to deal with his writing. There seems to be growing, therefore, even if slowly, a realisation that, contrary to T. S. Eliot's 1919 viewpoint, there was, and still is, both a Scottish literature, and especially in the case of MacDiarmid and his interwar companions, a Scottish modernism that deserves to be brought back into the transnational family of modernisms. One aim of this new book on MacDiarmid is to bring his poetry into just such a family reunion.

Endnotes

Introduction – Lyall and Palmer McCulloch

1. William Jeffrey, 'Is this a Scottish Poetry Renaissance?', *Bulletin* 17 January 1921, p. 6.
2. Lewis Spence, 'The Scottish Literary Renaissance', *Nineteenth Century*, July 1926, in Margery Palmer McCulloch (ed.), *Modernism and Nationalism: Literature and Society in Scotland, 1918–1939: Source Documents for the Scottish Renaissance* (Glasgow: Association for Scottish Literary Studies, 2004), p. 71.
3. Edwin Morgan, *Hugh MacDiarmid* (Harlow: Longman, 1976), p. 32.

Chapter 1 – Watson

1. 'Modern Fiction', in Virginia Woolf, *The Common Reader* (Harmondsworth: Pelican, [1925] 1938), p. 149. See also Roderick Watson, 'Introduction', in Roderick Watson and Alan Riach (eds), *Hugh MacDiarmid: Annals of the Five Senses and other Stories, Sketches and Plays* (Manchester: Carcanet, 1999).
2. C. M. Grieve, 'In Acknowledgement', Watson and Riach (eds), *Annals of the Five Senses*, p. 4.
3. G. Gregory Smith, *Scottish Literature: Character and Influence* (London: Macmillan, 1919), Chapter 1, 'Two Moods'.
4. See, for example, Mark Antliff, *Inventing Bergson* (Princeton: Princeton University Press, 1993). T. E. Hulme translated Bergson into English and there was much discussion of his ideas in *The New Age*.
5. Lev Shestov, *All Things Are Possible*, trans. S. S. Koteliansky (London: Martin Secker, [1905] 1920), pp. 90, 110, with a foreword by D. H. Lawrence, who shared some of his vitalist views. Also Shestov, *In Job's Balances*, trans. C. Coventry and C. A. Macartney (London: J. M. Dent, [1929] 1932), pp. 225–6.
6. J. M. Synge, 'Preface', *Poems and Translations*, in T. R. Henn (ed.), *The Plays and Poems of J. M. Synge* (London: Methuen, 1963), p. 288.
7. Iain Crichton Smith, 'The Golden Lyric', in Duncan Glen (ed.), *Hugh*

MacDiarmid: A Critical Survey (Edinburgh: Scottish Academic Press, 1972), p. 140.

8. Kenneth Buthlay, *Hugh MacDiarmid* (Edinburgh: Oliver and Boyd, 1964), p. 27.
9. David Daiches, 'Hugh MacDiarmid's Early Poetry', in Glen (ed.), *Hugh MacDiarmid: A Critical Survey*, p. 65.
10. See Monroe K. Spears, *Dionysus and the City: Modernism in Twentieth-Century Poetry* (New York: Oxford University Press, 1970).
11. Buthlay, *Hugh MacDiarmid*, pp. 46, 31–2.
12. Ezra Pound, 'A Few Don'ts by an Imagiste', first published in *Poetry*, March 1913.
13. Rule 3, from F. S. Flint's 'Three Rules', *Poetry* (March 1913); and Rule 1 from 'Six Rules' in the preface to the anthology *Some Imagist Poets* compiled by HD and Richard Aldington in 1915.
14. See Victor Shklovsky, 'Art as Technique' (1917), in L. T. Lemon and M. J. Reis (ed. and trans.), *Russian Formalist Criticism: Four Essays* (Lincoln: University of Nebraska Press, 1965).
15. 'A Theory of Scots Letters', *SP*, p. 20.
16. MacDiarmid's versions owe a lot to the translations by Babette Deutsch and Avrahm Yarmolinsky in their 1923 anthology *Modern Russian Poetry*.
17. Letter to Paul Démeny, 15 May 1871, in *Arthur Rimbaud, Selected Poems and Letters*, trans. John Sturrock and Jeremy Harding (Harmondsworth: Penguin, 2004), pp. 237–40.
18. This reading of desire is derived from Lacan. A readable account of desire from Lacan's post-Freudian position is provided in the chapter on 'Psychoanalysis' in Terry Eagleton's *Literary Theory: An Introduction*, 2nd edn (Oxford: Blackwell, 1996), pp. 142–8.
19. T. S. Eliot, 'Burnt Norton', from *Four Quartets*, in *Collected Poems (1909–1962)* (London: Faber and Faber, 1963), p. 191.
20. A useful introduction to the socio-political implications of Bakhtinian theory can be found in Tony Crowley, 'Bakhtin and the History of the Language', in Ken Hirschkop and David Shepherd (eds), *Bakhtin and Cultural Theory* (Manchester: Manchester University Press, 1989), pp. 68–90.
21. See Chapter 13 in Samuel Taylor Coleridge's *Biographia Literaria* (1817).
22. C. M. Grieve, 'A Four Year's Harvest', Watson and Riach (eds), *Annals of the Five Senses*, p. 42.

Chapter 2 – Grieve

1. Hugh MacDiarmid, *Whaur Extremes Meet*, LP (Alton: Tuatha Music, 1978).
2. Minutes of the London Robert Burns Club (7 June 1920); in Margery Palmer McCulloch (ed.), *Modernism and Nationalism: Literature and Society in Scotland, 1918–1939: Source Documents for the Scottish Renaissance* (Glasgow: Association for Scottish Literary Studies, 2004), p. 11.

3. C. M. Grieve, *Aberdeen Free Press* (15 December 1921 and 30 January 1922); in Margery Palmer McCulloch (ed.), *Modernism and Nationalism*, pp. 21–2.

4. C. M. Grieve, 'A Theory of Scots Letters', *The Scottish Chapbook* 1.7 (February 1923); in *SP*, p. 20. He first draws the comparison in a footnote to 'Following Rebecca West in Edinburgh', *The Scottish Chapbook* 1.3 (October 1922), where 'The Watergaw' also appears.

5. C. M. Grieve, 'Causerie', *The Scottish Chapbook* 1.3 (October 1922); in *SP*, p. 11.

6. C. M. Grieve, 'A Theory of Scots Letters', *The Scottish Chapbook* 1.8 (March 1923); in *SP*, pp. 22–3.

7. Richard Sheppard, 'The Crisis of Language', in Malcolm Bradbury and James McFarlane (eds), *Modernism: A Guide to European Literature 1890–1930* (Harmondsworth: Penguin, 1991), p. 324.

8. C. M. Grieve, 'Causerie', *The Scottish Chapbook* 1.3 (October 1922); in *SP*, p. 10.

9. David Murison, 'The Language Problem in Hugh MacDiarmid's Work', in P. H. Scott and A. C. Davis (eds), *The Age of MacDiarmid: Essays on Hugh MacDiarmid and his Influence on Contemporary Scotland* (Edinburgh: Mainstream, 1980), p. 88. 'Wan-shoggin'' is glossed as 'pale swinging' in *The Hugh MacDiarmid Anthology* ed. Michael Grieve and Alexander Scott (London: Routledge, 1972), p. 12.

10. James Barke (ed.), *Complete Poems and Songs of Robert Burns* (Glasgow: HarperCollins, 1995), p. 83.

11. Sir James Wilson, *Lowland Scotch as Spoken in the Strathearn District of Perthshire* (London: Oxford University Press, 1915).

12. Edwin Morgan, 'MacDiarmid at Seventy-Five', in *Essays* (Cheadle: Carcanet, 1974), pp. 216–7.

13. John Jamieson, *An Etymological Dictionary of the Scottish Language*, ed. John Longmuir and David Donaldson, 4 vols (Paisley: Alexander Gardner, 1879–82).

14. Ruth McQuillan, 'MacDiarmid's Other Dictionary', *Lines Review* 66 (September 1978), p. 13.

15. C. M. Grieve, '*Mannigfaltig*: Beyond Meaning', *The New Age* (26 June 1924 and 3 July 1924); in *RT1*, pp. 163, 165. C. M. Grieve, 'Art and the Unknown', *The New Age* (20 May 1926); in *SP*, p. 39.

16. C. M. Grieve, 'A Theory of Scots Letters', *Scottish Chapbook* 1.8 (March 1923), p. 210.

17. See, for example, PennSound <www.writing.upenn.edu/pennsound> or Poetry Archive <www.poetryarchive.org>

18. Hugh MacDiarmid, *A Drunk Man Looks at the Thistle*, ed. Kenneth Buthlay (Edinburgh: Scottish Academic Press, 1987), p. 196.

19. Kenneth Buthlay, 'Shibboleths of the Scots', *Akros* 12.34–5 (August 1977), p. 41.

20. C. M. Grieve, *The Scottish Educational Journal* (24 July 1925); in CSS, p. 46.
21. C. M. Grieve, *The Scottish Educational Journal* (18 September 1925); in CSS, p. 122.
22. David Daiches, 'Hugh MacDiarmid in his Context', *Library Review* 20.1 (Spring 1965), pp. 6–7.
23. Ibid., p. 6
24. Ruaraidh Erskine of Mar, '"Dominus Insularum"', *The London Mercury* 32.188 (June 1935), p. 176.
25. E. R. Dodds (ed.), *Journal and Letters of Stephen MacKenna* (London: Constable, 1936), p. 230.
26. James Joyce, *Ulysses* (London: Bodley Head, [1922] 1937), p. 175.
27. John Masters, *Bhowani Junction* (New York: Viking Press, 1954), p. 325.
28. Susan R. Wilson (ed.), *The Correspondence between Hugh MacDiarmid and Sorley MacLean: An Annotated Edition* (Edinburgh: Edinburgh University Press, 2010), p. 287.
29. Ibid., p. 130.
30. James Murray, quoted in K. M. Elisabeth Murray, *Caught in the Web of Words: James A. H. Murray and the* Oxford English Dictionary (Oxford: Oxford University Press, 1979), p. 83.
31. Ruth McQuillan, 'Hugh MacDiarmid's Shetland Poetry', in Laurence Graham and Brian Smith (eds), *MacDiarmid in Shetland* (Lerwick: Shetland Library, 1992), p. 12.
32. Kenneth Buthlay, 'Adventuring in Dictionaries', in Nancy K. Gish (ed.), *Hugh MacDiarmid: Man and Poet* (Edinburgh: Edinburgh University Press, 1992), p. 155.
33. David Purves, 'MacDiarmid's Use of Scots: Synthetic or Natural', *Scottish Language* 16 (1997), p. 85.
34. J. G. Outterstone Buglass, 'Arne Garborg, Mr Joyce, and Mr MacDiarmid', *The Northern Review* (September 1924); in RT1, p. 238. Cf. Mallarmé, 'for the first time in the literary history of any nation, along with the general and traditional great organ of orthodox verse which finds its ecstasy on an ever-ready keyboard, any poet with an individual technique and ear can build his own instrument, so long as his fluting, bowing, or drumming are accomplished – play that instrument and dedicate it, along with others, to Language': 'Stéphane Mallarmé from Crisis in Poetry 1886–95', in Vassiliki Kolocotroni, et al. (eds), *Modernism: An Anthology of Sources and Documents* (Edinburgh: Edinburgh University Press, 1998), p. 124.

Chapter 3 – Riach

1. Samples of Grieve/MacDiarmid's writing from all of the periodicals discussed in this chapter are to be found in SP, CSS and RT1, RT2, RT3. For further

contemporary essays and documents by others and samples of writing from the journals and books that engaged in the debates of this period, see Margery Palmer McCulloch (ed.), *Modernism and Nationalism: Literature and Society in Scotland, 1918–1939: Source Documents for the Scottish Renaissance* (Glasgow: Association for Scottish Literary Studies, 2004).

2. For a fully detailed account of Grieve's involvement with periodical publications see Glen Murray, 'MacDiarmid's Media 1911–1936', in *RT1*, pp. x–xix and 'MacDiarmid's Media 1937–1978', in *RT3*, pp. xiv–xxxiv. On *The Scottish Chapbook*, see Murray, *RT1*, p. xiii.

3. C. M. Grieve (ed.), *Living Scottish Poets* (London: Benn, 1931).

4. Ibid., p. 14.

5. C. M. Grieve, 'A Stone among the Pigeons', *The Student* 30.2 (25 October 1933).

6. The present author was informed of this in conversation with W. R. Aitken, and has adapted these paragraphs about *The Voice of Scotland* and MacDiarmid's friendship with Aitken from his 'Introduction' to the index to *The Voice of Scotland* in the Scottish Poetry Index to Periodicals at the Scottish Poetry Library, Edinburgh.

7. Editorial, *The Voice of Scotland: A Quarterly Magazine of Scottish Arts and Affairs*, 1.1 (June–August 1938); quoted in Murray, 'MacDiarmid's Media 1937–1978', *RT3*, p. xvi. For information on *The Voice of Scotland*, see also Bold's *MacDiarmid*, pp. 372–7.

8. Murray, 'MacDiarmid's Media 1937–1978', *RT3*, p. xvi.

9. Ibid., p. xvii.

10. Hugh MacDiarmid (ed.), *William Soutar, Collected Poems* (London: Andrew Dakars, 1948), p. 9.

11. See introduction by Carl MacDougall and Douglas Gifford, *Into a Room: Selected Poems of William Soutar* (Glendaruel: Argyll Publishing, 2000), p. 7.

12. '[Unsigned] Editorial: The Flytin' o' the Makars', *The Voice of Scotland* (March 1948); in *RT3*, p. 118.

13. Quoted in Murray, *RT3*, p. xxix.

14. Arthur Leslie, 'Jerqueing Every Idioticon: Some Notes on MacDiarmid's Joyce Poem', *The Voice of Scotland* 6.2 (July 1955); extracts reprinted in 'In Memoriam James Joyce', *SP*, pp. 231, 232.

15. '[Unsigned] Book Reviews', *The Voice of Scotland* (1958–9); in *RT3*, pp. 386–7.

16. Robert Henryson, *Henryson Selected by Hugh MacDiarmid*. Poet to Poet (Harmondsworth: Penguin, 1973).

17. Seamus Heaney, 'Tradition and an Individual Talent: Hugh MacDiarmid', in *Preoccupations: Selected Prose 1968–1978* (London: Faber and Faber, 1980), pp. 195–8; 'A Torchlight Procession of One: On Hugh MacDiarmid', in *The Redress of Poetry* (London: Faber and Faber, 1995), pp. 103–23.

Chapter 4 – Palmer McCulloch and Matthews

1. Edwin Muir, *Scott and Scotland: The Predicament of the Scottish Writer* (Edinburgh: Polygon, [1936] 1982), pp. 21–2.

2. In his *More Collected Poems* (1970), MacDiarmid footnoted 'Cencrastus' as 'the snake symbolizing the fundamental pattern of the universe' (p. 49). See also his letter to Helen Cruickshank, 'C. M. Grieve–Helen Cruickshank Correspondence', Edinburgh University Library, pp. 79–85.

3. The quotation from Tennyson's 'Ulysses' is in *LP*, p. 182, with other references on pp. 153, 379. There are a number of references to Tennyson elsewhere in MacDiarmid's writings, for example in *RT1* and *RT2*, and in *SP*. 'Ulysses' is in *The Poetical Works of Alfred Lord Tennyson* (London: Macmillan, 1899), pp. 95–6.

4. Robert Louis Stevenson, *Dr Jekyll and Mr Hyde* (London: Heinemann, 1926), p. 58.

5. See *The Scottish Chapbook* 1.3 (October 1922), pp. 74–6: 'Five Sonnets Illustrative of Neo-Catholic Tendencies in Contemporary Scottish Literature', including 'The Litany of the Blessed Virgin' by C. M. Grieve, p. 75.

6. Compare Nietzsche's aphorism concerning 'Man and Woman': 'What is great in man is that he is a bridge and not a goal'; reproduced in A. R. Orage, *Nietzsche in Outline and Aphorism* (Edinburgh: T. N. Foulis, 1907), p. 55.

7. Charles Darwin, letter to Asa Briggs, in J. M. Golby (ed.), *Culture and Society in Britain 1850–1890* (Oxford: Oxford University Press, 1986), pp. 45–6.

8. Tennyson, 'In Memoriam A. H. H.', *Poetical Works*, pp. 261, 282.

9. For readers new to MacDiarmid, Kenneth Buthlay's annotated edition of *A Drunk Man* (1987) is not only arguably the best guide to the poem itself, but is also helpful for its information about MacDiarmid's reading material and early indications of his 'borrowing' methodology in his work.

10. A. R. Orage, *Consciousness: Animal, Human, and Superman* (London and Benares: The Theosophical Publishing Society, 1907), pp. 13, 50, 52, 22, 52.

11. Ibid., pp. 70, 71, 72.

12. In his commentary on *A Drunk Man*, Buthlay reintroduces for discussion and teaching purposes the section titles MacDiarmid supplied for *Collected Poems* (New York: Macmillan, 1962). 'Letter to Dostoevsky' and 'Farewell to Dostoevsky' are two of these titles, or 'handrails' as MacDiarmid referred to them.

13. Virginia Woolf, *Times Literary Supplement* (22 February 1917), p. 91; Edward Moore [Edwin Muir], *We Moderns: Enigmas and Guesses* (London: George Allen and Unwin, 1918), pp. 148, 147.

14. It is unfortunate that both Ann Edwards Boutelle in her *Thistle and Rose: A Study of Hugh MacDiarmid's Poetry* (Loanhead: Macdonald, 1981), p. 148 and

Alan Bold in his biography of MacDiarmid (London: John Murray, 1988), p. 214 and his introduction to his anthology of MacDiarmid's writings, *The Thistle Rises* (London: Hamish Hamilton, 1984), p. xv, interpret this passage positively in relation to the thistle's (and Scotland's) power to rise above all obstacles, with Bold specifically commenting: 'This is a defiant declaration of faith in the political and spiritual future of Scotland.' It is very clear from the imagery of this section that the opposite is the case.

15. T. S. Eliot, *Collected Poems* (London: Faber and Faber, 1963), p. 190.
16. George Davie supports this interpretation in *The Crisis of the Democratic Intellect* (Edinburgh: Polygon, 1986).
17. *Clann Albann* was to be an autobiographical epic poem, or anthology of poems, in five books, the first of which dealt with MacDiarmid's childhood in Langholm. *First Hymn to Lenin and Other Poems* (1931), *Second Hymn to Lenin* (1932) and *Scots Unbound and Other Poems* (1932) were all identified by MacDiarmid as belonging to the first book of *Clann Albann*; however, when he published a detailed description of the *Clann Albann* project in the *Scots Observer* in 1933, MacDiarmid did not seem to have expected to complete the work. See 'Clann Albann: An Explanation', *The Scots Observer*, 12 August 1933, p. 10.
18. Peggy Grieve, letter to Helen Cruickshank. Edinburgh University Library, Gen.886, f.6.
19. For a detailed account of this period, see Alan Bold, *MacDiarmid: Christopher Murray Grieve: A Critical Biography* (London: John Murray, 1988), pp. 229–46.
20. Catherine Kerrigan, *Whaur Extremes Meet: The Poetry of Hugh MacDiarmid 1920–1934* (Edinburgh: Mercat Press, 1983), p. 160.
21. Harvey Oxenhorn, *Elemental Things: The Poetry of Hugh MacDiarmid* (Edinburgh: Edinburgh University Press, 1984), p. 106.
22. Margery [Palmer] McCulloch, 'The Undeservedly Broukit Bairn: Hugh MacDiarmid's *To Circumjack Cencrastus*', *Studies in Scottish Literature* 17 (1982), p. 182.
23. J. S. Buist, letter to John Tonge, 3 July 1931, Edinburgh University Library, Gen.171/10 (folios not numbered).
24. See Bold, *MacDiarmid*, pp. 119, 255.
25. See Rev. Patrick S. Dineen (ed. and trans.), *The Poems of Egan O' Rahilly* (London: Irish Texts Society, 1900), pp. 18–21 for the original poem.
26. See also Aodh de Blácam, *Gaelic Literature Surveyed* (Dublin: Talbot, 1929), p. 313.
27. 'The Caledonian Antisyzygy and the Gaelic Idea', *The Modern Scot* 2.2 (July 1931), pp. 141–54, and 2.4 (January 1932), pp. 333–7.
28. 'The Caledonian Antisyzygy and the Gaelic Idea' (July 1931), p. 152.
29. Ibid.

Chapter 5 – Lyall

1. Letter to Neil M. Gunn, 19 May 1933, L, p. 250.
2. Ibid.
3. David Craig, 'MacDiarmid the Marxist Poet', in Duncan Glen (ed.), *Hugh MacDiarmid: A Critical Survey* (Edinburgh: Scottish Academic Press, 1972), p. 159.
4. 'Lenin – The Man and his Message and Methods', *Montrose Review*, 13 February 1920; cited in Scott Lyall, *Hugh MacDiarmid's Poetry and Politics of Place: Imagining a Scottish Republic* (Edinburgh: Edinburgh University Press, 2006), p. 83.
5. Stephen Spender, *The Thirties and After: Poetry, Politics, People (1933–75)* (London: Macmillan, 1978), pp. 13, 17.
6. Samuel Hynes, *The Auden Generation: Literature and Politics in England in the 1930s* (London: Faber and Faber, 1979), p. 13.
7. Robert Crawford and Mick Imlah (eds), *The Penguin Book of Scottish Verse* (London: Penguin, 2006).
8. Robin Skelton (ed.), *Poetry of the Thirties* (Harmondsworth: Penguin, 1987), p. 15.
9. C. Day Lewis, *A Hope for Poetry* (Oxford: Basil Blackwell, [1934] 1944), pp. 51, 53, 51.
10. Spender, *The Thirties and After*, p. 23.
11. Hugh MacDiarmid, 'Robert Fergusson: Direct Poetry and the Scottish Genius', in Sydney Goodsir Smith (ed.), *Robert Fergusson 1750–1774: Essays by Various Hands to Commemorate the Bicentenary of his Birth* (Edinburgh: Nelson, 1952), pp. 67, 71, 74.
12. Hynes, *The Auden Generation*, p. 10.
13. Hugh MacDiarmid (ed.), *The Golden Treasury of Scottish Poetry* (London: Macmillan, [1940] 1948), p. xxv.
14. G. S. Fraser, 'Hugh MacDiarmid: The Later Poetry', in Glen (ed.), *Hugh MacDiarmid: A Critical Survey*, pp. 214 (emphasis in original), p. 227.
15. Kenneth Buthlay, *Hugh MacDiarmid* (Edinburgh: Scottish Academic Press, [1964] 1982), p. 96.
16. George Orwell, cited in John R. Harrison, *The Reactionaries* (London: Victor Gollancz, 1966), p. 55.
17. Valentina Bold (ed.), *Smeddum: A Lewis Grassic Gibbon Anthology* (Edinburgh: Canongate, 2001), p. 739.
18. 'Plea for a Scottish Fascism', *The Scottish Nation* (June 1923); in *RT1*, pp. 82–7. 'Programme for a Scottish Fascism', *The Scottish Nation* (June 1923); in *SP*, pp. 34–8. For MacDiarmid and Nazism, see 'The Caledonian Antisyzygy and the Gaelic Idea', in Duncan Glen (ed.), *Selected Essays of Hugh MacDiarmid* (London: Jonathan Cape, 1969).

19. Jimmy Ross, 'Hugh MacDiarmid', in Chris Bambery (ed.), *Scotland, Class and Nation* (London: Bookmarks, 1999), p. 186.
20. 'Arthur Leslie', 'The Politics and Poetry of Hugh MacDiarmid', *The National Weekly* (1952); in *SP*, pp. 213–14.
21. Scott Lyall, '"The Man is a Menace": MacDiarmid and Military Intelligence', *Scottish Studies Review* 8.1 (2007), pp. 37–52.
22. 'Spain', first published in 1937, was republished with changes in Auden's *Another Time* (1940); see Humphrey Carpenter, *W. H. Auden: A Biography* (London: George Allen and Unwin, 1981), p. 219.
23. Stephen Spender, in Richard Crossman (ed.), *The God that Failed: Six Studies in Communism* (London: The Right Book Club, 1949), p. 248. Spender is referring to André Malraux's *Man's Hope*, Ernest Hemingway's *For Whom the Bell Tolls*, Arthur Koestler's *Spanish Testament* and George Orwell's *Homage to Catalonia*.
24. George Orwell, 'Political Reflections on the Crisis', *The Adelphi*, December 1938, p. 110; cited in Bernard Crick, *George Orwell: A Life* (London: Secker and Warburg, 1980), p. 435.
25. Unsigned, 'The English Literary Left', *The Voice of Scotland* (June/August 1939); in *RT3*, p. 34; *LP*, p. 171.
26. Iain Crichton Smith, 'The Golden Lyric: An Essay on the Poetry of Hugh MacDiarmid', in Glen (ed.), *Hugh MacDiarmid: A Critical Survey*, p. 133.
27. Sorley MacLean, 'MacDiarmid 1933–1944', in P. H. Scott and A. C. Davis (eds), *The Age of MacDiarmid: Essays on Hugh MacDiarmid and his Influence on Contemporary Scotland* (Edinburgh: Mainstream, 1980), p. 18.
28. Neal Ascherson, 'MacDiarmid and Politics', in Scott and Davis (eds), *The Age of MacDiarmid*, p. 228.
29. Skelton, *Poetry of the Thirties*, p. 24.
30. Roderick Watson, *MacDiarmid* (Milton Keynes: Open University Press, 1985), p. 70.
31. Crichton Smith, in Glen (ed.), *Hugh MacDiarmid: A Critical Survey*, p. 131.
32. Catherine Kerrigan, *Whaur Extremes Meet: The Poetry of Hugh MacDiarmid 1920–1934* (Edinburgh: The Mercat Press, 1983), p. 156.
33. Ascherson, in Scott and Davis (eds), *The Age of MacDiarmid*, p. 229.
34. Burns Singer, 'Scarlet Eminence: A Study of the Poetry of Hugh MacDiarmid', in Glen (ed.), *Hugh MacDiarmid: A Critical Survey*, p. 50.
35. Alan Bold, *MacDiarmid: Christopher Murray Grieve: A Critical Biography* (London: John Murray, 1988), p. 347.
36. Fraser, 'Hugh MacDiarmid: The Later Poetry', in Glen (ed.), *Hugh MacDiarmid: A Critical Survey*, pp. 216, 221.
37. Letter to Iain Crichton Smith, 2 July 1967, *L*, p. 870.
38. Letter to Christopher Grieve [CMG's grandson, 1975], *NSL*, pp. 495–6.
39. Yevgeny Zamyatin, *We*, trans. Clarence Brown (Harmondsworth: Penguin, [1924] 1993), pp. 3, 207.

Chapter 6 – Gairn

1. Hugh MacDiarmid, 'The Future', in Lewis Grassic Gibbon and Hugh MacDiarmid, *Scottish Scene, or The Intelligent Man's Guide to Albyn* (London: Jarrolds, 1934), p. 336.
2. Hugh MacDiarmid, 'Poetry and Science', in Duncan Glen (ed.), *Selected Essays of Hugh MacDiarmid* (London: Cape, 1969), p. 243.
3. Patrick Geddes, *A Study in City Development: Park, Gardens, and Culture-Institutes* (Dunfermline: The Riverside Press, 1904), p. 113.
4. Written in the 1930s as part of *The Muckle Toon*, 'Whuchulls' was first published in 1966. See Hugh MacDiarmid, *Whuchulls: A Poem*, ed. Duncan Glen (Preston, Lancashire: Akros, August 1966).
5. Jonathan Bate, *The Song of the Earth* (London: Picador, 2000), pp. 42, 266.
6. Charles Darwin, *On the Origin of Species* (London: Wordsworth Classics of World Literature, 1998), p. 368.
7. MacDiarmid, *Scottish Scene*, pp. 337, 336.
8. T. C. Smout, 'The Highlands and the Roots of Green Consciousness', *Proceedings of the British Academy* 76 (1991), pp. 240–1.
9. Volker M. Welter, *Biopolis: Patrick Geddes and the City of Life* (Cambridge, MA and London: MIT Press, 2002), p. 220.
10. Letter to Neil M. Gunn, 14 October 1925, *L*, p. 201.
11. Letter to Arthur Geddes, 20 January 1948, *L*, p. 857.
12. Patrick Geddes, 'The Scots Renascence', *The Evergreen: A Northern Seasonal* (Spring 1895), pp. 136–7.
13. Hugh MacDiarmid, *The Company I've Kept: Essays in Autobiography* (London: Hutchison, 1966), p. 83.
14. Ibid., pp. 80, 79, 80–1.
15. Hugh MacDiarmid, 'In Memoriam James Joyce', *SP*, p. 224.
16. Patrick Geddes, 'Nature Study and Geographical Education', *Scottish Geographical Magazine* XIX (1903), p. 526.
17. Hugh MacDiarmid, *The Islands of Scotland* (London: Batsford, 1939), p. 18.
18. Ibid., pp. 43–4.
19. See Hugh MacDiarmid, 'Memorial to William Stewart', *Forward* (16 October 1948); in *RT3*, p. 134.
20. Robert Crawford, *The Modern Poet: Poetry, Academia, and Knowledge since the 1750s* (Oxford: Oxford University Press, 2001), pp. 214, 199.
21. Patrick Geddes, *Cities in Evolution*, ed. Edinburgh Outlook Tower Association and London Association for Planning and Regional Construction (London: Knapp, Drewett and Sons, [1915] 1949), p. 16.
22. Iain Crichton Smith, *The Golden Lyric: An Essay on the Poetry of Hugh MacDiarmid* (Edinburgh: Akros, 1967), pp. 22, 14.
23. Edwin Morgan, *Essays* (Cheadle: Carcanet New Press 1974), p. 220.
24. Letter to Iain Crichton Smith, 2 July 1967, *L*, p. 870.

25. Letter to Edwin Morgan, 15 January 1975, *L*, p. 677.
26. Ibid.
27. See Scott Lyall, *Hugh MacDiarmid's Poetry and Politics of Place: Imagining a Scottish Republic* (Edinburgh: Edinburgh University Press, 2006), pp. 116–50.
28. Ann Edwards Boutelle, *Thistle and Rose: A Study of Hugh MacDiarmid's Poetry* (Loanhead: Macdonald, 1981), p. 185.
29. Iain Crichton Smith, 'MacDiarmid and Ideas, with Special Reference to "On a Raised Beach"', in P. H. Scott and A. C. Davis (eds), *The Age of MacDiarmid: Essays on Hugh MacDiarmid and his Influence on Contemporary Scotland* (Edinburgh: Mainstream, 1980), p. 157.
30. Iain Crichton Smith, 'Introduction', *Duncan Ban Macintyre's Ben Dorain*, trans. Iain Crichton Smith (Newcastle: Northern House, 1988), pp. 4–7.
31. David Daiches, 'MacDiarmid and the Scottish Literary Tradition', in Scott and Davis (eds), *The Age of MacDiarmid*, p. 67.
32. Tim Ingold, *The Perception of the Environment: Essays in Livelihood, Dwelling and Skill* (London: Routledge, 2000), p. 89.
33. Ibid., p. 90.
34. Ibid., pp. 168–9 (italics in original).
35. W. N. Herbert, *To Circumjack MacDiarmid: The Poetry and Prose of Hugh MacDiarmid* (Oxford: Clarendon, 1992), p. 196.
36. Gaston Bachelard, *The Poetics of Space*, trans. Maria Jolas (Boston: Beacon Press, 1994), p. 32.
37. Jakob Jakobsen, *The Dialect and Place Names of Shetland* (T. and J. Mansen, 1897), p. 84. For a discussion of MacDiarmid's sources for Norn vocabulary, see Ruth McQuillan, 'MacDiarmid's Other Dictionary', *Lines Review* 66 (September 1978), pp. 5–14.
38. Herbert, *To Circumjack MacDiarmid*, p. 129.
39. MacDiarmid, *The Islands of Scotland*, p. xi.
40. 'Causerie', *The Scottish Chapbook* 1.3 (October 1922); 'Introducing "Hugh M'Diarmid"' in *SP*, p. 12.
41. Catherine Kerrigan, *Whaur Extremes Meet: The Poetry of Hugh MacDiarmid 1920–1934* (Edinburgh: Mercat Press, 1983), p. 217.
42. Theodor Adorno, cited in Bate, *The Song of the Earth*, p. 123.
43. Hugh MacDiarmid, 'Letter to a Young Poet' (1959), in Glen (ed.), *Selected Essays*, p. 186.
44. Martin Heidegger, cited in George Pattison, *The Later Heidegger* (London: Routledge, 2000), p. 100.
45. Greg Garrard, *Ecocriticism* (London: Routledge, 2004), p. 31.
46. C. M. Grieve, 'Towards a "Scottish Idea"', *The Pictish Review* (November 1927); in *RT2*, p. 40.
47. C. M. Grieve, 'The Caledonian Antisyzygy and the Gaelic Idea', *The Modern Scot* (Summer/Winter 1931); in Margery Palmer McCulloch (ed.), *Modernism and Nationalism: Literature and Society in Scotland, 1918–1939: Source*

Documents for the Scottish Renaissance (Glasgow: Association for Scottish Literary Studies, 2004), p. 283.

48. Letter to Neil M. Gunn, 10 December 1954, *L*, p. 271.
49. 'The MacDiarmids – A Conversation: Hugh MacDiarmid and Duncan Glen with Valda Grieve and Arthur Thompson, 25 October 1968'; in *RT3*, p. 566.
50. Lyall, *Hugh MacDiarmid's Poetry and Politics of Place*, p. 130.
51. Hugh MacDiarmid, 'Charles Doughty and the Need for Heroic Poetry' (1936); in *SP*, pp. 125–36.
52. Alan Bold, *MacDiarmid: Christopher Murray Grieve: A Critical Biography* (London: John Murray, 1988), p. 330. For fuller details of MacDiarmid's reliance on MacLean in his Gaelic translations, see Susan R. Wilson (ed.), *The Correspondence between Hugh MacDiarmid and Sorley MacLean: An Annotated Edition* (Edinburgh: Edinburgh University Press, 2010).
53. Alan Bold, *MacDiarmid: The Terrible Crystal* (London: Routledge and Kegan Paul, 1983), p. 132.
54. Sorley MacLean, letter to Christopher Murray Grieve (Hugh MacDiarmid), 13 June 1935, MSS 2954.13. Edinburgh University Library.
55. Sorley MacLean, 'On Realism in Gaelic Poetry', in William Gillies (ed.), *Ris a' Bhruthaich: Criticism and Prose Writings* (Stornoway: Acair, 1985), p. 34.
56. Frank Fraser Darling, *A Herd of Red Deer: A Study in Animal Behaviour* (London: Oxford University Press, 1937), p. 26.
57. Herbert, *To Circumjack MacDiarmid*, p. 179.
58. Sorley MacLean, 'Old Songs and New Poetry', in William Gillies (ed.), *Ris a' Bhruthaich: Criticism and Prose Writings*, p. 110.
59. Edwin Morgan, 'Roof of Fireflies', in W. N. Herbert and Matthew Hollis (eds), *Strong Words: Modern Poets on Modern Poetry* (Northumberland: Bloodaxe, 2000), p. 192; Bate, *The Song of the Earth*, p. 175.
60. Crichton Smith, *Duncan Ban Macintyre's Ben Dorain*, pp. 5–6.
61. MacDiarmid, 'Letter to a Young Poet', in Glen (ed.), *Selected Essays*, p. 186.

Chapter 7 – Whitworth

The author gratefully acknowledges the Leverhulme Trust for granting a research fellowship in support of his research project 'Science, Poetry and Specialisation, 1900–1942', from which the present chapter derives.

1. Ruth McQuillan, 'MacDiarmid's Other Dictionary', *Lines Review* 66 (September 1978), p. 5; Michael H. Whitworth, 'Hugh MacDiarmid and Chambers's Twentieth Century Dictionary', *Notes and Queries* 55 (2008), pp. 78–80.
2. 'C. M. G', 'The Assault on Humanism', *The Scottish Nation* (16 October 1923); in *RT1*, p. 111.
3. Hugh MacDiarmid, 'Art and the Unknown', *The New Age* (20 and 27 May 1926); in *SP*, p. 39.

4. Hugh MacDiarmid, 'Science and Culture', *New English Weekly* (27 April 1933); in *RT2*, p. 481.

5. Hugh MacDiarmid, 'Problems of Poetry Today', *New English Weekly* (21 September 1933); in *RT2*, pp. 484, 485.

6. Kenneth Buthlay, *Hugh MacDiarmid* (Edinburgh: Scottish Academic Press, 1982), p. 84.

7. See the review of Read's *English Prose Style*, *The Scottish Educational Journal* 11.43 (26 October 1928), pp. 1132–3, over the initials 'A. L.', which makes mention of *Reason and Romanticism*: MacDiarmid frequently contributed to the *TSEJ* as 'A. L.', i.e., Alistair Laidlaw. Another essay-review over the same initials, 'The Structure of the Novel', *The Scottish Educational Journal* 12.4 (25 January 1929), pp. 102–3, makes further mention of it.

8. Anon., *Times Literary Supplement* (1 June 1933), p. 372; Anon., *Times Literary Supplement* (2 May 1936), p. 378. For 'On a Raised Beach', see Whitworth, 'Three Prose Sources for Hugh MacDiarmid's "On a Raised Beach"', *Notes and Queries* 54 (2007), pp. 175–7.

9. David Balsillie, 'Contemporaneous Volcanic Activity in East Fife', *Geological Magazine* 64.11 (November 1927), pp. 481–94.

10. E. H. L. Schwarz, 'Cauldrons of Subsidence', *Geological Magazine* 64.10 (October 1927), pp. 449–57.

11. Balsillie, 'East Fife', p. 488.

12. Edwin Morgan, 'Poetry and Knowledge in MacDiarmid's Later Work', *Essays* (Manchester: Carcanet, 1974), p. 207 (note).

13. Balsillie, 'East Fife', pp. 487, 488.

14. Veronica Forrest-Thomson, 'Poetry as Knowledge: The Use of Science by Twentieth-Century Poets' (University of Cambridge, unpublished PhD thesis, 1971).

15. Ibid., pp. 64–5.

16. Ibid., p. 120.

17. Ibid., p. 82.

18. Ibid., p. 137.

19. Ibid., p. 145.

20. For the borrowings in 'Etika', see Michael H. Whitworth, 'Forms of Culture in Hugh MacDiarmid's "Etika Preobrazhennavo Erosa"', *International Journal of Scottish Literature* 5 (Autumn/Winter 2009), accessed online at <www.ijsl.stir.ac.uk>

21. The poem was first published in 1955; for the date of composition, see Ruth Pitter, letter to Hugh MacDiarmid, 20 August 1937, in John Manson (ed.), *Dear Grieve* (Glasgow: Kennedy and Boyd, 2011). I am grateful to John Manson and Margery Palmer McCulloch for drawing this information to my attention.

22. Patrick Manson, quoted in Philip H. Manson-Bahr and A. Alcock, *The Life and Work of Sir Patrick Manson* (London: Cassell, 1927), p. 108.

23. Ibid.
24. Ibid., pp. 109–10.

Chapter 8 – Sassi

1. See, amongst others, Susan Stanford Friedman, 'Periodizing Modernism: Postcolonial Modernities and the Space/Time Borders of Modernist Studies', in *Modernism/Modernity* 13.3 (2006), pp. 425–43 and Peter Childs, *Modernism and the Post-Colonial: Literature and Empire, 1885–1930* (London: Continuum, 2007).
2. Agnieszka Chmielewska, 'National Style in the Second Republic: Artists and the Image of the Newly Created State', in Jacek Purchla and Wolf Tegethoff (eds), *Nation, Style, Modernism* (Cracow: International Cultural Centre, 2006), p. 189; see also Éva Forgács, 'Enlightenment versus the "National Genius". Attempts at Constructing both Modernism and National Identity through Visual Expression in Hungary 1910–1990', in *Nation, Style, Modernism*, pp. 307–22.
3. Caren Kaplan, *Questions of Travel: Postmodern Discourses of Displacement. Post-Contemporary Interventions* (Durham, NC: Duke University Press, 1996), p. 30.
4. T. S. Eliot, 'In Memory of Henry James', *Egoist* 5.1 (January 1918), pp. 1–2.
5. Barbara Abou-El-Haj, 'Languages and Models for Cultural Exchange', in Anthony D. King (ed.), *Culture, Globalization, and the World-System: Contemporary Conditions for the Representation of Identity* (Basingstoke: MacMillan, 1991), p. 142.
6. C. M. Grieve, 'Scottish Nationalism versus Socialism', *The Scots Independent* (February 1929); in *RT2*, pp. 75, 77, 78.
7. Michael Grieve, 'Foreword', in Laurence Graham and Brian Smith (eds), *MacDiarmid in Shetland* (Lerwick: Shetland Library, 1992), p. 3.
8. Helen B. Cruickshank, *Octobiography* (Montrose: Standard Press, 1976), p. 75.
9. Alexander Scott, *The MacDiarmid Makars, 1923–1972* (Preston: Akros Publications, 1972), p. 3.
10. This has been recently highlighted by two seminal contributions to a rereading of the Scottish Renaissance: Margery Palmer McCulloch (ed.), *Modernism and Nationalism: Literature and Society in Scotland, 1918–1939: Source Documents for the Scottish Renaissance* (Glasgow: Association for Scottish Literary Studies, 2004) and Margery Palmer McCulloch, *Scottish Modernism and its Contexts 1918–1959: Literature, National Identity and Cultural Exchange* (Edinburgh: Edinburgh University Press, 2009).
11. John Manson, Dorian Grieve and Alan Riach (eds), *The Revolutionary Art of the Future: Rediscovered Poems by Hugh MacDiarmid* (Manchester: Carcanet in association with the Scottish Poetry Library, 2003), p. 63.

12. 'My Ambition', in Manson, Grieve and Riach (eds), *The Revolutionary Art of the Future*, p. 15.

13. Mary Louise Pratt, *Imperial Eyes: Travel Writing and Transculturation* (London: Routledge, 1992), p. 7.

14. Deborah E. Reed-Danahay, *Auto/Ethnography: Rewriting the Self and the Social* (Oxford: Berg, 1997), p. 2.

15. Barbara Tedlock, 'From Participant Observation to the Observation of Participation: The Emergence of Narrative Ethnography', in Norman K. Denzin and Yvonna S. Lincoln (eds), *The SAGE Handbook of Qualitative Research* (Thousand Oaks: Sage Publications, 2005), p. 467; originally published in *Journal of Anthropological Research* 47. 1 (1991), pp. 69–94.

16. Catherine Carswell and John Carswell, *Lying Awake: An Unfinished Autobiography and Other Posthumous Papers* (London: Secker and Warburg, 1950).

17. *A Scots Quair* was first published by Jarrolds (London, 1946). The *Quair's* three constitutive novels, *Sunset Song* (1932), *Cloud Howe* (1933) and *Grey Granite* (1934), had already been published separately by the same publishing house.

18. Christopher Whyte, *Modern Scottish Poetry* (Edinburgh: Edinburgh University Press, 2004), p. 94.

19. M. M. Bakhtin, *The Dialogic Imagination: Four Essays* (Austin: University of Texas Press, 1981), p. 67.

20. Louisa Gairn, *Ecology and Modern Scottish Literature* (Edinburgh: Edinburgh University Press, 2008), p. 99.

21. Edward Casey, 'Body, Self and Landscape: A Geo-philosophical Inquiry into the Place-World', in P. Adams (ed.), *Textures of Place: Exploring Humanist Geographies* (Minneapolis: University of Minnesota Press, 2001), p. 413.

22. The poem is included under the title 'Scotland' in *CP1*, p. 652.

23. Gairn, *Ecology and Modern Scottish Literature*, pp. 95–6.

24. For a survey of literary figurations of Scotland as the archetypal 'land of romance' see Andrew Hook, 'Scotland and Romanticism', in Andrew Hook (ed.), *The History of Scottish Literature, Vol. 2: 1660–1800* (Aberdeen: Aberdeen University Press, 1987), pp. 307–21.

25. Robert Crawford, 'MacDiarmid in Montrose', in Alex Davis and Lee M. Jenkins (eds), *Locations of Literary Modernism: Region and Nation in British and American Modernist Poetry* (Cambridge: Cambridge University Press, 2000), p. 33.

26. Scott Lyall, *Hugh MacDiarmid's Poetry and Politics of Place: Imagining a Scottish Republic* (Edinburgh: Edinburgh University Press, 2006), p. 135.

27. Hugh MacDiarmid, *The Islands of Scotland: Hebrides, Orkneys, and Shetlands* (London: B. T. Batsford, 1939), p. 6.

28. Ibid., p. 26.

29. Ibid., p. 136.
30. Edouard Glissant, *Traité du tout-monde* (Paris: Gallimard, 1997), p. 194.

Chapter 9 – Goldie

1. See, for example, Duncan Glen (ed.), *Hugh MacDiarmid: A Critical Survey* (Edinburgh: Scottish Academic Press, 1972), p. vii. Nancy K. Gish, *Hugh MacDiarmid: The Man and His Work* (London: Macmillan, 1984), p. 14. Alan Riach, *Hugh MacDiarmid's Epic Poetry* (Edinburgh: Edinburgh University Press, 1991), p. x.
2. See, among many others, Kenneth Buthlay, 'Adventuring in Dictionaries', in Nancy K. Gish (ed.), *Hugh MacDiarmid: Man and Poet* (Edinburgh: Edinburgh University Press, 1992) and Michael H. Whitworth, 'Forms of Culture in Hugh MacDiarmid's "Etika Preobrazhennavo Erosa"', *International Journal of Scottish Literature* 1.5 (2009) <http://www.ijsl.stir.ac.uk/issue5/whitworth.htm.>
3. 'Plea for a Scottish Fascism', *RT1*, pp. 82–7; 'Programme for a Scottish Fascism', *SP*, pp. 34–8. See also Alan Bold, *MacDiarmid: Christopher Murray Grieve: A Critical Biography* (London: Paladin, 1990), pp. 409–11.
4. Allan Campbell and Tim Niel (eds), *A Life in Pieces: Reflections on Alexander Trocchi* (Edinburgh: Rebel Inc., 1997), p. 151.
5. Letter to *The Scotsman*, 13 March 1964, *L*, p. 821.
6. 'Author's Note 1972', *LP*, p. xiii.
7. See, for example, his letter to the *Aberdeen Free Press*, 30 January 1922, *L*, pp. 754–6.
8. See Kenneth Buthlay, 'Hugh MacDiarmid's "Conversion" to Scots: Practice before Theory', in Horst W. Drescher and Hermann Volkel (eds), *Nationalism in Literature – Literarischer Nationalismus: Literature, Language and National Identity* (Frankfurt am Main: Peter Lang, 1989), p. 189.
9. See, for example, Catherine Kerrigan, *Whaur Extremes Meet: The Poetry of Hugh MacDiarmid 1920–1934* (Edinburgh: Mercat Press, 1983).
10. Roderick Watson and Alan Riach (eds), *Hugh MacDiarmid, Annals of the Five Senses and Other Stories, Sketches and Plays* (Manchester: Carcanet, 1999), p. 13.
11. David Daiches, 'Hugh MacDiarmid and the Scottish Literary Tradition', in P. H. Scott and A. C. Davis (eds), *The Age of MacDiarmid: Essays on Hugh MacDiarmid and his Influence on Contemporary Scotland* (Edinburgh: Mainstream, 1980), p. 60.
12. Christopher Whyte, *Modern Scottish Poetry* (Edinburgh: Edinburgh University Press, 2004), pp. 93–4.
13. MacDiarmid is quoting from John Willcock's biography of Urquhart, which itself embeds an unattributed quotation.

14. Peter McCarey, *Hugh MacDiarmid and the Russians* (Edinburgh: Scottish Academic Press, 1987), p. 171.
15. See MacDiarmid's letters to Routledge's Frederick Warburg, *L*, pp. 544–7.
16. See G. Gregory Smith, *Scottish Literature: Character and Influence* (London: Macmillan, 1919) and, for example, Edward J. Cowan and Douglas Gifford (eds), *The Polar Twins* (Edinburgh: John Donald, 1999).
17. *LP*, p. xi; Bold, *MacDiarmid*, p. 47. The Whitman quote can be found in Sculley Bradley et al. (eds), *Walt Whitman, Leaves of Grass. A Textual Variorum of the Printed Poems, Poems, 1855–1856*, 3 vols (New York: New York University Press, 1980), I: p. 82.
18. David Norbrook, 'What Happened to MacDiarmid', *London Review of Books* 8.18 (1986), p. 24.
19. It is perhaps wholly typical of MacDiarmid that he quotes MacCormick's attack on him at length in his *Burns Today and Tomorrow* (1959); see Alan Riach (ed.), *Hugh MacDiarmid, Albyn: Shorter Books and Monographs* (Manchester: Carcanet, 1996), p. 276.
20. Colin Kidd, *Union and Unionisms: Political Thought in Scotland, 1500–2000* (Cambridge: Cambridge University Press, 2008), pp. 2–5.
21. See Scott Lyall, *Hugh MacDiarmid's Poetry and Politics of Place: Imagining a Scottish Republic* (Edinburgh: Edinburgh University Press, 2006), pp. 163–4.
22. Hugh MacDiarmid, *The Company I've Kept: Essays in Autobiography* (London: Hutchinson, 1966), p. 56.
23. C. H. Sisson, 'MacDiarmid's Sticks', *London Review of Books* 6.6 (1984), p. 16.
24. Seamus Heaney, 'A Torchlight Procession of One', *Parnassus* 21.1/2 (1996), pp. 11–29.
25. Richard Aldington, *Portrait of a Genius, But . . . The Life of D. H. Lawrence 1885–1930* (London: William Heinemann, 1950).
26. Letter to George Bruce, 1 July 1964, *L*, p. 531.
27. Iain Crichton Smith, 'The Golden Lyric: The Poetry of Hugh MacDiarmid', in *Towards the Human: Selected Essays* (Edinburgh: MacDonald, 1986), p. 185.
28. Bold, *MacDiarmid*, p. 303.

Chapter 10 – Skoblow

1. Hugh MacDiarmid, *The Company I've Kept* (London: Hutchison, 1966; Berkeley: University of California Press, 1967), p. 174.
2. Hugh MacDiarmid, *At the Sign of the Thistle* (London: S. Nott, 1934), p. 110.
3. C. M. Grieve, 'On American Literature', *The New Age* (29 May 1924); in *RT1*, pp. 155–6.
4. Hugh MacDiarmid, interviewed by Nancy Gish, *Contemporary Literature* (1977); in *RT3*, p. 582.

5. Letter to Alan Bold, 4 September 1972, *NSL*, p. 476.
6. [Unsigned Editorial], 'The Neglect of Byron', *The Scottish Nation* (22 May 1923); in *RT1*, p. 75.
7. MacDiarmid's quotations from Whitman are from Whitman's *Democratic Vistas* and 'A Backward Glance Over Many Travel'd Roads'.
8. The Whitman quoted here is cobbled together from the 1855 preface to *Leaves of Grass*, 'Poem of Many in One' and 'Poem of the Singers, and of the Words of the Poem'.
9. Whitman quotation is from 'A Backward Glance Over Many Travel'd Roads'.
10. Ibid.
11. Whitman quotation is from the 1855 preface to *Leaves of Grass*.
12. From Robert Burns's 'Is There for Honest Poverty'.
13. MacDiarmid, *At the Sign of the Thistle*, pp. 15–16.
14. C. M. Grieve, 'Gertrude Stein', *The New Age* (18 February 1926); in *RT1*, p. 277.
15. Ibid.
16. Alan Riach and Michael Grieve (eds), *Hugh MacDiarmid, Selected Poetry* (Manchester: Carcanet, 1992), p. xxviii.
17. C. M. Grieve, 'Wallace Stevens, *Harmonium*', *The New Age* (7 August 1924); in *RT1*, pp. 180–1.
18. Recent seminar comment from Jessica Wohlschlaeger, student studying MacDiarmid's poetry as part of a senior (post-graduate and/or final under-graduate year) course on Global English, Southern Illinois University, Edwardsville (USA).
19. Ibid., Victoria Cernich.
20. Ibid., Travis Neel.

Chapter 11 – Palmer McCulloch

1. Margery Palmer McCulloch (ed.), *Modernism and Nationalism: Literature and Society in Scotland, 1918–1939: Source Documents for the Scottish Renaissance* (Glasgow: Association for Scottish Literary Studies, 2004), pp. 21, 23.
2. Derek Walcott, 'The Schooner *Flight*', in W. R. Owens (ed.), *Literature in the Modern World: The Poetry Anthology* (Milton Keynes: Open University Press, 1991), p. 216.
3. H. J. C. Grierson, *Edinburgh Essays on Scots Literature* (Edinburgh: Oliver and Boyd, 1933), p. vi.
4. Ibid., pp. v–vi, vii.
5. T. M. Devine, 'Educating the People', *The Scottish Nation 1700–2000* (Harmondsworth: Alan Lane /The Penguin Press, 1999), p. 400.
6. For further discussion of this influence, see Margery Palmer McCulloch, *Scottish Modernism and its Contexts 1918–1959: Literature, National Identity*

and Cultural Exchange (Edinburgh: Edinburgh University Press, 2009), pp. 29–52.

7. Edwin Muir, 'Scotland 1941', *Complete Poems of Edwin Muir* (Aberdeen: Association for Scottish Literary Studies, 1991), p. 100.

8. C. M. Grieve, Letter to *Aberdeen Free Press*, 30 January 1922; in McCulloch (ed.), *Modernism and Nationalism*, pp. 22–3.

9. William Wordsworth, 'London, 1802', *The Poetical Works of Wordsworth* (London: Oxford University Press, 1904), p. 244.

10. Robert Burns, 'On Fergusson', in James Kinsley (ed.), *Burns Poems and Songs* (Oxford: Oxford University Press, 1969), p. 258 (poem K 143); see *L*, p. 90.

11. MacDiarmid, *Albyn* (1927), in Alan Riach (ed.), *Albyn: Shorter Books and Monographs* (Manchester: Carcanet, 1996), p. 14.

12. C. M. Grieve, 'Scotsmen make a God of Robert Burns', *Radio Times* (17 January 1930), p. 137. Carswell responded in 'The "Giant Ploughman" Can Withstand his Critics', *Radio Times* (14 February 1930), p. 376.

13. See Margery Palmer McCulloch, 'Bad Sort but – Lovable': Catherine Carswell's *The Life of Robert Burns*, *The Bibliotheck* 22 (1997), p. 73.

14. C. M. Grieve, *Contemporary Scottish Studies* (London: Leonard Parsons, 1926), p. 317.

15. C. M. Grieve, 'The Scott Centenary', *The Free Man* 1.35 (1 October 1932), p. 5.

16. Neil M. Gunn, review of *Scott and Scotland*, *Scots Magazine* (26 October 1936), p. 73.

17. Lewis Spence, 'The Scottish Literary Renaissance', *Nineteenth Century* (July 1926); in *Modernism and Nationalism*, p. 71.

18. Edwin Muir, *Scott and Scotland* (Edinburgh: Polygon, [1936] 1982), pp. 4, 8–9.

19. Edwin Muir, *Bulletin* (27 January 1938), p. 18; reprinted in *Scottish Studies Review* 6.1 (2005), pp. 68, 70.

20. Alasdair Gray, 'A Modest Proposal for By-Passing a Predicament', *Chapman* 35–6 (1983), pp. 8–9.

21. Ian Duncan, 'On the Study of Scottish Literature', *Scotlit* 28 (Spring 2003), can be accessed at <http://www.arts.gla.ac.uk/Scotlit/ASLS>

22. James B. Caird, 'Hugh MacDiarmid', *Chapman* 22 (1978), p. 18.

23. Edwin Morgan, 'On Hugh MacDiarmid's *Complete Poems 1920–1976*', *Comparative Criticism* 3 (1981), p. 308.

24. MLA bibliographical listings accessed in early August 2010; Patrick Crotty, speaking on Yeats and MacDiarmid at the conference 'Scottish and International Modernism', University of Stirling, June 2009; Michael Schmidt, *40 Tea Chests: Hugh MacDiarmid and Shetland* (Lerwick: Shetland Amenity Trust, 2010), p. 12.

25. For information on translations of MacDiarmid's poems, see National Library of Scotland's Bibliography of Scottish Literature in Translation at <http://boslit.nls.uk>

26. Cairns Craig, 'Modernism and National Identity in Scottish Magazines', in Peter Brooker and Andrew Thacker (eds), *The Oxford Critical and Cultural History of Modernist Magazines, Volume 1: Britain and Ireland 1880–1955* (Oxford: Oxford University Press, 2009), pp. 759–84; Margery Palmer McCulloch, 'Scottish Modernism', in Peter Brooker, Andrzej Gasiorek, Deborah Longworth and Andrew Thacker (eds), *The Oxford Handbook of Modernisms* (Oxford: Oxford University Press, 2010), pp. 765–81. See also Margery Palmer McCulloch, *Scottish Modernism and its Contexts 1918–1959: Literature, National Identity and Cultural Exchange* (Edinburgh: Edinburgh University Press, 2009).

Further Reading

Primary Materials

Bold, Alan (ed.), *The Letters of Hugh MacDiarmid* (London: Hamish Hamilton, 1984).
— (ed.), *The Thistle Rises: An Anthology of Poetry and Prose* (London: Hamish Hamilton, 1984).
Buthlay, Kenneth (ed.), *Hugh MacDiarmid, A Drunk Man Looks at the Thistle*. An Annotated Edition. The Association for Scottish Literary Studies (Edinburgh: Scottish Academic Press, [1926] 1987).
Calder, Angus, Glen Murray and Alan Riach (eds), *Hugh MacDiarmid, The Raucle Tongue: Hitherto Uncollected Prose, Volume I: 1911–1926* (Manchester: Carcanet, 1996).
— (eds), *Hugh MacDiarmid, The Raucle Tongue: Hitherto Uncollected Prose, Volume II: 1927–1936* (Manchester: Carcanet, 1997).
— (eds), *Hugh MacDiarmid, The Raucle Tongue: Hitherto Uncollected Prose, Volume III: 1937–1978* (Manchester: Carcanet, 1998).
Glen, Duncan (ed.), *Selected Essays of Hugh MacDiarmid* (London: Jonathan Cape, 1969).
Grieve, C. M., 'Scotsmen make a god of Robert Burns', *The Radio Times* (17 January 1930).
—, 'The Scott Centenary', *The Free Man* 1.35 (1 October 1932).
—, 'A Stone among the Pigeons', *The Student* 30.2 (25 October 1933).
—, C. M. Grieve–Helen Cruickshank Correspondence, Edinburgh University Library.
Grieve, Dorian, Owen Dudley Edwards and Alan Riach (eds), *Hugh MacDiarmid, New Selected Letters* (Manchester: Carcanet, 2001).
Grieve, Michael and W. R. Aitken (eds), *Hugh MacDiarmid, Complete Poems: Volume I* (Manchester: Carcanet, [1978] 1993).
— (eds), *Hugh MacDiarmid, Complete Poems: Volume II* (Manchester: Carcanet, [1978] 1994).
Kerrigan, Catherine (ed.), *The Hugh MacDiarmid – George Ogilvie Letters* (Aberdeen: Aberdeen University, 1988).

McCulloch, Margery Palmer (ed.), *Modernism and Nationalism: Literature and Society in Scotland, 1918–1939: Source Documents for the Scottish Renaissance* (Glasgow: Association for Scottish Literary Studies, 2004).

MacDiarmid, Hugh, *At the Sign of the Thistle* (London: S. Nott, 1934).

—, *The Islands of Scotland: Hebrides, Orkneys, and Shetland* (London: B. T. Batsford, 1939).

—, 'Robert Fergusson: Direct Poetry and the Scottish Genius', in Sydney Goodsir Smith (ed.), *Robert Fergusson 1750–1774: Essays by Various Hands to Commemorate the Bicentenary of his birth* (Edinburgh: Nelson, 1952), pp. 51–74.

—, *The Company I've Kept: Essays in Autobiography* (London: Hutchison, 1966).

— and Lewis Grassic Gibbon, *Scottish Scene, or The Intelligent Man's Guide to Albyn* (London: Jarrolds, 1934).

— and Owen Dudley Edwards, Gwynfor Evans and Ioan Rhys, *Celtic Nationalism* (London: Routledge and Kegan Paul, 1968).

—, and Campbell Maclean and Anthony Ross, *John Knox* (Edinburgh: Ramsay Head Press, 1976).

Manson, John, Dorian Grieve and Alan Riach (eds), *The Revolutionary Art of the Future: Rediscovered Poems by Hugh MacDiarmid* (Manchester: Carcanet in association with the Scottish Poetry Library, 2003).

Riach, Alan (ed.), *Hugh MacDiarmid, Selected Prose* (Manchester: Carcanet, 1992).

— (ed.), *Hugh MacDiarmid, Scottish Eccentrics* (Manchester: Carcanet, [1936] 1993).

— (ed.), *Hugh MacDiarmid, Lucky Poet: A Self-Study in Literature and Political Ideas, Being the Autobiography of Hugh MacDiarmid (Christopher Murray Grieve)* (Manchester: Carcanet, [1943] 1994).

— (ed.), *Hugh MacDiarmid, Contemporary Scottish Studies* (Manchester: Carcanet, [1926] 1995).

— (ed.), *Hugh MacDiarmid, Albyn: Shorter Books and Monographs* (Manchester: Carcanet, 1996).

— and Michael Grieve (eds), *Hugh MacDiarmid, Selected Poetry* (Manchester: Carcanet, 1992).

Watson, Roderick and Alan Riach (eds), *Hugh MacDiarmid, Annals of the Five Senses and Other Stories, Sketches and Plays* (Manchester: Carcanet, 1999); first published as C. M. Grieve, *Annals of the Five Senses* (Montrose: C. M. Grieve, 1923).

Books Edited by C. M. Grieve/Hugh MacDiarmid

Northern Numbers, Being Representative Selections from Certain Living Poets (Edinburgh: T. N. Foulis, 1920; 2nd series, Edinburgh: T. N. Foulis, 1921; 3rd series, Montrose: C. M. Grieve, 1922).

Robert Burns 1759–1796. Augustan Books of Poetry (London: Benn, 1926).

Living Scottish Poets (London: Benn, 1931).

The Golden Treasury of Scottish Poetry (London: Macmillan, [1940] 1948).
William Soutar, Collected Poems (London: Andrews Dakers, 1948).
Robert Burns: Poems (London: Grey Walls Press, 1949).
Selections from the Poems of William Dunbar. The Saltire Society (Edinburgh: Oliver and Boyd, 1952).
Selected Poems of William Dunbar (Glasgow: Maclellan, 1955).
Robert Burns: Love Songs (London: Vista Books, 1962).
Henryson. Poet to Poet (Harmondsworth: Penguin, 1973).

Books Translated by Hugh MacDiarmid

Tenreiro, Ramon Maria, *The Handmaid of the Lord* (London: Secker, 1930). Anonymous translation.
Martinson, Harry, *Aniara: A Review of Man in Time and Space* (London: Hutchison, 1963). Adapted from Swedish by MacDiarmid and Elspeth Harley Schubert.
Brecht, Bertolt, *The Threepenny Opera* (London: Eyre Methuen, 1973).

Periodicals Edited by C. M. Grieve/Hugh MacDiarmid

The Scottish Chapbook. Montrose 1.1 (August 1922) – 2.3 (November/December 1923). Monthly.
The Scottish Nation. Montrose 1.1 (8 May 1923) – 2.8 (25 December 1923). Weekly.
The Northern Review. Edinburgh 1.1 (May 1924) – 4 (September 1924). Monthly.
The Voice of Scotland. 1.1 (June/August 1938) – 9.2 (August 1958): Dunfermline (1938–9); Glasgow (1945–9); Edinburgh (1955–8). Quarterly (irregular).
Poetry Scotland. 4: Guest Editor (Edinburgh: Serif Books, 1949).
Scottish Art and Letters. Fifth miscellany. PEN Congress Number. Literary Editor (Glasgow: Maclellan, 1950).

Audio

MacDiarmid, Hugh, *Whaur Extremes Meet*, LP (Alton: Tuatha Music, 1978).

Secondary Materials

Biography

Bold, Alan, *MacDiarmid: Christopher Murray Grieve: A Critical Biography* (London: John Murray, 1988).
Wright, Gordon, *MacDiarmid: An Illustrated Biography* (Edinburgh: Gordon Wright, 1977).

Criticism

Monographs

Baglow, John, *Hugh MacDiarmid: The Poetry of Self* (Kingston and Montreal: McGill-Queen's University Press, 1987).

Bold, Alan, *MacDiarmid: The Terrible Crystal* (London: Routledge and Kegan Paul, 1983).

Boutelle, Ann Edwards, *Thistle and Rose: A Study of Hugh MacDiarmid's Poetry* (Loanhead: Macdonald, 1981).

Buthlay, Kenneth, *Hugh MacDiarmid (C. M. Grieve)* (Edinburgh: Scottish Academic Press, [1964] 1982).

Gish, Nancy K., *Hugh MacDiarmid: The Man and his Work* (London: Macmillan, 1984).

Glen, Duncan, *Hugh MacDiarmid (Christopher Murray Grieve) and the Scottish Renaissance* (Edinburgh: Chambers, 1964).

Herbert, W. N., *To Circumjack MacDiarmid: The Poetry and Prose of Hugh MacDiarmid* (Oxford: Clarendon Press, 1992).

Kerrigan, Catherine, *Whaur Extremes Meet: The Poetry of Hugh MacDiarmid 1920–1934* (Edinburgh: Mercat Press, 1983).

Lyall, Scott, *Hugh MacDiarmid's Poetry and Politics of Place: Imagining a Scottish Republic* (Edinburgh: Edinburgh University Press, 2006).

McCarey, Peter, *Hugh MacDiarmid and the Russians* (Edinburgh: Scottish Academic Press, 1987).

Morgan, Edwin, *Hugh MacDiarmid*. Writers and their Work (Harlow: Longman, 1976).

Oxenhorn, Harvey, *Elemental Things: The Poetry of Hugh MacDiarmid* (Edinburgh: Edinburgh University Press, 1984).

Riach, Alan, *Hugh MacDiarmid's Epic Poetry* (Edinburgh: Edinburgh University Press, 1991).

Schmidt, Michael, *40 Tea Chests: Hugh MacDiarmid and Shetland* (Lerwick: Shetland Amenity Trust, 2010).

Watson, Roderick, *Hugh MacDiarmid* (Milton Keynes: Open University Press, 1976).

—, *MacDiarmid* (Milton Keynes: Open University Press, 1985).

Collections of Critical Essays

Duval, Kulgin D. and Sydney Goodsir Smith (eds), *Hugh MacDiarmid: A Festschrift* (Edinburgh: Duval, 1962).

Gish, Nancy K. (ed.), *Hugh MacDiarmid: Man and Poet*. Modern Scottish Writers (Edinburgh: Edinburgh University Press, 1992).

Glen, Duncan (ed.), *Selected Essays of Hugh MacDiarmid* (London: Jonathan Cape, 1969).

— (ed.), *Hugh MacDiarmid: A Critical Survey* (Edinburgh: Scottish Academic Press, 1972).

Graham, Laurence and Brian Smith (eds), *MacDiarmid in Shetland* (Lerwick: Shetland Library, 1992).

Scott, P. H. and A. C. Davis (eds), *The Age of MacDiarmid: Essays on Hugh MacDiarmid and his Influence on Contemporary Scotland* (Edinburgh: Mainstream, 1980).

Essays in Journals and Chapters in Books

Aitken, W. R., 'A Bibliography of Hugh MacDiarmid', in Nancy K. Gish (ed.), *Hugh MacDiarmid: Man and Poet*. Modern Scottish Writers (Edinburgh: Edinburgh University Press, 1992), pp. 297–323.

Ascherson, Neal, 'MacDiarmid and Politics', in P. H. Scott and A. C. Davis (eds), *The Age of MacDiarmid: Essays on Hugh MacDiarmid and his Influence on Contemporary Scotland* (Edinburgh: Mainstream, 1980), pp. 224–37.

Boutelle, Ann E., 'Language and Vision in the Early Poetry of Hugh MacDiarmid', *Contemporary Literature* 12.4 (Autumn 1971), pp. 495–509.

Buthlay, Kenneth, 'Shibboleths of the Scots in the Poetry of Hugh MacDiarmid', *Akros* 12.34–5 (August 1977), pp. 23–47.

—, 'Hugh MacDiarmid's "Conversion" to Scots: Practice before Theory', in Horst W. Drescher and Hermann Volkel (eds), *Nationalism in Literature – Literarischer Nationalismus: Literature, Language and National Identity* (Frankfurt am Main: Peter Lang, 1989), pp. 189–200.

—, 'Adventures in Dictionaries', in Gish (ed.), *Hugh MacDiarmid: Man and Poet*, pp. 147–69.

Byrne, Michel, 'Tails o the Comet? MacLean, Hay, Young and MacDiarmid's Renaissance', *ScotLit* 26 (Spring 2002), pp. 1–3. Also at <http://www.arts.gla.ac.uk/scotlit/asls/Tails_o_the_comet.html>

Caird, James B., 'Hugh MacDiarmid', *Chapman* 22 (1978), pp. 18–21.

Craig, Cairns, 'Modernism and National Identity in Scottish Magazines', in Peter Brooker and Andrew Thacker (eds), *The Oxford Critical and Cultural History of Modernist Magazines, Volume 1: Britain and Ireland 1880–1955* (Oxford: Oxford University Press, 2009), pp. 759–84.

Craig, David, 'MacDiarmid the Marxist Poet', in Glen (ed.), *Hugh MacDiarmid: A Critical Survey*, pp. 155–67.

Crawford, Robert, 'MacDiarmid in Montrose', in Alex Davis and Lee M. Jenkins (eds), *Locations of Literary Modernism: Region and Nation in British and American Modernist Poetry* (Cambridge: Cambridge University Press, 2000), pp. 33–56.

—, *The Modern Poet: Poetry, Academia, and Knowledge since the 1750s* (Oxford: Oxford University Press, 2001), pp. 170–222.

Crichton Smith, Iain, 'The Golden Lyric: An Essay on the Poetry of Hugh MacDiarmid', in Glen (ed.), *Hugh MacDiarmid: A Critical Survey*, pp. 124–40.

Crotty, Patrick, 'From Genesis to Revelation: Patterns and Continuities in Hugh MacDiarmid's Poetry in the Early Thirties', *Scottish Literary Journal* 15 (1988), pp. 5–23.

Forrest-Thomson, Veronica, 'Poetry as Knowledge: The Use of Science by Twentieth-Century Poets' (University of Cambridge, unpublished PhD thesis, 1971), pp. 132–45.

Fraser, G. S., 'Hugh MacDiarmid: The Later Poetry', in Glen (ed.), *Hugh MacDiarmid: A Critical Survey*, pp. 211–27.

Gairn, Louisa, *Ecology and Modern Scottish Literature* (Edinburgh: Edinburgh University Press, 2008), pp. 77–104, 128–33.

Heaney, Seamus, 'Tradition and an Individual Talent: Hugh MacDiarmid', in *Preoccupations: Selected Prose 1968–1978* (London: Faber and Faber, 1980), pp. 195–8.

—, 'A Torchlight Procession of One: On Hugh MacDiarmid', in *The Redress of Poetry* (London: Faber and Faber, 1995), pp. 103–23.

Lyall, Scott, '"Genius in a Provincial Town": MacDiarmid's Poetry and Politics in Montrose', *Scottish Studies Review* 5.2 (2004), pp. 41–55.

—, 'Hugh MacDiarmid and Scottish Identity', *International Review of Scottish Studies* 29 (2004), pp. 3–28.

—, '"The Man is a Menace": MacDiarmid and Military Intelligence', *Scottish Studies Review* 8.1 (2007), pp. 37–52.

McClure, J. Derrick, *Language, Poetry and Nationhood: Scots as a Poetic Language from 1878 to the Present* (East Linton: Tuckwell, 2000), pp. 84–100.

McCulloch, Margery [Palmer], 'Modernism and the Scottish Tradition: The Duality of *A Drunk Man Looks at the Thistle*', *Chapman* 25 (1979), pp. 50–6.

—, 'The Undeservedly Broukit Bairn: Hugh MacDiarmid's *To Circumjack Cencrastus*', *Studies in Scottish Literature* 17 (1982), pp. 165–85.

McCulloch, Margery Palmer, 'Towards a Scottish Modernism: C. M. Grieve, Little Magazines and the Movement for Renewal' and 'Hugh MacDiarmid and Modernist Poetry in Scots', in *Scottish Modernism and its Contexts 1918–1959: Literature, National Identity and Cultural Exchange* (Edinburgh: Edinburgh University Press, 2009), pp. 11–28 and pp. 29–52.

—, 'Scottish Modernism', in Peter Brooker, Andrzej Gasiorek, Deborah Longworth and Andrew Thacker (eds), *The Oxford Handbook of Modernisms* (Oxford: Oxford University Press, 2010), pp. 765–81.

MacLean, Sorley, 'MacDiarmid 1933–1944', in Scott and Davis (eds), *The Age of MacDiarmid*, pp. 15–21.

McQuillan, Ruth, 'MacDiarmid's Other Dictionary', *Lines Review* 66 (September 1978), pp. 5–14.

Manson, John, 'The Poet and the Party', *Cencrastus* 68 (2000), pp. 35–8.

Morgan, Edwin, 'Poetry and Knowledge in MacDiarmid's Later Work', in *Essays* (Manchester: Carcanet, 1974), pp. 203–13. First published in K. D. Duval and S. G. Smith (eds), *Hugh MacDiarmid: A Festschrift* (1962).

Morgan, Edwin, 'MacDiarmid at Seventy-Five', in *Essays* (Manchester: Carcanet, 1974), pp. 214–21.

—, 'On Hugh MacDiarmid's *Complete Poems 1920–1976*', *Comparative Criticism* 3 (1981), pp. 303–9.

Murison, David, 'The Language Problem in Hugh MacDiarmid's Work', in Scott and Davis (eds), *The Age of MacDiarmid*, pp. 83–99.

Murray, Glen, 'MacDiarmid's Media 1911–1936', in Angus Calder, Glen Murray and Alan Riach (eds), *Hugh MacDiarmid, The Raucle Tongue: Hitherto Uncollected Prose, Volume I: 1911–1926* (Manchester: Carcanet, 1996), pp. x–xix.

—, 'MacDiarmid's Media 1937–1978', in *Hugh MacDiarmid, The Raucle Tongue: Hitherto Uncollected Prose, Volume III: 1937–1978* (Manchester: Carcanet, 1998), pp. xiv–xxxiv.

Norbrook, David, 'What Happened to MacDiarmid', *London Review of Books* 8.18 (1986), pp. 24–6.

O'Connor, Laura, *Haunted English: The Celtic Fringe, the British Empire, and De-Anglicization* (Baltimore: The Johns Hopkins University Press, 2006), in particular, Chapter 3, 'Hugh MacDiarmid's Poetics of Caricature', pp. 111–51.

Ross, Jimmy, 'Hugh MacDiarmid', in Chris Bambery (ed.), *Scotland, Class and Nation* (London: Bookmarks, 1999), pp. 177–96.

Singer, Burns, 'Scarlet Eminence: A Study of the Poetry of Hugh MacDiarmid', in Glen (ed.), *Hugh MacDiarmid: A Critical Survey*, pp. 35–57.

Whitworth, Michael H., 'Three Prose Sources for Hugh MacDiarmid's "On a Raised Beach"', *Notes and Queries* 54 (2007), pp. 175–7.

—, 'Culture and Leisure in Hugh MacDiarmid's "On a Raised Beach"', *Scottish Studies Review* 9.1 (Spring 2008), pp. 123–43.

—, 'Hugh MacDiarmid and Chambers's *Twentieth Century Dictionary*', *Notes and Queries* 55 (2008), pp. 78–80.

—, Forms of Culture in Hugh MacDiarmid's "Etika Preobrazhennavo Erosa"', *International Journal of Scottish Studies* 5 (Autumn/Winter 2009), accessed online at <www.ijsl.stir.ac.uk>

Whyte, Christopher, *Modern Scottish Poetry* (Edinburgh: Edinburgh University Press, 2004), pp. 92–102.

Notes on Contributors

Louisa Gairn is the author of *Ecology and Modern Scottish Literature* (2008) and a contributor to *The Edinburgh Companion to Contemporary Scottish Literature* (2007) and other essay collections. She lives and works in Helsinki, Finland.

David Goldie is Senior Lecturer in the School of Humanities at the University of Strathclyde. He is the editor, with Gerard Carruthers and Alastair Renfrew, of *Beyond Scotland: New Contexts for Twentieth-Century Scottish Literature* (2004) and the forthcoming *Scotland in the Nineteenth-Century World*.

Dorian Grieve is a postgraduate doctoral student attached to the AHRC-funded Corpus of Modern Scottish Writing project in the School of Critical Studies at the University of Glasgow. He has previously co-edited MacDiarmid's *New Selected Letters* (2001).

Scott Lyall is Lecturer in Modern Literature at Edinburgh Napier University, having taught previously at Trinity College, Dublin and the University of Exeter. He is the author of *Hugh MacDiarmid's Poetry and Politics of Place: Imagining a Scottish Republic* (2006).

Margery Palmer McCulloch is the author of monographs on Neil M. Gunn (1987) and Edwin Muir (1991), and co-editor of a collection of essays on Lewis Grassic Gibbon (2003). Her most recent books are *Modernism and Nationalism* (2004) and *Scottish Modernism and its Contexts* (2009). She is Senior Research Fellow at Glasgow University and co-editor of *Scottish Literary Review*.

Kirsten Matthews is a graduate of Cambridge and Glasgow Universities and from March 2009 to December 2010 was a Literature Curriculum Developer for the University of the Highlands and Islands. Her publications include

'Life and Aesthetic Containment in Hugh MacDiarmid's *Lucky Poet*', in *Material Worlds* (2007) and 'A Democracy of Voices', in *The Edinburgh Companion to Contemporary Scottish Poetry* (2009).

Alan Riach is Professor of Scottish Literature at Glasgow University, general editor of the *Collected Works of Hugh MacDiarmid*, and author of *Hugh MacDiarmid's Epic Poetry* (1991), *The Poetry of Hugh MacDiarmid* (1999), *Representing Scotland in Literature, Popular Culture and Iconography* (2005) and *Homecoming* (2009). He co-authored *Arts of Resistance: Poets, Portraits and Landscapes of Modern Scotland* (2008).

Carla Sassi is Associate Professor of English Literature at the University of Verona and specialises in Scottish and Postcolonial Studies. Among her publications are *Why Scottish Literature Matters* (2005) and, as co-author, *Caribbean-Scottish Relations* (2007). She was a Royal Society of Edinburgh Visiting Research Fellow in 2008.

Jeffrey Skoblow is Professor of English at Southern Illinois University, Edwardsville (USA), and author of the books *Dooble Tongue: Scots, Burns, Contradiction*, and *Paradise Dislocated: Morris, Politics, Art*, as well as scholarly articles on various subjects (Scottish and otherwise), fiction and poetry.

Roderick Watson is Professor Emeritus at the University of Stirling. He has lectured and published widely on modern Scottish literature and currently co-edits the *Journal of Stevenson Studies*. His books include *Hugh MacDiarmid* (1976; 1985), *The Poetry of Norman MacCaig* (1989), *The Literature of Scotland* (1984; 2006) and *Into the Blue Wavelengths* (poetry, 2004).

Michael H. Whitworth is a University Lecturer in the English Faculty, University of Oxford and a Tutorial Fellow of Merton College, Oxford. He is the author of *Einstein's Wake: Relativity, Metaphor, and Modernist Literature* (2001), *Virginia Woolf* (2005) and *Reading Modernist Poetry* (2010); and the editor of *Modernism* (2007).

Index

189